Epistolary Practices

· · · · · · · · · · · · · · · · · · · ·

Epistolary Practices
Letter Writing in America before Telecommunications

· ·

William Merrill Decker

The University of North Carolina Press

Chapel Hill and London

© 1998
The University of
North Carolina Press
All rights reserved
Designed by Richard Hendel
Set by Keystone Typesetting, Inc.
Monotype Garamond
Manufactured in the
United States of America
The paper in this book meets the guide-
lines for permanence and durability of the
Committee on Production Guidelines for
Book Longevity of the Council on Library
Resources.
Library of Congress
Cataloging-in-Publication Data
Decker, William Merrill.
Epistolary practices : letter writing in America
before telecommunications / by William Merrill
Decker.
p. cm.
Includes bibliographical references and index.
ISBN 0-8078-2438-0 (cloth: alk. paper) —
ISBN 0-8078-4743-7 (pbk.: alk. paper)
1. American letters—19th century—History and
criticism. 2. Letter writing—United States—
History—19th century. I. Title.
PS417.D43   1998   98-5270
816'.309—dc21   CIP
A portion of this work appeared earlier, in
somewhat different form, as " 'A Letter Always
Seemed to Me Like Immortality': The
Correspondence of Emily Dickinson," *ESQ:
A Journal of the American Renaissance* 39 (1993):
77–104, and is reprinted here with permission
of the Board of Regents, Washington State
University.

02   01   00   99   98   5   4   3   2   1

For Marion Culp Decker

Contents

· · · · · · · · · ·

Illustrations

· · · · · · · · · · · · ·

Preface

. . . .

It is fitting that a book on letter writing should itself have been fostered at every stage of its development by conversations conducted through the mail, and it is a pleasure to acknowledge two correspondents whose friendship and letters have sustained not only this project but many other inquiries and pursuits. With Charles (Tony) Stoneburner, professor emeritus at Denison University, I have conversed by letter sheet now for nearly a quarter century, and this continuing exchange figures among those cycles of affirmation, large and small, by which life goes forward. As I celebrate the open-ended longevity of this conversation, I mark the loss of my other steady correspondent, Sherman Paul, with whom I studied at the University of Iowa, and thereafter through the mails on every conceivable subject. Even in his final letter, written two weeks before his death, he had suggestions, leads, and considerations for this project.

For what emerged as this book's ambition I am deeply indebted to Charles Vandersee, with whom I have conversed on the subject of letter writing for a decade and who closely and responsively read the completed manuscript. Joanne Jacobson and Joel Myerson read the manuscript for the Press, and to both I am grateful for perceptive, specific, and suggestive readings.

Many other colleagues and friends have contributed directly or indirectly to this project. For their various acts of assistance and encouragement I thank Eric Gary Anderson, Edward Chalfant, James Cox, Sarah and Lewis Dabney, Brian Evenson, Margaret Ewing, Earl Harbert, Eric Nye, James Olney, John Orr, Ann Ratcliffe, Jane Remus, James Showalter, and Cindy Weinstein. Five of my Oklahoma State University graduate students have been gracious in allowing me to talk out ideas in their presence as well as instructive in their response, and for such generosity I thank Deborah Lee Ames, Charla Cook, Andrea Frankwitz, Michael Pratt, and Melanie Springer.

Jeffrey B. Walker, head of the English Department at Oklahoma State University, and Carol Lynn Moder, associate head, have been steady sources of collegial encouragement and facilitators of institutional support. Departmental staff members Cecilia Austell and Shirley Bechtel have provided much indispensable assistance. To the College of Arts and Sciences, Oklahoma State University, I am grateful for two Dean's Incentive Grants, and I thank the Oklahoma Foundation for the Humanities (and its sponsor, the National Endowment for the Humanities) for three grants that sustained this project in its early and later stages.

It has again been a great privilege to work with the staff at the University of North Carolina Press. I thank Kate Douglas Torrey for her abiding interest in the idea of this project, Barbara Hanrahan for her helpfulness in its earliest stage, and Sian Hunter for her perception and counsel through numerous stages subsequent. For a second time I thank Ron Maner for his expertise and good humor.

My family has often surprised me by their interest in and enthusiasm for this project. My brother, Thomas Decker, and sister-in-law, Barbara LaVaque Decker, have never failed to inquire about its progress, nor for that matter have my niece and nephew, Kathryn and James Decker. To Kathryn I am indebted for a memorable conversation on the subject of pioneer correspondence. My in-laws, Lester and Jane S. Grubgeld, have likewise demonstrated a kindly ongoing interest. My sons and good friends, Edward and Robert, have graciously put up with a lot of overheard conversation on the subject of letter writing as well as the visual clutter of stacks and stacks of books that never seem to move. Elizabeth Grubgeld, colleague, wife, partner in unending discussion, championed this project from its outset and read large portions of the manuscript in progress.

I dedicate this book to my mother, Marion Culp Decker, exemplary sustainer of family correspondence.

Excerpts from letters of Washington W. McDonough (John McDonough Papers) and Abream Scriven (Charles Colcock Jones Papers) are quoted by permission of the Howard-Tilton Memorial Library, Tulane University. An excerpt from a letter of Thaddeus Capron (Thaddeus Capron Papers) is quoted by permission of the American Heritage Center, University of Wyoming.

Abbreviations & Note on Quotations

. . . .

ABBREVIATIONS

Editions that are cited frequently in the text and notes have been identified by the following abbreviations. In citations, page references appear after the abbreviations.

AFC: *Adams Family Correspondence*. Ed. L. H. Butterfield, Marc Friedlaender, and Richard Alan Ryerson. 6 vols. Cambridge, Mass.: Harvard University Press, 1963–93.

CEC: *The Correspondence of Emerson and Carlyle*. Ed. Joseph Slater. New York: Columbia University Press, 1964.

CW: *Collected Works of Ralph Waldo Emerson*. 5 vols. to date. Cambridge, Mass.: Harvard University Press, 1971– .

J: Indicates Johnson's numbering of Dickinson's poems in *The Poems of Emily Dickinson*. Ed. Thomas H. Johnson. 3 vols. Cambridge, Mass.: Harvard University Press, 1955.

JMN: *The Journals and Miscellaneous Notebooks of Ralph Waldo Emerson*. Ed. William H. Gilman et al. 16 vols. Cambridge, Mass.: Harvard University Press, 1960–82.

LED: *The Letters of Emily Dickinson*. Ed. Thomas H. Johnson and Theodora Ward. 3 vols. Cambridge, Mass.: Harvard University Press, 1958.

LHA: *The Letters of Henry Adams*. Ed. J. C. Levenson, Ernest Samuels, Charles Vandersee, and Viola Hopkins Winner. 6 vols. Cambridge, Mass.: Harvard University Press, 1982–88.

LRWE: *The Letters of Ralph Waldo Emerson*. Ed. Ralph L. Rusk (vols. 1–6) and Eleanor M. Tilton (vols. 7–10). 10 vols. New York: Columbia University Press, 1939, 1990–95.

NOTE ON QUOTATIONS

Nonstandard spelling and grammar as well as inscription error are endemic to familiar letter writing. In quoting from published correspondence and unpublished holographs, I have made no attempt to identify departures from standard usage or to correct obvious oversight.

In quoting from *The Journals and Miscellaneous Notebooks of Ralph Waldo Emerson* and *The Letters of Ralph Waldo Emerson*, both of which offer genetic text transcriptions of holographs, I have not reproduced struck words and phrases or typographical indications that a word or phrase was inserted, although my modified clear-text versions preserve Emerson's spelling, capitalization, punctuation, and abbreviation.

Epistolary Practices

What is it that instructs a hand lightly created,

to impel shapes to eyes at a distance, which for them

have the whole area of life or of death?

> *Emily Dickinson to Louise Norcross,*
>
> *September 1880*

Introduction

. . . .

In much of the world, from the fifteenth century on, spaces widened between people who wished to remain in contact with one another. Citizens of colonizing European countries had to learn to communicate over distances that were inconceivable by the light of a prior geographic experience. An efficient post had extended to the frontiers of the Roman Empire and for centuries messages flowed along ancient and medieval trade routes; with the Renaissance, however, separations commonly assumed the magnitude of an oceanic or continental expanse. The means of exchanging words between a far-off seaboard settlement and a home country were tenuous at best. In America, the task of establishing postal connections within colonized but still unmapped territories was fraught with difficulties that persisted well into the early national period.[1] In the ample interiors of what was to become the United States, where families typically scattered across hundred- and thousand-mile tracts and where regional as well as federal polity remained for long periods in doubt, efforts to enhance communication were highly motivated. Migration and mobility in eighteenth- and nineteenth-century America created a desire for instantaneous contact that technology steadily aimed to meet. That communications technology became ever more refined and increasingly pervasive of the culture that it served is apt to strike us as the inevitable development of a continental nation determined to maintain political, economic, and social cohesion. It is not surprising that global telecommunications have proceeded all along from American models.[2]

Telecommunications have altered, and continue to alter, our experiences of space and time, of interpersonal presence and absence. Although letters made of paper and ink continue to flow, the practice of writing and awaiting a reply is not what it was before the emergence of the telegraph, telephone, and electronic mail. In a crisis even the most traditional epistolarian seeks access to faster modes. Until quite recently, however, no mesh of overhead and underwater cables—much less a "worldwide" electronic network—existed to eliminate the time it took for messages to cross the space between persons. Distances were more formidable, the presence and absence of one person to another possessed fewer gradations than what they assume in a world of beamed simulacra, and separated parties more commonly created elaborate texts of their relationships. Reading pre-telecommunication-age letters requires acts of imagination and empathy, but even casual attention to their commonplace expressions reveals a sense of space and time different from our own. In addition, then, to examining the diverse rhetoric and underlying tropology of epistolary texts, this study inquires into the cultural transformations that such writing manifests—changes that involve no less than the parameters of a society's spatiotemporal orientation.

As archival documents, letters have never suffered neglect: they have long been read as primary sources of biography and history, as texts brimming with informational content. Yet the performative, fictive, and textual dimensions of letter writing, and the artifacticity of the personally inscribed holograph, have only recently attracted serious notice. In examining letters written to bridge the geographic and interpersonal spaces that separated people prior to the electronic age, I investigate a discursive practice to which people of nearly every class and level of literacy had recourse, however unequal. My chief questions are these: What role does letter writing have in the literate as well as the self-consciously literary culture of pre-twentieth-century America, and how has that role changed in the past hundred years? What is the relationship between letter writing and speech, and what is the relationship between letter writing and composition in other genres? What did correspondents feel that they could say in letters but nowhere else? What manner of narrative arose in the exchange of letters? What do letters tell us about what formerly it meant for people to be present and absent to one another? What possibilities for the creation of human relationship were (and for some people still are) promoted by a practice that negotiates distance between persons through the comparatively slow material exchange of written texts? And finally, to bring the inquiry home to our own time: In view of our increasing reliance on telephone contact and e-mail, what possibilities for the creation of human relationship are served by the minimal materiality and virtual instantaneity of electronic mediation?

Although a large portion of epistolary communication has always been businesslike and relatively impersonal, letters are inevitably associated with intimacy. Perhaps the most fundamental fiction of letter writing is that the epistolary utterance, despite the absence of addresser to addressee, if not precisely because of that absence, speaks with an immediacy and intimacy unavailable in the face-to-face conversation that letter writing typically takes as its model. Such intimacy commonly assumes the existence of a certain confidentiality as its enabling condition. The fact that this study enlists us as readers of other people's mail, which we not only read but interrogate in pursuit of knowledge answerable to interests foreign to the concerns of the correspondents, compels us to ponder the pretexts by which scholarship, no less than the popular media, erases the line between public and private domains. Arguably that line is always in the process of being erased; particularly in an electronic age, we are inured to the betrayal of "privacies" to the genres of public spectacle. As voyeurs of lives preserved in the letter genre's continuous present tense, we may justify our more scholarly intrusions by arguing that our inquiry focuses not on persons so much as on systems of representation—that it is concerned less with disclosures per se than with discourse that generates disclosure. It is accurate to state that one writer's confidence encodes itself much like another's. And we can generally affirm that, in the absence of a grossly prurient interest, the object of such study is no more susceptible to exploitation than the object of any other.

But this argument may not free the analyst from claims the notion of privacy is apt to make on anyone who in everyday life must distinguish between a private and a public sphere. It may not prepare the reader of old correspondences to deal impersonally with such enduringly painful documents as Dickinson's "Master" letters, the missives Emerson dispatched to announce the death of his son, or those Adams penned in the hours following his wife's suicide. A theoretical interest may not always avert the sense of moral contamination before the racist and sadistic musings that Adams, Jack London, and Ernest Hemingway committed to the epistolary page, may not absolve one of embarrassment before the erotic letters of James Joyce. Even the most serious student of letters is bound to ask from time to time whether a particular text ought not to have seen print. Because study of correspondence involves the invasion of what we perceive as someone else's privacy (albeit an erstwhile privacy, a privacy that, at a certain remove, deconstructs as an individual-centered ideology), theoretical and ethical considerations are more than usually in order.[3]

One writer's confidence does in fact encode itself much like another's; what we identify as the private life is a conventionalized and hence public construction. It is impossible, however, to read extensively in the literature of personal correspondence without becoming aware of the conditions of human isolation that generate such texts, and of the vulnerability, sorrow, folly, and crudity, as well as the invention, eloquence, and lyricism, that such conditions bring out. In formulating an ethical stance for the analyst of letters, it is important to remember that one is party to an intervention that has imposed a market consumability if also a public answerability on texts that were never necessarily intended to endure such reification and bear such exposure. As the epistolary text becomes the object of scrutiny, one can consciously achieve an empathy (if not always a sympathy) with the stultifying and tragic dimensions of human experience that letter writers frequently articulate. One can choose—as I have chosen throughout this study, in ways that I trust will become clear as I proceed—to honor the occasion of epistolary inscription. As for the morally reprehensible expressions that occur in letters: although private attitudes are never without public consequence, and although common standards of human decency will never allow us to be anything but appalled at Adams's anti-Dreyfusard rants or London's cold-blooded disowning of family members, we can hardly expect correspondents not to articulate moments of imaginative and ethical failure. Subjected to interrogation, the writings of the most enlightened writers predictably manifest ventings of small-mindedness and residues of bigotry. Even when we come upon the intensely virulent expression, it may be productive to suppose that there is a place for musings that are not willfully published.

Consideration of the privacy and intimacy of personal correspondence leads to the recognition that readers not party to a correspondence customarily encounter only the published texts of the exchange, already something other than what the writers in most cases intended them to be. With some exceptions, this study discusses letters that have been collected, printed, and bound between book covers, and my commentary makes reference to a published and hence widely accessible body of texts. Editions of letters are so much a fixture of literate culture that it is easy to forget that in its published state a correspondence leads the second of two distinct generic lives. Constituted initially by conventions that regulate the composition and exchange of autograph manuscripts addressed to specific people, a correspondence is reconstituted in becoming the printed letters of a historical person or persons, a publication intended for readers who have no part in what is now a chronologically distant exchange. Although I will recurrently explore the private exchange of autograph manuscripts— the genetic condition of epistolary writing—this study (as my table of abbreviations makes clear) would not exist in the absence of letters that have been transcribed, annotated, and published, and that have been rematerialized in the process. At the outset, then, I wish to identify the immediate object of criticism as for the most part published letters in which the events of editing and publication not only figure prominently but refer to and shape our position as readers.

The massive publication of personal correspondence merits recognition as one of the major events—indeed, one of the great capital investments—of twentieth-century humanities scholarship. Not only have the letters of prominent individuals appeared in print but also those of men and women of lesser fame as well as those of people whose histories remain obscure beyond what their letters tell us. As will be discussed at length in the first chapter, such publications have become more and more committed to printing whole, unexpurgated letters, and advances in print technology have permitted an increasingly faithful representation of revisions found in the autograph copy. Volumes of letters have appeared steadily since the sixteenth century, but nothing compares with the scale of letter publication over the course of the twentieth. Although ample selections of correspondence were made available to receptive readerships throughout the eighteenth and nineteenth centuries, it is only since the First World War that editors have aspired to reproduce an author's total surviving epistolary output, the stock purchase, the one-line thank-you, the erotic fantasy not excepted, printed with the assumption that any text produced by a particular hand may potentially mean something to someone's reading or scholarship.

This interest in the epistolary writing of the past itself commands interest, especially because in its published state that writing is reconstituted by our efforts to preserve and access it. Anything as assiduously and expensively pursued as the scholarly publication of letters rests on the assumption that an object of inestimable value is at stake, and it will be an ongoing task of this book to clarify what that object and its value are. We may begin that task with two observations. First, as works of scholarship conforming to high (if not necessarily uniform) standards of verification, modern academic letter volumes commend themselves as a species of historical documentation, offering information about the past as the past may be known from contemporary records of individual letter writers or sets of correspondents. The past to be known may be that of the letter writer or the age; it may be a biographical, literary, or political past. Whatever emphasis a reader wishes to develop, letter volumes are published as primary sources that, variously interrogated, will support a range of interpretive narratives. Maintaining a posture of scholarly detachment, the editorial voice that introduces, annotates, and otherwise defines the occasion of the letters' printing can always justify the publication of the most personal, confidential, and compromising utterances. Committed to disciplined inquiry, and avoiding too warm an homage to the author (although publication itself commonly represents homage), letter volumes of our century tend to avoid the idealized memorials of many nineteenth-century volumes: the heavily edited eulogistic selection, the heroic life-and-letters.

The twentieth-century reaction against the volume of letters edited with a view to idealizing the image of its usually deceased author prompts my second observation. As publications arising in a culture that valorizes individuals, our own period's letter volumes derive much of their aesthetic fascination from their status as texts that say "I"; even when the "I" says unacceptable things there generally remains a qualified idealization of the individual life. Not all letter volumes cultivate that fascination. Whereas the recent Harvard *Letters of Henry Adams* groups letters in chapters that represent a biographical reading of Adams's life, the Rusk and Tilton *Letters of Ralph Waldo Emerson*, beyond lengthy biographical introductions, offers little more than annotated transcriptions of letters clustered by year. Still, this edition can assume readerly interest in Emerson the unique consciousness, whose every missive bears a possible value to an author-valorizing scholarship. In ways that appeal as well to the guiding ideology of many readers' experience as letter authors, letter volumes preserve the idea of writing as something that emanates from a singular consciousness, an author who signs his or her name in guarantee of the writing's authentic issue. Letter volumes preserve that idea even as they encourage a view of the letter exchange as intertextual and multiauthorial— blurring the boundaries between addresser and addressee.

In short, letter volumes are valued and continue to be produced not only for what they allow us to construct of the past but for their capacity to tell the stories (heroic, scandalous, or pathetic) of individuals, their ability to create the illusion of individuals telling their own stories. In the language of truisms, we may say that letter volumes make for sound knowledge and enjoyable reading: they make history "come alive" in the daily circumstances of men and women.[4] This is but a preliminary and superficial answer to the question of why letters are valued, but it may clarify our expectations of published letters and put us in view of the problems that attend those expectations. Although their value as primary documents is indisputable, letters do not really provide transparent access to history; nor do they generally conform to anything like self-evident story lines. A major problem in the reading of letters has in fact to do with the way letters are made to cohere as narrative. Letters tell stories centered in the experience of historically real individuals, but the stories they tell depend on the context in which they are read, the manifest interventions of editors and readers. As we read letters in a published volume, and consider the ways in which a letter writer addresses a reader, an editorial enterprise addresses us as members of a posterior readership (Janet Gurkin Altman speaks usefully of published letters being "readdressed").[5] Much of a letter's story may be invisible, buried, or lost. In any reading, some narrative possibilities are bound to be privileged above others, and readers of published letters expect to be prompted by an editorial hand.

What we do as members of a posterior readership figures in the larger story: that certain letter writers (such as Emerson and Adams) accept and even welcome the probability of our interventions while others (such as Dickinson) conceal their letters from readers they themselves have not inscribed compels scrutiny of the role our reading plays. As participants in our own century's disclosure of the epistolary past, we assert contested prerogatives as possessors of texts not in the first instance addressed to us, texts that are inscribed "Burn after reading," whose publication would have mortified the parties in the exchange. The flame has often figured as the ultimate defense of epistolary privacy and many invaluable correspondences have vanished by its agency. In examining published letters we incur, I believe, a moral obligation to keep such contestations in view and to provide some account of the literary and scholarly culture that makes it possible for these texts to command an enduring posthumous public. We are obliged, in other words, to substantiate the claim that something of great public value resides in these once private documents. It is the intent of this book to substantiate that claim in a variety of ways: by exploring the ever tenuous boundaries between private and public discourse, by distinguishing the insight into the nature of language that certain writers gain as practitioners of the genre, and especially by identifying the commonalities and reciprocities that correspondents must work repeatedly to establish.

Mindful as it must be of the invasive media that permit its scholarship, this book will focus mainly on historical practices to which the labors of countless editors have provided access, and I must now outline its overall scheme and explain my selection of specific cases.

Chapters 1 and 2 provide overviews respectively of the genre of familiar letter writing and epistolary practices that coincide with American experiences of space, settlement, separation, and reunion. My consideration of the genre in chapter 1 is necessarily restricted. It makes reference to the history of letter writing, to the letter's capacity to assimilate other genres (poem, essay, travel narrative, confession), and to the letter's own susceptibility to assimilation (verse epistle, epistolary novel, travelogue, polemic). But it is principally aimed at defining the genre as practiced within a conventionalized exchange of inscribed letter sheets. Following a discussion of the ways in which the autograph missive has been assimilated to the genres of printed and published letter collections, this chapter aims to clarify the relationship between the letter as artifact and the letter as text, and to view the inscribed artifact as a multivalent negotiation of human separation.

With the materiality of the letter exchange in mind, chapter 2 examines instances in which the American experience of space is articulated by epistolary artifacts. Such artifacts are frequently predetermined both as objects of exchange and as texts that repeat what other letters have previously said and repeated, but they nevertheless bespeak ruptures of traditional structures of coherence and in so doing evince novel experiences of space, time, presence, and absence. By "American experience" I primarily refer to the adventure of speakers of European languages, and their European and non-European heirs, among the expansive horizons known as the New World. It would be difficult and purposeless to argue that there arise distinctively "American" epistolary modes, and the subtitle of this book in no way refers to developments in letter writing unique to American correspondents. It adverts rather to a theater of usage, one in which two conditions, not exclusive to America but prominent in American experience, may be remarked: first, that in what was to become the United States, distance from spouses, family members, and friends has always been a common experience given the unprecedented mobility of the population, and second, that the pervasive if often marginal literacy of the population (itself the reflection of a democratic republic's recognition of the necessity of common schools) has made writing a resource on which a large portion of the population could draw in attempting to preserve communications over distance.

The circumstance of being vastly separated from family and friends was shared by men and women who could articulate their conditions with facility and invention and those who could but woodenly manipulate a narrow repertoire of formulas; the letters that register such experience are variously inscribed in free-flowing ink on high-quality stationery or scrawled on scrap paper. As obvious as one may find the differences between the letters of the highly literate and those of the barely literate, the materially advantaged and the materially disadvantaged (although literacy and affluence do not always correlate), resemblances to one another of a tropological character are even more impressive. In chapter 2 I examine letters written by well-known and comparatively well-educated persons such as Christopher Columbus, John Winthrop, Benjamin Franklin, Thomas Jefferson, and John and Abigail Adams; I also examine the letters of writers who, except in their letters, were not writers at all: those of indentured servants, New England factory workers, slaves, and Western pioneers. The second chapter, in sampling a popularly practiced genre, seeks to identify a culturally pervasive activity that contains themes and narrative possibilities that literarily and theoretically astute writers like Ralph Waldo Emerson, Emily Dickinson, and Henry Adams could realize with high degrees of self-consciousness.

Chapters 3 through 5 are devoted to the letter writing of Emerson, Dickinson, and Adams. As will be seen, they have much in common with correspondents who were not authors by vocation, and for all of their illustrative differences they have much in common with one another. Emerson, Dickinson, and Adams are alike New Englanders of upper-middle-class origin born within a span of thirty-five years. Each began exchanging letters with members of an epistolarily active family long before identifying his or her vocation as a specifically literary one; in the biographies of each, letter writing figures as a formative literary activity. Each provides abundant evidence that the familiar letter served as an important channel of cultural transmission. Each confirms the central place of the letter exchange in daily life not only by participating prolifically in it but also by regarding such practice as a metaphor for language use, human contact, and communal enterprise generally. As self-reflexive students of what transpires in the epistolary act, all three learn as correspondents what are for them fundamental lessons about the capacity of language to mediate social relations; they at once make use of and think through the structures of the genre. Letter writing also provides all three with occasions to speculate about other genres and to consider the obstacle that genre presents to their respective authorial aims. Each was aware that, as an aesthetic formation and economic commodity, genre is invested with powers to constrain what may be written for a paying public. Our sense of literary history is enhanced by the recognition that the letter, for these authors as for others, serves both as the medium of initial trial and last resort—averted from the exposure, and disengaged from the market economy, of public performance.

With all that they have in common, Emerson, Dickinson, and Adams bring distinct temperaments and worlds of experience to the occasions of writing and receiving letters; moreover, they practice the genre amid contexts that register the diversity and changefulness of a regional and national culture. The sequence begins with Emerson, who intermittently characterizes himself as a reluctant letter writer but whose epistolary output documents an extraordinary effort to formulate and achieve what he describes as ideals of conversation elsewhere unattainable in the spoken and written discourse of his time. His pursuit of such ideals reflects his disaffection from the political and economic culture of antebellum New England, while his later falling-off as a letter writer signals alterations in his friendships and measures his general decline as an author. With Dickinson I examine the practice of one for whom letter writing would become the exclusive medium of many friendships and whose letters probe with exceptional lucidity the spatial and temporal separation of correspondents; in her letters and poems about letter writing, as I will argue, Dickinson achieves an incomparable theoretical understanding of what it means to send and to receive letters. I follow with Adams, undoubtedly the most ambitious of American letter writers, whose achievement must be seen in several contexts: his eminent family's diplomatic and personal correspondence; the Augustan example on which he modeled his early efforts; and the chronicle of disappointment, disaffection, and bereavement that his writings generally constitute. Throughout a long and active life, Adams's letter writing complicates the boundaries between public and private, political and personal; in each of his several phases as a correspondent, questions concerning the public value of an initially confidential body of writing are implicitly and sometimes explicitly raised.

My decision to devote chapter-length attention to Emerson, Dickinson, and Adams is thus made in view of the depth and pervasiveness of their epistolary self-reflexivity—their constant monitoring of the possibilities of writing in the letter genre and of the possibilities of language as the letter genre manifests them. Other authors demonstrate a comparable self-reflexivity, and this book might alternatively have been sustained by extended study of the letters of Abigail Adams, John Adams, Thomas Jefferson, Nathaniel Hawthorne, Margaret Fuller, Henry David Thoreau, Samuel Clemens, Henry James, and Alice James, to cite authors whose correspondences I also discuss. As well, this book would undoubtedly have been enriched by consideration of the correspondences of James Fenimore Cooper, Lydia Maria Child, William Gilmore Simms, Edgar Allan Poe, Harriet Beecher Stowe, Harriet Jacobs, Sidney Lanier, Herman Melville, Walt Whitman, and William Dean Howells, to cite authors whose epistolary practices are not discussed at all. Arbitrary as my selection inevitably must be, I believe that detailed conceptions of the diversity of this genre and of the amplitude of insight generated by its practice emerge from close study of Emerson, Dickinson, and Adams, and that focused inquiry into exemplary instances will do more to represent the history of a genre than an overtly encyclopedic coverage. To be sure, the three featured writers share a regional culture, and each may be said to exhibit traits of a post-Calvinist "New England Mind." Yet with such common ground they serve all the more to demonstrate the genre's diverse aspect and multifaceted life.

In the conclusion, I inquire into the conditions under which letters continue to be written and exchanged and the altered orders of time and space through which a global postmodern culture communicates. Accordingly, the closing pages reconsider the ways in which telecommunication has prompted us to reconceive our presence and absence to one another, and address the manner in which human relationships have been transformed in the process.

Various theoretical developments in contemporary literary scholarship inform this book. Pursuing lines of interrogation that have come to be identified with the New Historicism, my inquiry is concerned with the ways in which texts come into being, under what social, economic, and technological conditions, with what challenge to established power relations or what confirmation of the status quo. Although ideological analysis per se is seldom the immediate goal of my commentary, such questions are central to the study of texts that rely—as letters so obviously do—on particular embodiments and schemes of exchange. The foregoing discussion has already articulated an interest in letters as textual objects that assume one form within the context of the epistolary exchange and quite another for those who read them in books. The obvious material differences reflect more subtle differences and tensions: marketable as published texts, letters arise within private economies that call for personal exchange "in kind," and nearly all the professional authors herein treated relished the evasion of commodified writing that personal correspondence seemed to allow. For professional and nonprofessional authors alike, letters serve as the material evidence and agency of social power and class attainment. Often they exist as the token of a self-satisfied class identity, but they also exist as scenes of subversion and insurgency, a claiming of power that may or may not achieve effective social form. The letter is ever a locus of class markers: masteries of protocol, refinements of taste, levels of cultivation, grades of literacy. There is almost no portion of society to which the letter at some time does not belong.[6]

As a study of letters that in initial form were inscribed by hand and dispatched through a space organized by various economies and technologies, this book examines the peculiar conjunction of artifacts and texts. The performative, paratactic, metonymic writings borne by these artifacts find a receptive and appreciative interpretive vocabulary among poststructuralist theories of language. Indeed, it would be virtually impossible not to approach the epistolary text as writing that exemplifies the unboundedness, undecidability, and endless complication of the binary opposition of presence to absence theorized by Barthes and Derrida. In one way or another, nearly all contemporary literary study reflects the challenges to old assumptions of textual presence, unity, authorship, and consensually stable meanings, mounted by Barthes, Derrida, Foucault, Bakhtin, and a host of followers, and it has long been conventional to regard texts as animated by the play of unanchorable and unbounded signifiers, exceeding the borders that authors attempt to impose on them. Likewise, it has become commonplace to speak of the reader's revision of the text; to view the text as multiauthored, dialogic, pliable. As references make clear, my study is enabled by such perspectives. I am also indebted to those (Derrida and Lyotard, but more particularly Landow) who have applied the theorization of textuality to the task of interrogating postal, telephonic, and digital technologies—the networks of electronic signification—that appear to confirm poststructuralist notions of the text in what is increasingly a postprint civilization.[7]

Throughout this study the term *metonymy* figures prominently. If, as Roman Jakobson suggests, metonymy is the determining tendency of language in realist literature, then familiar letter writing is an intensely metonymic discourse inasmuch as it typically abounds in the registry of quotidian "realist" minutiae that become more or less explicitly significant in reference to the addressee's absence (the occasion of the letter's composition).[8] The metonymic function of language, according to Jakobson, is to establish contiguity and contexture. Such precisely is the function of epistolary writing, which undertakes the task of establishing addresser and addressee in one or another condition of contiguity despite some measure of geographic separation, and which often has recourse to affirming a contiguity of soul to soul (or a unity in God) while the body of one correspondent is separated from that of the other by an ocean or a continent. Pre-electronic correspondences make frequent reference to a provisional contiguity of body and soul: a contiguity of inscribing hand to letter sheet, which receives and bears a text whereby one soul speaks to another by virtue of the artifact's eventual contiguity with the addressee's body and (hence) soul. Such paradoxes are deeply ingrained in Western epistolarity; the Pauline epistles—well-known to almost every writer considered in this book—provide a kind of keynote when the apostle characterizes his position as one in which he is "absent in body, but present in spirit" (1 Corinthians 5:3), and mortal existence as one marked by division and disconnection: "Whilst we are at home in the body, we are absent from the Lord" (2 Corinthians 5:6).

The contiguities offered by language generally and the epistolary text in particular are always threatened by the possibility that the letter will not arrive, will become a dead letter; a possibility that for Derrida in *The Post Card* is inevitable destiny. The death that is the space between correspondents—a geographic space but also the space between signifier and the mirage of consensual meanings—haunts letter writers, although in actual practice there is much to suggest that for many correspondents the metonymic function of language succeeds in establishing contiguities and that a complex social contexture is built and sustained despite the miscarriage of mail and the specter of the dead-letter office.[9] In her discussion of the letter as a genre that dwells on the margins of discourse, Barbara Herrnstein Smith affirms the capacity of the letter to reflect and thereby sustain a linguistic and social context. Taking issue with the subordinate status that Smith assigns to the letter genre as a "natural" as opposed to "fictive discourse," Bruce Redford makes a stronger case for the argument that letters create context. Epistolary writing, he writes, "fashions a distinctive world at once internally consistent, vital, and self-supporting."[10] Redford primarily has in mind the "letters of a master," yet examples will follow in which the tropological density of letters written by correspondents who write mainly in clichés and who have never mastered standard written forms likewise succeeds in fashioning distinctive worlds.

The broadening interest in autobiographical writing has also enabled this book. I have benefited in particular from theorists such as Paul de Man and Louis Renza who have examined the ways in which the forms of lifewriting constrain as they invite the telling of a life; few forms are as constraining yet inviting as the letter in its various subgenres.[11] Moreover, I share the satisfaction others have taken in recovering the literary complexity and social interest found in writings of people who were not authors by profession and who mostly led lives of obscurity. My more sustained focus does attach to canonical figures, yet here I direct attention to what have been regarded as peripheral texts, a subliterature traditionally considered ancillary to major achievement. As much as a language of literary self-consciousness and accomplishment, I explore a language of daily conversation, observe the major literary figure's participation in the epistolary discourse of the period, and examine the bond between that figure and his or her literate if not so literarily self-conscious correspondent.

This study, then, concerns a literature that exists in a multiauthorial context and that reflects everyday usage, even as it enables moments of invention and eloquence. It concerns a literature that is overtly dialogic and that serves to mediate and embody community metonymically. And it concerns a form of writing that, perhaps for more persons than any other, has provided the occasion for autobiographical acts. Although it presents itself as a study of the historical practice of a particular genre, this book is impelled by tendencies to think beyond genre. "Mixture," writes Derrida, "is the letter, the epistle, which is not a genre but all genres, literature itself."[12] There is justice to this, but it is also true—when we speak more exactly—that "the letter" refers to a historically stable genre object and genre practice of which we may give some account. Certain rhetorical features typify all letter writing, although social conditions and aesthetic expectations (conscious and unconscious) vary widely from period to period as well as within given historical times. Letter writers themselves struggle hard to define the epistolary genre, conflating it with other forms and rhetorical frames of reference. The problem of letters and generic definition must now command our attention.

I

Burn This Letter
Autograph Missive and Published Text

· ·

"I really did not mean when you asked me for a letter to write a homily" (LRWE 7:352). So Ralph Waldo Emerson apologizes to H. G. O. Blake toward the close of a letter that he fears may exceed the more concise response that Blake probably expects. Perhaps Emerson genuinely felt that his reply, for which he had apologized in the first place because it was belated, had become a rather long-winded metaphysical harangue. The communication was nevertheless sent: such apologies, in Emerson's letters and in those of many others, are largely a matter of form. Henry Adams likewise adverts to the tendency of letter writing to overrun foreseen bounds. "At length I expect to conclude this species of autobiography which is becoming a volume," he observes toward the end of a rambling dispatch to his British friend C. M. Gaskell (LHA 2:55). He does not really regret the long diary-like entries or the delay in getting the matter closed and posted. What there is of apology is muted by the perception—evident throughout Adams's epistolarium—that letters ever require apology as the self-indulgent discourse of the first person, but that they will always in any case be written and sent. "They are books rather than letters," Adams prefaces a bundle of letters to Elizabeth Cameron during his visit to

Samoa, "and they are written only on the chance that they may give you half an hour's amusement. If they bore you, burn them." Although he was correct in perceiving that what he sent was the substance of books, they were not, as he well knew, books but letters, subject to the perils and ephemeral life span that attends letters but not books. "They are for you," he goes on to remark, "and not meant to be preserved" (LHA 3:328).

A homily, a species of autobiography, books—so Emerson and Adams characterize what as letter writers they have produced: letters of a sort, apologies for letters, but not letters in the strict sense. What, strictly speaking, did these writers call a letter? Both suggest that the real thing would not burden, disappoint, or bore the recipient, whereas a homily or book likely would. A letter is what they feel obliged to fear (or pretend to fear) they have not written, but the ideal for them is less a matter of form than of effective content: writing that can please or otherwise fulfill the recipient's expectations. In the context of the epistolary exchange, a true letter is communication that figures successfully in an interpersonal relationship. Where there is doubt concerning the relationship, or of the rapport mediated by letter sheet, there is particular occasion for apology. But such occasion is endemic to the epistolary task, in which to apologize in anticipation of a letter's failure is to plead the terms of its success. Given the spatial and temporal separations that such colloquy must negotiate, it can hardly surprise us that letter writers affect not to meet what they project as the addressee's expectations. "You know it is customary for the first page to be occupied with apologies," Emily Dickinson observes to Abiah Root (LED 1:65). Letter writers apologize—for letters too long, letters too short, late letters, letters that are not letters.

Apologies aside, the communications that Emerson, Dickinson, and Adams deprecate but still send *are* letters, produced under common epistolary conditions, dependent on the same ink, letter sheet, and mails and generated by the same social, psychological, and economic needs as the outpourings of writers whose letters are less apologetic, less sophisticated, less likely to have survived on their literary merits alone.[1] "They are for you, and not meant to be preserved," writes Adams, conscious that they almost certainly will be preserved, but also aware of the privacy and disposability of what he has produced. The literarily self-conscious letter writers examined at length in this study participate as correspondents in an activity that is popularly practiced, and although they are aware of the possibility of literary excellence in letters and may be well-read in the published works of such canonized practitioners as Madame de Sévigné and Horace Walpole, they write their letters, much as nonliterary authors write theirs, to transact one or another kind of interpersonal business. Even when they generate texts that mimic homilies, diaries, novels, or poems, even when they provide the substance of books, as correspondents they write within a framework that serves the ends of short-term private communication and that does not necessarily favor, much less guarantee, the preservation of what is written or its ultimate possession by an anonymous readership. However much the letters of an Emerson, Dickinson, or Adams transcend, singly and as assembled lifeworks, the productions of less accomplished letter writers, their works amply reflect the protocol, conversationality, license, and hazard commonly found in this form.

An inquiry into a genre must specify the characteristics of that genre; although the foregoing paragraphs suggest some features of the familiar letter, a working definition of the objects and practices to be examined is in order. Most criticism directed to letters in English has concerned the eighteenth-century British practitioners, yet the epistolary works of the Augustan writers, which aspired to literary canonization even in their own time, have been marked off as literature in ways that the letters of American writers have not. There are advantages to approaching epistolary texts as a category of writing irrespective of the literary quality of specific instances; my definition will therefore conserve something of the conception of letters as a marginal literary form. In *The Converse of the Pen: Acts of Intimacy in the Eighteenth-Century Familiar Letter*, Bruce Redford ponders the "critical neglect" that has been the genre's fate even after a period of concerted attention to many other forms of autobiographical nonfiction prose. "The explanation," Redford writes, "has much to do with the vexed issue of generic placement: how can we do more than talk impressionistically about the letter until we can fix a category for it and then formulate appropriate aesthetic criteria?"[2] To place the letter generically and to assume a perspective from which to theorize its variant aesthetic aims involves, as Redford suggests, avoiding the merely impressionistic response elicited by particular examples and resisting habits of reading that focus on a writer's life and personality. But the task also involves viewing the letter as a cultural as well as a specifically literary form.

To this task I would apply a fundamentally materialist conception of genre, one that embraces literary and nonliterary writing, text and artifact, autograph manuscript and printed page—a conception that repudiates traditional genre hierarchies. "Genres," Fredric Jameson writes, "are essentially literary *institutions*, or social contracts between a writer and a specific public, whose function is to specify the proper use of a particular cultural object."[3] Emphasizing the conventions that govern rhetorical relations, and contextualizing those conventions within the dynamics of a society's system of exchange, such a definition is valuable because it posits the genre-object as the vehicle of a genre-practice; it encourages us to recognize that a genre-practice assimilates to a contemporary culture while preserving certain structures and themes historically associated with the genre. A materialist view of genre encourages us to account for the generally confidential life a letter leads as a private autograph text as well as the transformations it undergoes in becoming a document published in a collection intended for what is usually a posthumous readership. To account for the letter's multiple rhetorical lives compels a consideration of whether, in passing from the autograph state to the print transcription, the letter undergoes a genre change, or whether the contracts by which letter exchanges go forward and those by which letters are appropriated for publication are so interdependent as to mark different phases of one generic practice.

Jameson's definition requires two modifications before we apply it to the study of letters. First, within the context of the epistolary exchange, the contractual parties are correspondents who alternate in the readerly and writerly roles, and for whom reading and writing are inextricable activities. Second, with respect to volumes of published letters, editors normally figure as intermediary if not preemptive presences in the relationship between writers and nonepistolary readerships; to them fall the tasks of appropriating letters to the institution that is the letter volume and of redefining, from time to time, the contract between the letter volume and its public. Equally applicable to texts that are literarily self-conscious and those that are not (granted, the distinction is often far from self-evident), a materialist conception of genre resists confining the criticism of letters to a single aesthetic. In addition, it encourages recognition of the varied conventions that occur within letter writing as a cross-cultural practice. Whereas even the most naïve letter writing embodies ancient notions as to the agency of inscribed utterance, it more immediately reflects expectations that arise within a particular culture at a particular time. To the degree that such expectations lend themselves to revision, they may foster idiosyncratic utterances peculiar to specific epistolary relationships.

As the forms the familiar letter can take and the uses to which it can be put are so numerous, it is well to propose a minimal definition. By familiar letter, then, I wish to designate texts that at some point in their histories are meant to pass in accordance with some postal arrangement from an addresser to an addressee, and that in some way inscribe the process by which an author personally addresses a specific readership.[4] Addresser and addressee need not be singular; particularly among family correspondences, letters are written in collaboration to addressees who often collaborate as readers. Postal arrangements may include everything from a government postal service to the conveyance of a letter by someone happening to travel in the direction of the addressee. Letters that are meant to pass from a writer to a designated recipient do not always arrive and sometimes are not posted, and they are notoriously subject to becoming lost in transit. Yet even letters that are never mailed or that exist only in the roughest drafts usually bear in their rhetorical structure a clear epistolary intent. The process of addressing a specific readership enters the letter text in a number of ways, most obviously in certain stock gestures: dating, salutation, and complimentary close. It enters more profoundly, however, in a number of genre-reflexive themes found in correspondences at every level of literariness. The most prominent are those of separation, loneliness, and apprehension that death will intervene before the parties can reunite—a fear that letter sheet, mail, and language are inadequate to the task of maintaining relations.

Such themes commonly arise in meditations on the time and space that divide correspondents, in the anxiety expressed over the state of those whose absence prompts the letter's composition, and in the anguish registered over delayed replies. To be sure, not all personal correspondence concerns itself with these themes; letters exchanged within a locality between persons who have access to one another are not apt to reflect upon spatiotemporal division, and examples may be found of letter writers for whom distance from friends and relatives excites little evident anxiety.[5] Nevertheless, the occasion of letter writing as represented by many correspondents before the twentieth century is one in which the temporary (but always potentially permanent) loss of the addressee figures prominently. Moreover, the apprehension of that loss commonly generates a nostalgic or otherworldly fantasy of future reunion in which parties are compensated for the pain of endured separation. As we will see, the epistolary construction of utopian scenes that restore the full presence of the lost or absent friend is one of the most pervasive and interesting motifs in pre-twentieth-century letter writing. These themes inform the many occasions of correspondence, yet they arise with particular force in letters of condolence—those messages that address the void a death has produced in a family or among a circle of friends. Recurrently I will discuss condolence letters as expressions that most fully articulate the common epistolary themes of loss, separation, and reunion "in this world or the next," that foreground the awareness of mortality that constitutes a dimension of much routine letter writing.

By defining letters as texts that pass from an addresser to an addressee and that in some way inscribe the process by which an author addresses a specific readership, I would exclude the letters of epistolary fiction. Such fiction, as Janet Altman, Linda Kauffman, and others have shown, develops possibilities for narrative inherent in the letter exchange, especially those exchanges in which letters serve as a medium of erotic relationships.[6] Fictive and authentic letters are in some respects inseparable; both validate the importance of individual daily experience, and, as Altman and English Showalter Jr. suggest, affirm the broadly realist aesthetic that emerges throughout the eighteenth century and is associated with the rise of the novel.[7] Writers of epistolary fiction (many of whom are themselves prolific correspondents) draw on the experience of writing authentic letters, while literate correspondents practice within a frame of reference that includes epistolary fiction. But fictional letters and the stories they tell are created under circumstances that differ markedly from the reciprocal exchanges that produce authentic letters. The present of authentic letter writing is a condition missing from the composition of epistolary fiction, which requires a synchronic structure in which the open-ended process of ongoing correspondences is imaged but not engaged. A long-time correspondence may indeed generate its own synchronic structures— paradigmatic responses to recurrent situations, anticipations of how the corresponding partner will reply, or how a reply may resonate within the shared experience of epistolary composition. Emerson, Dickinson, and Adams all have letters that they write again and again throughout their lives, and that assert a power to predetermine experience. However, authentic correspondences, unlike their fictional counterparts, can only provisionally forecast closure.[8]

In addition to epistolary novels, the present study also excludes a variety of texts that proceed in the more or less elaborate fiction— generally reflected in the title—that they are letters, but that do not engage a genuinely epistolary process. Examples range from conduct books such as Lydia Sigourney's *Letters to Young Ladies* (1837)—which share with epistolary fiction a common ancestor in the letter-writer (or letter-writing manual) with its model letters and moral precepting, pioneered by Samuel Richardson's *Familiar Letters on Important Occasions* (1741)—to instructional tracts like John Young's *The Letters of Agricola on the Principles of Vegetation and Tillage* (1822), a text that addresses farming practices appropriate to Nova Scotia.[9] Another major genre of such writing is the philosophical letters of travel, real and imagined. Examples include J. Hector St. John de Crèvecoeur's *Letters of an American Farmer* (1782), John La Farge's *An Artist's Letters from Japan* (1899), William Dean Howells's *Through the Eye of the Needle* (1907), and, more recently, Alphonso Lingis's *Abuses* (1994)—all developments of a genre framed by Montesquieu's *Lettres Persans* (1721). An additional category of writing not covered by this study that does engage something of a genuine epistolary process is the public letter published in a newspaper or as a pamphlet. Examples range from John Dickinson's *Letters from a Farmer in Pennsylvania to the Inhabitants of the British Colonies* (1767) to David Walker's *Appeal* (1829) and Sarah Moore Grimke's *Letters on the Equality of the Sexes, and the Condition of Women* (1838). Writing of this kind often grows out of, leads to, and overlaps with private correspondence, and the public letter is adept at mimicking the confidential tone of the private exchange. Yet the conventions and expectations that distinguish the private from the public occasion remain firm.[10]

In describing letters as texts that at some point in their history are meant to pass from an addresser to an addressee, I anticipate a further qualification of what the letter can be as a cultural object. Letters have histories, even those (by far the vast majority) that duly arrive at their destination to be read and, sooner or later, abandoned, discarded, or destroyed. What the addressee does with a letter received constitutes a crisis in a letter's existence. Always more than its text, the holograph is an artifact of potential fetish value; the meaning of a letter within the economy of a correspondence emerges not only in the textual response that it draws but in the physical disposal of the holograph. To preserve or destroy a personally inscribed manuscript determines what the letter, beyond the initial cycle of exchange, may become as a cultural object. As it is preserved in a private or public archive the letter undergoes transformation: for the addressee it becomes an aging object that speaks to an evolving sense of the interpersonal past; to readers outside the epistolary exchange it becomes a document to be read for its various levels of biographical, historical, and literary interest. Although later readers may peruse autograph manuscripts in research libraries or on microfilm, they commonly encounter the texts of letters in books that have been constructed from archival materials. Presented to a book readership in the context of other letters that, in the unity of their compilation, are supposed to represent the totality of an author's epistolary output or of a specific correspondence, the transcribed and annotated text of a letter is by no means the cultural object that began life as an autograph document addressed to a specific reader.

Apprehension that such objects may come under the scrutiny of unauthorized readers is registered by writers at all levels of sophistication: "I bege you not to let this scrabling be seen," writes Sarah Hodgdon, a sixteen-year-old mill worker, to her mother in 1830.[11] The more literary or prominent the letter writer, the more cognizant the writer is apt to be of the potential interception or preservation of a holograph and its subsequent transformation into published text.[12] The letter writer's plea that the recipient burn the letter after it has been read is commonplace in printed volumes of letters; nothing so drives home the ironic relationship that readers of published letters bear to these texts than the appearance of this request amid the material evidence of its disregard. As we shall see, "Burn upon reading" occurs in letters of authors who are nonetheless ambitious to address a posterity beyond the letter's specified initial readership, and who, when requesting that a letter be destroyed, do not always require utter obliteration. Yet many authors wish just what they ask. As such extreme measures to maintain the privacy of these documents make clear, the proper use of the familiar letter is subject to debate. Accurately speaking, there exist conflicting if equally proper uses of the letter, specified by conventions that sort into two basic sets: those that govern the composition of holographs in a private correspondence and those that preside over the transformation of private letters into published books.[13]

We may wish in fact to consider whether distinct uses compel the recognition of distinct genres: on the one hand the autograph missive in all of its varied subgenres (love letter, condolence, thank-you note, and so on); on the other, the published letter in all of its subgeneric variations (the complete letters of a single author, the correspondence of two or more, the "newly discovered" letter that appears in an academic journal). Such material differentiation decidedly alters the status and character of such texts. However, because I wish to emphasize certain thematic continuities, and as I would affirm the contractual interdependence of autograph missive and published letter, I will approach these various manifestations as phases of a cohesive cultural practice. From the perspective taken in this study, letters ultimately contribute to a dialogue that transcends specific forms and individual participants. The isolated private letter is ever a token of a widely practiced generic discourse; it always already speaks to nonaddressees, to the contingency of being intercepted and published. The mailing of the letter to a known addressee and the publication of its text to an unknown and anonymous readership are different material realizations of its potential as a language-bearing artifact.

Within these two divisions—autograph missive and published letter—there are endless variations of subgeneric practice, both within and across historical periods. Perhaps the first observation to make of the autograph missive is that, for many writers on many occasions, composing a letter is largely a fulfillment of form. In Europe, letter-writing manuals begin to appear during the sixteenth century, a period of increased literacy that brought a concomitant increase in familiar correspondence.[14] Although the conventions that prescribe letter writing for members of the seventeenth-century French aristocracy differ from those that pertain to nineteenth-century middle-class Americans, for both groups the formal structures of the letter can be made to serve the occasion with or without the letter writer's investment of unique subjectivity. Even the invention and expressiveness that accomplished writers infuse in the genre conform by and large to period expectations, but what exist as conventions are apt to be challenged in a practice that privileges individual expression. As English Showalter Jr. observes, "the letter writer brings an individual mind, perhaps one of genius, to bear on the problem of encoding an experience and a set of referents within the forms available. The letter writer normally enjoys unusual freedom, both because the genre is loosely defined and because the communication need please (or produce the desired effect upon) one person, usually well-known to the writer."[15] Beyond the set forms of prescribed occasion, the uses that the letter serves are as various as the requirements correspondents place on it.

Upon the available forms, correspondents more or less consciously impose their own conventions and expectations. This superimposition is itself often the subject of negotiation. Extolling the letter's ability to perpetuate "the innocent pleasures that flow from social love," Samuel Richardson represents to Sophia Westcomb his own expectations as exemplifying the proprieties to be observed in the potentially dangerous correspondences between young women and men, a matter the author of *Clarissa* had meditated much upon. Richardson manages to be erotically playful even as he calls attention to the platonic virtue of the epistolary relationship; in so doing he foregrounds the constraints that ostensibly guide this particular exchange.[16] Correspondents may indeed cultivate an outlawry of content and form, but they are obliged to do so collaboratively. While appearing absolutely to abandon constraint, the explicitly sexual prose that characterizes the exchange James and Nora Barnacle Joyce conduct for several months exhibits nonetheless a seeking of assurances that the two correspondents agree on the matter of what constitutes mutually perpetuating discourse.[17] In the first years of their thirty-seven-year correspondence, Emerson and Carlyle struggle to define acceptable terms for the lapses in communication for which each was alternately responsible, and the understanding they achieve enables the exchange to survive in its later years Emerson's growing epistolary aphasia.

Letter publication likewise resists fixed form. The conventions that preside over the conversion of autograph missives into books have undergone great change since the sixteenth century and much of it has occurred in the past hundred years. Such development reflects evolving views of the purpose letters serve as published texts as well as the advancing capacity of the printed page to represent minute features of manuscript documents. Whereas letter publication in the past was mostly devoted to eulogistic memory, it is now more often directed to the ends of academic research; where formerly editors emended texts to enhance the image of an author's life, they now more commonly view their task as reporting in detail the autograph document as both text and artifact. Under the stewardship of scholarly editors, letters are presented not only as writings that reflect a social and intellectual context but also as objects grounded in a culturally significant materiality of ink, letter sheet, and postal conveyance. The idea of the letter volume as "the commemoration of an individual life," which Altman identifies as the "Renaissance vision" of these books, has proved the most enduring conception behind the publication of letters, although what should be remembered about an individual, and why, and what individualizes a life, are questions that have produced varying answers according to whose letters have become part of the print record and the means by which they have done so.[18]

In the United States, the correspondences of the Founding Fathers were the focus of the earliest publication of letters. Jared Sparks's twelve-volume *Diplomatic Correspondence of the American Revolution* (1829–30) compiles a collective epistolary enterprise; other editions, like Sparks's three-volume *Life and Correspondence of Gouverneur Morris* (1832), twelve-volume *The Writings of George Washington* (1834–37), and ten-volume *The Works of Benjamin Franklin* (1836–40), or like William Jay's *Life of John Jay* (1834), variously integrate correspondence with other documents and a narrative of the life. Charles Francis Adams's two-volume *Letters of Mrs. Adams* (1840), like his later *Familiar Letters of John Adams and His Wife, during the Revolution* (1875), provide a view of the domestic inner life behind Revolutionary-era public experience and suggest the public office of the private female correspondent. Sparks, William Jay, and C. F. Adams freely corrected and sanitized; Abigail Adams's phonetic spellings and accounts of a family prostrated by dysentery do not appear in the grandson's edition of her letters. Serving the dual purpose of commemorating heroic lives and the United States' increasingly mythological founding, nineteenth-century efforts to publish documents pertaining to the nation's history more often constituted exercises in filiopiety than what a later era would consider professional scholarship.[19]

Before the twentieth century, the letter per se had little significance as a text with its own history and integrity; its interest consisted rather in the historical and biographical moment that could be extracted from it. The life-and-letters biography, a genre in vogue in England and America from the latter part of the eighteenth century through the early decades of the twentieth, published passages of letters in a mostly unilinear narrative that did especial violence to the integrity of particular letters as well as to the epistolary context in which they appeared. Such productions were apt to conform to a predetermined thesis, at times baldly announced on the title page, as in *The Life and Letters of John Brown, Liberator of Kansas, and Martyr of Virginia* (1885). Fashioning public soliloquy out of private documents, they proceeded according to rigid principles of selection that might involve the wholesale suppression of certain kinds of evidence. In *Memoirs of Aaron Burr with Miscellaneous Selections from His Correspondence* (1836–37), letters become the material for the exoneration of Burr's military if not always his political and personal reputation; the editor in fact boasts of having "committed to the fire" his subject's illicitly amorous correspondence.[20] Yet as serious a scholar as Henry Adams, inspired in part by Sir George Trevelyan's well-received *Life and Letters of Lord Macaulay* (1876), produced *The Life of Albert Gallatin* (1879) by piecing together passages from letters with a view to creating a portrait of the public but not the private man.[21]

Throughout the nineteenth century, as Americans sought to formulate and codify their past, amateur and academic historians edited documents for publication. No generally accepted procedures for the transcription of documents existed, much less special consideration of the problems posed by the publication of letters, which were frequently printed with other papers associated with some figure or event. Yet the discipline that academic historians increasingly brought to the editing of state papers promoted a fidelity to the document irrespective of whatever exalted impression a publication might be intended to uphold. In the preface to his eight-volume *Letters of Members of the Continental Congress* (1921–36), Edmund C. Burnett states that "all possible pains have been taken to have the texts conform to the originals in every essential of accuracy"; such essentials include spelling, capitalization, punctuation, and paragraphing. They do not include the antiquated abbreviations which Burnett has expanded; but the difference between common late-nineteenth-century practice and the new documentary scholarship is that Burnett makes it clear to the reader that he has done so, and why.[22] Statements identifying the scope of an editor's intervention—by no means obligatory in older editing—become a standard feature in twentieth-century editions of historical papers, and sponsorship by such agencies as the National Historical Publications Commission compelled system and consensus with regard to matters of editorial principles.[23] Life-and-letters biographical treatment of such political and military figures as Alexander Hamilton, Thomas Jefferson, John Paul Jones, and James Garfield would appear in the first third of the twentieth century, but the scholarly publishing of historical documents (including letters and other private writings) had emerged as a distinct enterprise.

The letters of American literary figures before the second half of the twentieth century were likewise apt to appear in heavily edited excerpts framed by a thesis driven narrative. *Memoirs of Margaret Fuller Ossoli* (1852), a volume of personal writings hastily put together by Emerson, William Henry Channing, and James Freeman Clarke following Fuller's 1850 shipwreck, is a notorious example of how diaries and letters can be presented in such a way as to create a distorted impression of a life; the very title endeavors to suppress the scandal of Fuller's later years by the spurious attribution of Count Ossoli's surname. Martha Gilbert Bianchi's *Life and Letters of Emily Dickinson* (1924) likewise attempts to create an inoffensive profile from a body of writing that did not always conform to genteel expectations. Both publications were aimed at general readerships, as were the life-and-letters treatments of Washington Irving (1862–64), Oliver Wendell Holmes (1897), Harriet Beecher Stowe (of her there are two, 1891 and 1897), Edgar Allan Poe (1903), and William Dean Howells (1928). Although letter publication in the form of a correspondence was a well-established method of representing political discussion—examples include *Correspondence between Daniel Webster and His New Hampshire Neighbors* (1850), *Correspondence between Lydia Maria Child and Governor Wise and Mrs. Mason, of Virginia* (1860), as well as such historic exchanges as Sparks compiled—the literary correspondence did not importantly arise from American sources before Charles Eliot Norton's 1883 *Correspondence of Thomas Carlyle and Ralph Waldo Emerson*.

The transition from old-fashioned to modern forms of letter publication is indeed well illustrated by the printing of Emerson's correspondences, beginning with Norton's edition of the Emerson-Carlyle exchange and concluding, in 1995, with Eleanor Tilton's final supplement to the volumes edited by Ralph L. Rusk. Although Emerson was predictably the subject of a life-and-letters biography in James Elliot Cabot's *A Memoir of Ralph Waldo Emerson* (1887), his well-known exchange with Carlyle and other men of letters stimulated a fortunate interest in his many longstanding epistolary friendships. *The Correspondence of Thomas Carlyle and Ralph Waldo Emerson*, the first substantial offering of Emerson's letters, was followed by volumes of his exchanges with John Sterling, Herman Grimm, Samuel Gray Ward, William Henry Furness, and Arthur Hugh Clough. Except for the Furness, edited by H. H. Furness and published in 1910, and the Clough, coedited by Howard Lowry and Ralph Rusk and published in 1934, the editions of Emerson's correspondences were aimed at an educated but not a rigorously scholarly audience who would require a literal text; in the Sterling, Grimm, and Ward as well as in the Carlyle one finds false starts eliminated, ampersands rendered as "ands," proper names suppressed, and paragraphs detailing quotidian and business concerns left out, often without indication of excise.[24]

Building on what, for all its limitations, was still a progressive legacy of letter publication, Ralph L. Rusk's six-volume *Letters of Ralph Waldo Emerson* (1939) printed documents not previously published or published only fragmentarily. Working almost exclusively from holographs, Rusk endeavored "to print a literal text, with no interpolated corrections or apologies" (LRWE 1:v). Such method contrasted conspicuously with that of Norton, yet Rusk did not reprint the letters to Carlyle already published in the 1883 edition of the Carlyle-Emerson correspondence even though the rigor that he was bringing to *The Letters of Ralph Waldo Emerson* must have made the inadequacies of Norton's efforts painfully clear. The task of reediting and supplementing the Carlyle-Emerson correspondence was completed in 1964 by Joseph Slater, who, while acknowledging that Norton's previous edition of the letters was "well suited to its time and purpose," claims in turn to have treated the letters "as if they were sacred scripture" (CEC v). Emerson letters continued to appear after Rusk and Slater had published their volumes; moreover, there were texts previously printed in many other publications that Rusk had cited but not included in his edition. In an effort to collect the new and previously unincluded Emerson letters, Eleanor Tilton contributed the supplementary volumes 7 through 10 of *The Letters of Ralph Waldo Emerson* between 1990 and 1995. Working with a technologically more resourceful page, Tilton is able to represent the genetic condition of the text more fully than does Rusk. With her four volumes, more than a century of complementary editing and reediting of Emerson's letters has reached a tentative conclusion.

The editions of Slater, Rusk, and Tilton print "genetic text": the fullest possible representation of the uncorrected holograph wherever the holograph is available. The printed text reports the compositional features of the manuscript (false starts, deletions, insertions, misdatings, misspellings) with commentary that accounts for the manuscript's history and identifies its location—standard practice in publications meant to facilitate research. *The Letters of Ralph Waldo Emerson* additionally provides a running catalogue of nonextant letters known or thought to have existed. Genetic text is not the only modern editorial option, however. In editing the Adams letters, Samuels, Levenson, Vandersee, and Winner elect a "clear text" method of transcription in which inscription errors ("*to* for *too*, *it* for *at*") are corrected silently, while Adams's own corrections—of which there are few—are noted but not represented in what is printed as the letter text (LHA 4:xxx).[25] The clear-text presentation of Adams's letters is consistent with the "control" ("not a single serious crossed-out passage") that is everywhere "evident in the way the letters are inscribed" (LHA 1:xxx). The editors of *The Letters of Henry Adams*, while supplying the apparatus for further research, print, group, and introduce letters in such a way as to convey a belief that what they publish is on a par with Adams's supreme literary accomplishments.[26] Constrained by budgetary considerations to exclude 1,767 of 4,652 extant letters, they have made choices that reflect the range and literary quality of Adams's correspondence and that contribute to the collection's overall narrative continuity.

Like the Slater, Rusk, and Tilton editions of the Emerson letters, the Johnson edition of the Dickinson letters are printed as genetic text (her nonstandard capitalizations, spellings, and contractions are printed as they appear in the holograph), although new scrutiny of the subtleties of the Dickinsonian manuscript has prompted reevaluations of Johnson's representation of the holograph.[27] Whatever their differences, proponents of genetic-text, clear-text, or what the editors of the innovative *Mark Twain's Letters* call "plain text" methods mostly concur in what constitutes the basic integrity of the documentary unit from which letter volumes are built.[28] What distinguishes these approaches from earlier letter publication is the methodology with which they proceed, in which scrupulous reference is made to the holograph that is the text's source. Variously represented in the print medium, the holograph is routinely identified as an artifact that readers may examine in an archive. All of these volumes print whole letters or as much of a letter as survives.

The difference between modern and antiquated editing is more immediately obvious in the treatment of individual letters than in the scheme that compiles and groups them. As productions meant to foster research as well as appreciation, modern academic letter volumes have been produced on various scales and according to a variety of organizational principles. What at a given time can be printed of an author's epistolary writing is not determined on scholarly grounds alone; production costs and anticipated sales nearly always constrain editorial choices. The scale of letter volumes ranges from the complete correspondence (including letters received) of a prolific writer to the selected letters of an occasional writer. When publishing an author's correspondence, editors must decide whether to group letters in discrete correspondences (as in the forty-two-volume *Horace Walpole's Correspondence*) or to merge all letters in a single chronological sequence. Although volumes of letters usually focus on the practice of one author, two or more authors on occasion share equal billing; less frequently, volumes of letters are published that represent a community of letter writers. Henry Adams is represented in all three configurations: as a member of an epistolarily active family in *A Cycle of Adams Letters, 1861–1865*, as a single prolific author in the six-volume Harvard *Letters of Henry Adams* (an edition that supersedes a two-volume edition of the same title), and as a partner in *The Correspondence of Henry James and Henry Adams, 1877–1914.*

All three placements serve modern purposes in the publication of personal correspondence. Yet alternate contextualizations of a writer's letters raise questions—not only concerning which context exhibits letters to best advantage (and what in fact constitutes "best") but also in regard to this genre's unusual dependence on context. What in view of contextualizations made possible by CD-ROM we might call the multiple interface of a letter is a central fact of its genre identity, its aesthetic possibility, and its scholarly value as an artifact of cultural memory. How to represent the community of utterance with which letters, as overtly conversational texts, once connected is a problem that has produced no definitive solution. However the boundaries of such a context are marked, it can never be documented in its totality—much of it in any event will have vanished without a trace—but only synecdochized through various strategies of suggestion. Again, inclusivity has emerged as the preeminent objective in the modern academic publication of letters, but editors have been more successfully inclusive in their attempt to print whole single letters than in their design to print the entirety of a surviving epistolary output or correspondence, where scale must conform to budget.

Where editors have been innovative and budgets generous, the trend toward greater inclusivity has produced striking results. A publication like *Mark Twain's Letters* (part of the massive project known as the Mark Twain Papers) redefines what is meant by inclusive, for what distinguishes these volumes is not only an effort to print all of Clemens's personal and business letters but an attempt—well served by digital-age typography and graphics—to register the fine details of autograph copy in the transcribed text and textual commentary. Surviving envelopes likewise receive account. Although it has long been the custom to represent the holograph by transcribing words as authors misspelled them or by including a photograph (in older publications, a facsimile) of a manuscript, the Twain volumes attempt to represent all letters in something approaching their total artifacticity. An ambition that might easily have resulted in pages cluttered with struck passages and superscribed afterthoughts has instead produced a print artifact that is both extremely complex and highly intelligible, once one has mastered an extensive typographical code. We are thus unusually challenged to note the art with which the editing, transcription, and print setting has proceeded and to consider the aesthetic and ideology of what the volumes achieve.

What purposes are served by such broad inclusivity and micro-representation? Clearly *Mark Twain's Letters* commends itself to scholars who wish to examine letters as objects that signify as much by what has been erased or struck out as by what has been legibly inscribed or by the various pen styles an author might adopt on a given occasion. Yet there may be more to such a project than providing specialists far from an archive with research material. What a publication like this compels is the examination of reading habits that have become receptive to writings that are unfinished by the standards normally applied to published texts. These writings are preserved in a state of irresolution by editors who not only refuse to smooth phrases and regularize spellings but who, by printing canceled lines and superscribed insertions, represent a literary artifact in a way that encourages readers to construct the narrative of how the text proceeded through its various, if (by virtue of such inclusions) undiscarded, stages of refinement. In a production like the Twain volumes, we are presented not only with letters but with the process of their writing. Owing wholly to the existence of the volume of letters, and through no design on the part of their author, that process becomes performance as readers observe the author pen a word, reconsider it, strike it out, and write another.

In consequence of our intensified documentation of literary artifacts an aesthetic has evolved in appreciation of the performative dimensions of the "unfinished" text, an aesthetic that prizes the foregrounding of the compositional process. How we come at any moment to represent a genre like the letter exhibits the range of our changing attitudes toward literary discourse: preference of the unretouched text is consistent with the postmodern suspicion of the romantic and high-modernist ideologies of the organic and perfect verbal icon. And yet, postmodern as a publication like *Mark Twain's Letters* is, there are ways in which even the most sophisticated collections of letters conserve older notions of literary production. As scholars have become increasingly committed to publishing letters in their entirety, and as print technology has become proficient in representing both the autograph text and its genetic context (biographical and historical references, excerpts from correspondence to which a letter responds), the resulting publications give greater evidence of a discourse that exceeds anything containable within book covers or anything to be explained in terms of a single life. Still, new letter volumes, like old letter volumes, emplot that discourse with reference to an author's biography and contain it within an artifact that, howsoever raised to new powers of representation, is nevertheless the bound book: an object that differs from the autograph missives generated by the unbounded discourse of the epistolary exchange.

The life and the book: these remain the organizing principles of our greatly expanded print capacity to represent the products of epistolary practice. The more inclusive the scheme, the more manifest the tension between the texts and the strategies that would embrace them. The transcribed texts of letters are ever at odds with the unities of the book and the life: they refer constantly to the dialogical process, the multiauthorial exchange that constitutes their primary private context. Insofar as they address others, even the letters of a single-author volume lead away from the view of a life as singular; the texts persist as fragments of an unbounded and ever collaborative discourse. The argument of an edition like *Mark Twain's Letters* is that the value of its contents rises in proportion as the book is able to construct a memory of the manuscript artifact, whose discursive space is not that of the book that would contain it. While documenting the existence of that space, and foregrounding the artifice of its containments, *Mark Twain's Letters* nevertheless affirms the presumed biographical coherence that is the completed life of Samuel Clemens, whom the transcriptions—printed with photographs of the author and his family, contemporaries, and residences—insistently reify. What results is a kind of print reliquary of the author.

Inasmuch as our increasingly inclusive letter volumes put us in view of an unbounded and seldom fully recoverable exchange, we must approach the problem of formulating an aesthetic of the letter with reference to the discourse that letters indicate beyond the most technologically impressive volume's powers of representation. This is something that much recent literary theory, emphasizing the systemic discursive practice over the reified instance, prepares us to do. An expanded vision of epistolary discourse is encouraged, moreover, by new modes of publication that produce a quantum increase in the representation of unboundedness.[29] If, in the advent of electronic retrieval systems, we are well along in a transitional period that will see the obsolescence of the book, we may confidently predict that the multivolume edition of letters will be one of the first bound publications to go. Ultimately, epistolary discourse extends beyond what even hypermedia formats have the capacity of offering as the manifold interface of a letter within a body of multiple intersecting correspondences. Yet electronic publication will doubtless enhance our ability to recover the dialogicity of a letter's occasion, and transform our habits and experience of reading authentic epistolary works.

Letters on CD-ROM will not change the fact that we come to these texts as nonreciprocating readers of other people's mail, and there will remain as always the question of whose aesthetic defines this genre: that of the letter writers, insofar as we can reconstruct it, or that of the nonreciprocating reader—or, more truly, what combination of the two. That many readers of correspondence on screen are apt to be electronic mail correspondents with little experience of the rhythms of a conversation conducted by letter sheet may itself offer problems of aesthetic interference. Yet, however much we attempt to reconstruct a letter's history, it is impossible not to appropriate the productions of an earlier period according to the values of a present reading. Given the situationality of their poetics, the multicontextuality of their potential placements, and the material transformations they undergo in becoming published texts, letters commend themselves to a broad range of readerly protocols. Epistolary texts extend through various fields of aesthetic expectation and possibility; letter publication increasingly represents the diversity of those fields in addition to constituting new fields themselves.

Ultimately, then, we must place the familiar letter amid an intertextuality that exceeds any one aesthetic or generic field and that does not readily answer to the containments of the life or the book. Admittedly, such a placement may appear like a refusal to place, and to fall back on the argument that genre categories belie the intertextual, unstable, and transgressive behavior that language consistently exhibits. No utterance is wholly contained by the recognizable form and instituted use of a particular genre; words, phrases, and the texts that comprise them always exist among frames of reference that far exceed the purview of any user or specific application. In its intersubjectivity, its habit of quotation, its liquid form, its propensity to act as a solvent in its contact with other genres, the letter, perhaps more than any other form of writing, enacts a recognition of the tendency of language to leak from established placements into the interstitial space of informal occasion, trial and error, play, and reinvention.

Still, individual letters are inscribed *objects*, and as we imagine the discursive expanse, we must keep in mind the material artifacts whose dialogue invokes it. Letters, like letter writers, exist as bodies in time and space, and the manner in which the letter text refers to the artifact's materiality articulates the material and indeed mortal condition of the letter writer. The holograph exchange profoundly determines the thematic emphases of letter writing as a generic practice. To these material dimensions we must now turn.

THE MATERIALITY OF THE LETTER EXCHANGE

"I write you many letters with pens which are not seen," Emily Dickinson remarks to Elizabeth and Josiah Holland in November 1854. "Do you receive them?" (LED 1:309). A longing for transcendental or telepathic contact—mind speaking to mind without the intermediary of paper and ink—appears in numerous nineteenth-century correspondences. The motif draws attention to what letter writers often perceive as the discouragingly material condition of epistolary relations. That condition is most obviously reflected in the perilous conveyance of messages fashioned to cross the expanse of space and time that separates correspondents. Yet even when letters do arrive there is no assurance that they will be read in the spirit in which they are written, that the words themselves will not compound the geographic distance. Consciously projecting an impossible ideal, the letter writer's fantasy of unmediated converse proposes an intersubjective accord beyond the complications of time and space, spoken and written language.

Dickinson's "pens which are not seen" alludes to 2 Corinthians 4:17–18, verses that affirm a compensatory other world: "For our light affliction . . . worketh for us a far more exceeding and eternal weight of glory; while we look not at the things which are seen, but at the things which are not seen: for the things which are seen are temporal; but the things which are not seen are eternal." Parodic of pulpit discourse as Dickinson's paraphrase may be, it articulates a fear often expressed in letters of this period that correspondents may at any time find themselves abruptly separated by more than geographic space. "Where in the world art thou?—or hast thou flown away to Paradise, naughtiest Dove, without bidding thy husband farewell?" So Nathaniel Hawthorne begins a letter of May 1840 to his fiancée Sophia Peabody, whose exact location is unknown to him although he is quite certain that she is somewhere in Boston visiting friends: "my spirit knows not whereabout to seek thee, and so it shivers as if there were no *Thou* at all—as if my Dove had been only a dream and a vision, and now had vanished into unlocality and nothingness." A viable correspondence is grounded in a reciprocal sense of locality and somethingness; lacking confirmation of that sense, the text of this letter focuses entirely on the apparent disruption of the exchange. "I know not whereabouts this letter will find thee; but I throw it upon the winds," Hawthorne writes, "in the confidence that some breeze of Heaven will bear it to thee; for I suppose heart never spoke to heart, without being heard, and sooner or later finding a response."[30]

The pen that is not seen, the heart that speaks inerrantly, are metaphors for an intent to communicate that would defy the materiality and mortality of the world. Besides expressing a tentative faith in telepathic channels, such figures acknowledge the extent to which letter writing is constituted by the material means of epistolary transmission. Far from being extrinsic to the text, the materiality of the letter exchange is an abiding component in the poetics and narrative of epistolary relations. Intensely present to correspondents in the form of hand-inscribed letter sheet that arrives to the relief, dread, ecstasy, annoyance, or indifference of the recipient, across a vastly variable spatial and temporal expanse that contributes its own decided (if often irrecoverable) inflection to the letter's initial meanings, that materiality is inevitably absent in published volumes of letters, where, amid pages of transcribed text, it is but meagerly represented by various genetic-text protocols and by photographs or facsimiles of sample holographs.

The holograph speaks as no transcription can. Letter sheet freshly drawn from the envelope at once reifies a correspondent's presence and the absence that has motivated the epistolary exchange. A letter's materiality consists most evidently in the inscribed document itself but also, if less tangibly, in the circumstances of its inscription, transmission, and reception, considerations that involve the education and socioeconomic standing of correspondents, postal technologies, and many other contingent conditions. Still, in the holograph we confront the correspondence in its greatest material density, and much of that density derives from the fact that letters embody their authors. In *A Lover's Discourse*, Barthes discusses the semiosis of the epistolary manuscript, citing such features as the tear blot's certification of the lover's sorrow.[31] Although love letters intensively cultivate contiguities between the bodies of correspondents and the body (and text) of correspondence, it is by no means only the erotic exchange that fetishizes the letter object. The letter's materiality affords many opportunities for exporting the bodily trace. The author's embodiment in the letter and the text's reference to the material condition of the exchange occur in all manner of letters and take various form in the spatiotemporal meditations to which such reference gives rise. What the letter signifies as an artifact embodying its author is apt, moreover, to change over time, and an important material consideration has to do with what often exists for letter writers as the troubling existence of an accumulated correspondence: the manuscript exfoliation of the epistolary relationship.

The progressive dematerialization of epistolary media in our own time puts us in a unique position to recognize the place of the body in older correspondence. Letter writing in pre-electronic eras would have been unthinkable in the absence of a body of correspondence that, for those engaged in the epistolary exchange, existed in a state of contiguity with the bodies, minds, and souls of correspondents. Although one could always make a copy of a letter—Emerson, for example, copied passages into his journals from many letters sent and received—and although letters might be transcribed and published after a correspondence had run its course, text was not routinely abstracted from the usually singular body (ink, letter sheet, sealing wax, envelope) to which it was consigned. In pre-electronic mailings, the reproduction of a text did not figure in the process of transmission; what correspondents sent was an object that passed from one set of hands to another. Like the telegraph before it, the fax removes the materiality of the exchange: as a facsimile appears on the recipient's paper, the original document remains with the sender. Messages that pass from one visual display terminal to another—in the next room or on another continent—take the process of epistolary dematerialization a step further.

By contrast, the inscribed letter often communicates in ways that depend absolutely on the conceit of the sender's embodiment in the artifact sent. Having received a letter from Sophia Peabody at the Boston Custom House, Hawthorne portrays himself as responding first to the power it exerts as an artifact; Sophia's message, the essential meaning of which is in any case mutely conveyed by the substance of the epistolary object, is of secondary concern. "Belovedest," he writes in what he represents as the pleasure of its initial reception, "I have folded it to my heart, and ever and anon it sends a thrill through me; for thou has steeped it with thy love—it seems as if thy head were leaning against my breast."[32] In the text of the letter the correspondent's embodiment typically comes across in metonymic turns of phrase whereby the letter artifact becomes identified with its sender and/or recipient: "Here *you* are, *your Christmas letter!*" writes Henry Adams to

Elizabeth Cameron (LHA 3:596; italics added); "I kiss *my paper* here *for you*," Emily Dickinson writes Elizabeth Holland, ". . . would it were cheeks instead" (LED 2:330; italics added). The figural identification of the absent correspondent with the mailed object takes as its occasion the theatrical presence of the object; for correspondents, that object constitutes the actual bodily extension of the sender or recipient.

In eras when letters were always handwritten, the bodily trace of a correspondent stood before one on the sheet, so that the state of a partner's health might be read in the steadiness of his or her inscription. "I rejoice to think from the tone of your letter," writes Margaret Fuller to a convalescent Caroline Sturgis, "and still more the appearance of your hand-writing that *you* must be better."[33] Handwriting images actual bodily presence.[34] Responding to the sight of a hand familiar to him for thirty-six years, Thomas Carlyle writes Emerson in 1870: "Three days ago I at last received your Letter. . . . Indeed it is quite strangely interesting to see face to face my old Emerson again, not a feature of him changed, whom I have known all the best part of my life" (CEC 561). No doubt Carlyle refers here in part to the consistently gracious character of his correspondent's epistolary attention, an attention the more impressive as it came between lengthening intervals of silence. To speak of seeing one's correspondent "face to face," moreover, is in keeping with what has been a commonplace of epistolary relationships at least since the seventeenth century: that an exchange of letters should imitate—or provide the written equivalent of—conversation between two individuals physically present to one another.[35] Such a remark may also have been prompted by the fact that the features of Emerson's handwriting remained virtually unchanged over nearly four decades, and that Carlyle possesses letter sheet freshly bearing Emerson's inscribing presence.

"Hand" commonly served as a synonym of "penmanship" and "signature." It is in view of an exchange of handwritten communication that we should read Emily Dickinson's response to a letter from a cousin of Judge Otis Lord the year after Lord's death: "To take the hand of my friend's friend, even apparitionally, is a hallowed pleasure" (LED 3:860). Letter writing, Dickinson recognizes, may be an exchange of apparitions; to receive the handwritten note of her (deceased) "friend's friend" is not quite the same as grasping his hand, just as contact with Lord's cousin is not the same as contact with Lord. Yet what she speaks of as a "hallowed pleasure" is not apparitional. Lord's presence, although mediated by the handwriting of his cousin, is nevertheless real for her: the inscribed letter sheet palpably manifests the writer's nodal location amid an inclusive spiritual network. For Dickinson, material letters may have existed as the confirmation of absences for which one might wish telepathic compensation, but the artifact possessed a physicality of a piece with the body that shaped it, a body that moved at the behest of a soul subject to various intimations. A letter bespoke its author in diverse ways. In an early epistolary performance, Dickinson ascribes her maculate letter sheet to the wickedness of her character: "Dont see the *blot*, Susie. It's because I *broke the Sabbath!*" (LED 1:183). Defiantly, she calls attention to the blemish and lets it stand.

Some Dickinson holographs bear the imprint of flowers pressed for enclosure within the leaves of the letter, and a significant portion of her surviving epistolarium consists of notes that accompanied gifts of flowers and bread—the gift often cited, in the accompanying note, as indicative (metonymically) of sender, receiver, or both.[36] The insistent artifacticity of communications that would embody themselves not only in the expressive strokes of the pen—blots and all—but in nontextual objects that the sender has selected or made contrasts strikingly with Dickinson's well-known characterization of the epistolary interchange: "A Letter always feels to me like immortality because it is the mind alone without corporeal friend" (LED 2:460). To the extent that the geographic separation of correspondents prefigures their mutual death to one another, a letter anticipates the life that persists beyond the body's deprivation. Throughout Dickinson's surviving letters, the relationship to be established in the absence of the corporeal friend alternates between protocols of embodiment and a disembodiment that insists upon "the mind alone"—that would prefer letters written "with pens which are not seen," signifying the correspondents' "immortality." Consistently she designates the corporeality of her often mixed epistolary media as coextensive with the bodies of the correspondents, yet almost as consistently does she withdraw from the notion that the relationship depends on materials akin to the flesh.

Dickinson is not alone in associating epistolary contact with immortality, and immortality with an unmediated, sympathetic contact of which the best letters give a foretaste. Writing to George and Georgiana Keats with news of brother Tom's death, John Keats conflates the distance that now separates him from Tom with the oceanic expanse that divides him from George and Georgiana, recent émigrés to America: "sometimes I fancy an immence separation, and sometimes, as at present, a direct communication of Spirit with you. That will be one of the grandeurs of immortality—There will be no space and consequently the only commerce between spirits will be by their intelligence of each other—when they will completely understand each other." In other letters Keats is less interested in commerce between spirits, and the material dispatch becomes instrumental for utterances that invoke the medium of the body in its erotic aspect—invoke it while mourning its absence. Thus he implores Fanny Brawne to write a letter to him: "make it rich as a draught of poppies to intoxicate me—write the softest words and kiss them that I may at least touch my lips where yours have been."[37] In a letter to Fanny's mother written as Keats waited out his ship's quarantine in Naples Harbor shortly before his death, the degree to which the material letter counts as an extension of the body becomes grimly manifest in the poet's remark that the ship's letters were "liable to be opened for the purpose of fumigation at the Health Office." The holograph's discoloration suggests that measures were indeed taken to render it an uncontagious medium.[38]

Immortality, mortality, and the tenuous character of earthly contacts constitute a principal theme of letter writing, a theme that is metonymically reinforced in the text's reference to the letter's artifacticity and to its imperiled passage through time and space. Space between letter writers, particularly in older correspondences, is commonly imaged, and the images do much to remind us that such intervening distance, and the time required for people or letters to traverse it, offered a density whose resistance has been mitigated by instantaneous telecommunication and by the fact that it now takes hours where it once took days or weeks to make a transcontinental or transoceanic passage. These images are moments in the unfolding self-reflexive narrative of the letter exchange that correspondents more or less explicitly create and that functions as a metonym of their continuing relationship. Not surprisingly, the material frailty of a discourse that depends on complex, accident-prone postal procedures becomes a fixation, reflecting the contingent state of the letter writer's daily circumstance. "It is a long time since I have seen or heard from you," Betsy Bayley writes from Oregon to her sister in Ohio, "and I don't know whether I am writing to the dead or the living. There is a vast distance between us; the Rocky mountains separate us." At the close of this long letter detailing the trials of emigration over the Oregon Trail in 1845, she writes, conscious of the conditionality of the exchange: "If you receive this write me."[39]

Space between correspondents is measured less by miles than by their respective accessibility to one another. Thus Emily Dickinson, an agoraphobe who only selectively entertained visitors in Amherst, might receive a letter with a Boston postmark and marvel over the "immortality" that the letter intimates insofar as all space for her has become unnegotiable, all distant persons physically inaccessible unless they come to her. And yet any experience of confinement to a place where the absence of others is acutely felt can render intervening space metaphysical. In a letter written in 1830 from Lowell, Massachusetts, to her parents in Rochester, New Hampshire, Sarah Hodgdon, the teen-age mill worker cited earlier, quotes the following verses:

Although we are so far apart
if you die there and I die here
before one God we shall apeare.[40]

Commonplace as these sentiments are, they evince a habit of viewing the world as held together by a divinity whose omnipresence recalls individuals from a living death in which sorrow is identified with separation. In the next chapter, we will see how pervasive such views are and how often the letter becomes their occasion for utterance.

Even for the comparatively cosmopolitan Emerson, already a seasoned traveler in young manhood, vast expanses make for daunting images, particularly when the means of epistolary contact fail of their purpose, for in a world that lacks telecommunication such failures occur in a void that forbids explanation. "I am concerned at not hearing from you," Emerson writes Carlyle in April 1836.

I have written you two letters one in October, one in November, I believe, since I had any tidings of you. Your last letter is dated 29 June '35. I have counted all the chances of delay & miscarriage of letters and still am anxious, lest you are ill, or have forgotten us. . . . I thought I had made the happiest truce with sorrow in having the promise of your coming—I was to take possession of a new kingdom of virtue & friendship Let not the new wine mourn. Speak to me out of the wide silence. (CEC 142)

Emerson has not heard from Carlyle: in the unpleasant but common experience of letter writers his dispatch has not brought the reply called for in the unwritten epistolary contract that, following the model of conversation, obliges one to respond when addressed. But neither has a second letter brought the desired reply. Skeptical that two letters should have miscarried, Emerson considers other explanations: that Carlyle is ill, that Carlyle has "forgotten" his American friends—that he no longer takes such thought of them as would uphold their existence for him. With the suspension of correspondence, Emerson's plans for Carlyle's American visit (a proposition that, as Emerson may have suspected, commanded little of Carlyle's actual enthusiasm) fall in abeyance. The narrative that from Emerson's perspective binds their friendship is at a crisis; having speculated on how the story is to continue, Emerson, as he must, appeals to Carlyle, and through exactly those means that so worrisomely appear to have failed. In the concluding image, space for Emerson becomes wide with the absence of the partner's inscribed voice, without which the correspondence must catastrophically end.

In time, correspondents adjust their expectations of one another if the writing is to go forward. Emerson and Carlyle soon became inured to lapses in exchange; ultimately it would be Emerson rather than Carlyle who would require multiple appeals to reply. Both recognized that delay and loss of contact were possibilities intrinsic to epistolary relations, and, in the manner characteristic of much letter writing of their period, both perceived such disruption as one more feature of the death experience of the phenomenal world. Each successful exchange of letters represented a triumph prophetic of the final victory of spirit over death. From the start, the Emerson-Carlyle correspondence was conceived sub specie aeternitatis as contact between "brother souls": "Judge," Carlyle asks in his first reply to Emerson, "if I am glad to know that there, in Infinite Space, you still hold by me" (CEC 101). In a letter of September 1836 to Carlyle, the same Emerson who so recently felt neglected apologizes in the following terms for what he perceives as his own delay: "My Dear Friend,—I hope you do not measure my love by the tardiness of my messages. I have few pleasures like that of receiving your kind and eloquent letters. I should be most impatient of the long interval between one and another, but that they savor always of Eternity, and promise me a friendship and friendly inspiration not reckoned or ended by days or years" (CEC 147). Later in life, wholly accustomed to their irregularity of contact, Carlyle and Emerson would agree that the lapses themselves should be a form of speech—that their bond depended not at all on letter sheet and human language. "You must always thank me for silence," Emerson writes in July 1851, "be it never so long, & must put on it the most generous interpretations" (CEC 469). Breaking a three-year silence in 1869, Carlyle writes to

Emerson: "That you made no answer I know right well means only, 'Alas, what can I say to him of consolatory that he does not himself know!'" (CEC 554). Herein the correspondents affect an ultimate, space-defying, if not quite telepathic understanding, a mutual sympathy that tacitly suppresses the friends' irreconcilable political and philosophical differences. Yet such declarations of confidence in the partner's active remembrance of the other are utterances by which the correspondence audibly reassures itself, and the silence admits of generous construction only within the context of a continuing, paper-borne dialogue.

Such dialogue is truly sustained only by the dramatic and generally affirming event of a letter's arrival at its destination. The attempt on the part of Emerson and Carlyle to deny their friendship's dependence on a material exchange is a provision taken against anxieties that gather in the long intervals between letters. That space can be crossed by such material objects is in fact a marvel that encourages transcendental views of friendship: "as the Atlantic is so broad and deep," Carlyle asks early in the correspondence, "ought we not rather to esteem it a beneficent miracle that messages can arrive at all; that a little slip of paper will skim over all these weltering floods" to arrive at last in the postman's hand "like green leaf in the bill of Noah's Dove?" (CEC 112). But an arrangement that at some moments appears miraculous and capable of world-renewing effect seems, at other moments, a terrible constraint on human relationship, and what is celebrated as the continued presence of the friend out *there* in infinite space is in other moods dolefully mourned as the friend's absence *here*. In the midst of a recitation of troubles that had kept him from writing sooner, Carlyle observes, "I must not speak of these things. How can I speak of them on a miserable scrap of blue paper? Looking into your kind eyes with my eyes, I could speak: not here" (CEC 172). The paper—no "green leaf" in this instance but a much more material and degraded "miserable scrap"—is the metonymic figure of Carlyle's separation from Emerson's kindness (imaged corporeally as his "kind eyes"), and is represented as a token of the distance between them that enforces Carlyle's isolation. This passage contrasts strikingly with one quoted earlier in which Carlyle, on receiving Emerson's letter sheet—and hence finding himself in the role of one with whom a connection is completed—speaks of seeing his friend "face to face."

The difference between the ideal communion that correspondents ask of epistolary relations and the uncertain communication they generally receive appears memorably in the correspondence of Thoreau, for whom the arrival of a letter was no very reassuring event. "However slow the steamer," he affirms on receiving a transatlantic letter from Emerson, "no time intervenes between the writing and the reading of thoughts," but the phenomenal medium of those thoughts' conveyance is a matter of troubled fascination and a source, finally, of metaphysical dissonance. "It is hard to believe that England is so near as from your letters it appears," he writes in his next letter to Emerson, "and that this identical piece of paper has lately come all the way from there hither, begrimed with the English dust which made you hesitate to use it; from England, which is only historical fairyland to me, to America, which I have put my spade into, and about which there is no doubt."[41] Like Carlyle, Thoreau marvels over the fact that letter sheet may pass from one person to another over a great distance, but whereas Carlyle regards his incoming mail as an object guided by, and perhaps invested with, powers that defy the perdition that must otherwise claim such vessels of human purpose, Thoreau interrogates the vessel's credentials. In speaking of "this identical piece of paper," he exhibits a suspicion that an object's identity must cease when removed from its original neighborhood, and the ghostly or apparent identity that the letter sheet suggests to him becomes an occasion to meditate on difference and misconnection. The begrimed English paper is not reconcilable to its American destination. What being, Thoreau asks, may the exanimate "dust" of a "historical fairyland" share with the live indubitable soil into which, in the radical present of the New World, he sinks his spade? Is it possible, Thoreau seems implicitly to question, that Emerson can write back from such a place and still be Emerson? Communication between the two men is in any case degraded and disrupted. "You must excuse me," Thoreau writes in closing, "if I do not write with sufficient directness to yourself, who are a far-off traveler. It is a little like shooting on the wing, I confess."[42] Against his previous affirmation that letter reader and letter writer unite in the universal mind, Thoreau verifies that time, dust, paper, and incredulity—a basic distrust of the epistolary genre—very much intervene between the writing and reading of thoughts.

Represented in the text of the letter, then, the materiality of the letter exchange reifies the correspondents' absence to one another and the distance between them, even as it embodies the letter writer to the far-off reader, offering something of the addresser's "here" to the addressee's "there." Exchange of letter sheet thus articulates and sub-

stantiates the central paradox of epistolary discourse: that the exchange of personally inscribed texts confirms even as it would mitigate
separation. As much as correspondents affirm their transcendence of
geographic distance or affect, in their letters, a series of sociable visits,
the fact of separation remains and excites the suspicion that separation
between friends is a condition that neither written nor spoken language can bridge. This recognition, driven home by the occasion of
letter writing, prompts Thoreau ultimately to suspect any mediation of
human solitude that does not arise from a profound and nonverbal
consensus antedating all attempts at textual communication. "Dear
Waldo," he begins his next letter to Emerson, the far-off traveler, "For
I think I have heard that that is your name. . . . Whatever I may *call* you,
I know you better than I know your name, and what becomes of the
fittest name—if in any sense you are here with him who *calls*, and not
there simply to be called."[43] This is Thoreau's extreme statement of the
problem: that the "here" and "there" that are not already dissolved in
the correspondents' abiding presence to one another mark a distance
that no amount of letter sheet can effectively bridge. Happily, Thoreau
proceeded in the faith that his correspondents were in some sense with
him "here," or else his letter writing (if not indeed all his writing)
should have been in jeopardy; but his scruple may have combined with
other causes to discourage a prolific epistolary output.

Hawthorne offers a further variation of the proposition that there
exists a universal mind that nullifies the workings of geographic space,
such space as figures in so much pre-twentieth-century letter writing as
a realm of separation and death. The divine *and* human intentionality
to communicate exceeds the merely human medium it has at its disposal. "I am ashamed of this letter," Hawthorne writes to Sophia
Peabody in September 1840: "there is nothing in it, worthy of being
offered to my Dove; but yet I shall send it; for a letter to one's beloved
wife ought not to be kept back for any dimness of thought or feeble-
ness of expression, any more than a prayer should be stifled in the soul,
because the tongue of man cannot breathe it eloquently to the Deity.
Love has its own omniscience; and what Love speaks to Love is com-
prehended in the same way that prayers are."[44] For Hawthorne letter
writing is not only a redundant activity but one that dramatizes the degree to which all language degrades what it is asked to represent. "We
have left expression—at least, such expression as can be achieved with
pen and ink—far behind us," he writes in January 1842. "Even the
spoken word has long been inadequate. Looks—pressures of the lips

and hands, and the touch of bosom to bosom—these are a better language; but, bye-and-bye, our spirits will demand some more adequate expression even than these. And thus it will go on; until we shall be divested of these earthly forms, which are at once our medium of expression, and the impediments to full communion. Then we shall melt into another, and all be expressed, once and continually, without a word—without an effort."[45] Letters, language, the body erotic: all for Hawthorne become emblems of epistolary failure and human mortality.

Other writers inscribe separation in other ways. Writing to Martha and Susan Gilbert during her 1855 absence from Amherst, Dickinson asks, "Which had you rather I wrote you—what I am doing here, or who I am loving *there*?" (LED 2:317). The conversational intimacy with which she poses the question does much to annihilate the distance that the utterance confirms, and the letter as a whole is written in the faith that to be writing here is to be loving the readers there, as the readers in good time must see, and that space may be dominated by such simple grammatical structure as can convert the reader into an object of the writer's verb. Elsewhere Dickinson mitigates the distance by making metaphor of the letter's passage—by assimilating the space between correspondents to the narrative of the epistle's successful journey. At a loss for something poetic to send Susan Gilbert—some conceit in which their sympathies might fully join—Dickinson proclaims that "there will be romance in the letter's ride to you—think of the hills and the dales, and the rivers it will pass over, and the drivers and conductors who will hurry it on to you; and wont that make a poem such as can ne'er be written?" (LED 1:181–82). For Dickinson, however, all such efforts are directed at repressing a fear of separation that commonly comes out in pleas to her correspondent not to die before they can be together again. Fatality haunts the space of separation. In time, Dickinson would act as though death has always virtually overtaken those who are not in physical proximity with her, and thus propose that immortality of one friend to another that had little occasion to declare itself outside the epistolary dimension of the relationship.

Even for the less transcendentally minded, death serves as the occasion of epistolary expression, the condition with which letter writing exists in implicit reference and animating tension. A sentence in a letter Alice James wrote to William James in January 1886, a month after the suicide of Marian (Clover) Hooper Adams, significantly merges the event of Clover's death with the event of Alice James's receiving a letter from Ellen Hooper Gurney, Clover's sister and Alice's friend: "Poor

Clover Hooper's death is sad indeed, a dreadfull shock—it has enabled Ellen, however, to write to me, as Kath. says it evidently takes an immense emotion to make it possible for her to express a lesser one."[46]

A source of everything from vague anxiety to acute anguish, space between correspondents holds immanent if ever uncertain danger, for, short of loss to actual death, there is the possibility of the deathlike loss of a partner to indifference, to a silence that cannot explain itself. What one writes at any moment may deal the correspondence a fatal blow. Having received, in Tautira, Tahiti, a long letter from Elizabeth Cameron in Washington, D.C., Henry Adams fears that any gratitude he expresses for her epistolary attentions must run the risk of culminating in a distinctly unwanted protestation of love. As he registers that fear, he adumbrates the protestation, all the while apologizing for his sentiment's triteness, "which, at a seven thousand mile dilution, is exasperatingly stupid; but you can at least to some degree imagine what sort of emotion I might be likely to feel at having you take me by the hand and carry me on with your daily life till I feel as though I had been with you all the month" (LHA 3:423). Seven thousand miles is as objective a measure of the distance separating correspondents as we are likely to meet with; in this correspondence it has an additional significance deriving from the fact that one of Adams's principal motives for traveling to the South Seas is to remove himself, at Cameron's request, from a nearer proximity to her.[47] The expanse of miles is but one measure of a separation that presents other obstacles to navigation, and what Adams fears is that by stating his love he will write words whose alienating properties cannot be weakened by intervening space.

And for good reason, as he himself testifies to the power of Cameron's letter to abrogate separation, to take him by the hand and lead him through her life as though he had spent the month in Washington with her rather than far away in Tahiti.[48] Had he actually been in Washington, the friends might never have been so fully present to one another, but in his gratitude Adams does not pause to consider the utopian cast of his imagined month with Cameron, and he ventures to secure his attempt to bridge the space between them by an appeal to her powers of empathy: "you can at least to some degree imagine what sort of emotion I might be likely to feel," he writes—and she must imagine it, because for Adams to articulate that emotion is to risk a breach in an intimacy that remains intact as long as the seven thousand miles do not tempt the correspondents into uttering unacceptable if obvious longings. Or, as Adams has in effect devised a means of uttering them, as long as the distance does not prompt correspondents to make such statements without articulating in the same breath bounds that must always be observed. Yet there are limits to how ironically you can inform someone of your love, and Adams posts the letter in full recognition of the danger it invests in their already perilous separation.

Letter exchanges proceed incrementally, against the constant possibility of being discontinued without notice. Even the most placid correspondences inscribe and enact their own ongoing crises and largely live from one letter to the next. Whatever public ambitions an author might have for his or her epistolary writing, autograph letters are written to be read by specific addressees in ephemeral time frames. Only briefly may the materials of a letter seem animated by the contemporaneous spirit of the person who inscribed it; when Carlyle speaks joyfully of beholding Emerson "face to face," it is the freshly arrived letter that he has before him, not any of Emerson's many previous letters filed away in Carlyle's drawer. For others, the intention to communicate may already be betrayed by the deadness of the letter sheet, as Thoreau demonstrates on receiving a letter from Emerson. But however timely or belated letters seem on their arrival, beyond their initial perusal they become documents that make for reading altogether different from the recipient's eager consumption of the text, impelled as that is by an alertness to the text's occasions for anguish and gratification, its running and largely implicit reference to the rapport between correspondents. No subsequent reading of a letter duplicates the first reading, tied as it is to the scene of its reception, its moment in the unfolding narrative of a correspondence. When that scene has dissolved, the addressee may reread; when the narrative has run its course, the letters may disappear, wholly or in part, and the correspondence be forgotten. Or, in what are always exceptional instances, some more or less ample fragment may be preserved in an archive or between book covers or on CD-ROM for nonreciprocating readers.

In the life of an ongoing epistolary relationship, a great deal of paper typically accumulates, and the fate of holographs after they have played their part in a continuing exchange can be a matter of ambivalence, even to authors who have all along expected their letters to be published someday for readers outside the exchange. As crafted as a letter may be—and as much as its craft reflects the published work of canonized letter writers—it exists in reference to a still private relationship. As much as the intimacy of that relationship may reflect intimacies publicized in authentic letters and epistolary novels, its artifacts have yet to be converted into the print medium of a public world. As constituted by an exchange of letters, the private relationship may still be in process of unfolding along various narrative lines, intersecting with other relationships; or, if concluded, it may have arrived at no settled interpretation in the view of its participants. As yet there is probably no unitary text of the correspondence, only exchanged manuscript documents, the halves of conversation. Such documents may exist as the stuff of books, but until that transformation occurs they remain privately signifying artifacts that form no necessary part of anyone else's historical narrative. If they remain in another's possession, letters may represent and objectify a life over which the letter writer may feel an increasing loss of control.

Even among the nonfamous, the practice of preserving letters in view of returning them eventually to their authors or to their authors' heirs was common throughout the nineteenth century. The letters of celebrated personalities constituted property of a more fluid order. Emerson, Carlyle, and their families never doubted that the correspondence between the two great men would be published to a buying readership, and the monetary value of the holographs is confirmed by the black market trade in a number of Emerson's letters that had been stolen from Carlyle's files. Still, while anticipating the publicity of their private correspondence, the celebrated author must continue to address specific recipients and the circumstances of the occasion for writing. The exigencies of the correspondence come first, and this becomes especially evident when authors wish to speak without record of having spoken. In 1872 Emerson advises Carlyle to avoid saying too much to Moncure Conway, "who (this in your private ear,) cannot, in my experience, report a fact or speech as it fell. . . . But he is a good fellow, & bright, & I owe him only good will. So pray burn this note or blot it" (CEC 586). Carlyle did neither, and the confidence utters itself to posterity, accompanied by the footnote that, after Emerson's death, Conway's London detective work resulted in the recovery of most of the purloined Emerson holographs.[49] One never has to look far for such examples of the letter writer's loss of control over the preservation and printing of epistolary remains.

The isolated letter of a celebrated personality may be the subject of intriguing if largely unfounded speculation. Such has been the fate of a note written by Samuel Clemens to my great-grandmother, Franke Carpenter Culp (1850–1937), in response to her evident query regarding Clemens's use of the word *chute* in *Life on the Mississippi*:

Elmira, N.Y. July 28/83
(It is easily forgivable, Madam, anyway!)
It is the French *chute* (fall,) applied in the sense of "short cut." To go
up or down the narrow passage (or *chute*) behind an island is generally a much briefer road than to follow the wide main river around
the *other* side of it—just as it's shorter to shoot past London on the
Thames than it is to travel *around* the city.
        Truly yours
        Mark Twain

Because the recipient had formerly resided in Elmira, and because she
would later establish her own local literary reputation as a contributor
of poetry to newspapers in central and western New York, for years
her descendants spoke of her "correspondence," and even of her
"friendship," with Mark Twain. The text of the letter, however, suggests only that Clemens politely responded to a reader's question; one
notes the omission of a salutation (uncharacteristic of Clemens's letters to friends) as well as an impulse to parade, in the reference to the
Thames, his knowledge of the world. Yet it is hardly surprising that
such a document should give rise to family folklore.

A ready answerer of fan mail, Clemens probably gave no thought to
the conjectural narratives to which a short impersonal dispatch might
give rise. Henry James, by contrast, was far less easy about old un-
destroyed mail, incoming and outgoing. Responding to an inquiry into
his possession of letters written by Sarah Orne Jewett, James writes
that her letters to him have been submitted to the law that in advanced
age he has made absolute: that "of not leaving personal and private
documents at the mercy of any accidents, or even of my executors! I
kept almost all letters for years—till my receptacles would no longer
hold them; then I made a gigantic bonfire and have been easier in mind
since."[50] The bonfire did not consume James's own voluminous output, but so thoroughly are the texts of one practice embedded in those
of another that he could take more than vicarious satisfaction in destroying documents that had originated at other writers' desks. In a
letter written two years before his death, James would declare his "utter
and absolute abhorrence" at the notion that anyone should publish
"any part or parts of my private correspondence."[51] His use of the
words "personal" and "private" articulates his view that a clear distinction exists between private and public discourse—or at least between
his private and his public discourse, for James, in one of the first
reviews of the Emerson-Carlyle correspondence, praised its specifi-

cally literary merits.[52] Yet letter writers commonly view their letters as so close to the self as to require the absolute silencing of the flame. "Please," Emily Dickinson writes to Mary Bowles during a period of frequent exchange, "now I write so often, make lamplighter of me, then I shall not have lived in vain" (LED 2:359); and we cannot doubt that Dickinson directed her sister to destroy her correspondence along with the poems that Lavinia chose rather to preserve.[53] The history of the letter is one marked by famous fires; certainly there have been significant burnings about which little or nothing is known.

The ambivalence of a writer to the accumulating documents of a prolific correspondence is especially pronounced in the case of Adams. Reared in a family in which private papers were retained for their public worth, and which twice published editions of the private correspondence of John and Abigail Adams, Henry Adams brought to his writing desk the consciousness that his letters too should one day reach a public readership. His sense of the ultimate publicity of his correspondence is registered in a letter that Adams addresses to his brother Charles in December 1860 at the onset of the secession crisis. "I propose to write you this winter a series of private letters," he declares in Washington, D.C., ". . . and though I have no ambition nor hope to become a Horace Walpole, I still would like to think that a century or two hence when everything else about us is forgotten, my letters might still be read and quoted as a memorial of manners and habits at the time of the great secession of 1860" (LHA 1:204). To write with the notion that one's letters might be read and quoted "when everything else about us is forgotten" is to be driven by a large ambition indeed, one confirmed by the six large volumes of the Harvard *Letters of Henry Adams* that even so are not a complete collection.

Yet one must be struck by their author's inconstant pursuit of this ambition. Always a voluminous letter writer, Adams is known to have only twice made copies; his part in correspondences carried on with a number of persons has vanished. In several instances he explicitly asks his correspondent to destroy the letters he has sent. "Yesterday your letter arrived, only about a week old," he writes Elizabeth Cameron from the South Seas in 1891 during one of his richest epistolary periods. "Naturally I was pleased, for it was all good news, as your letters always are; whereas mine are so disagreeable, egotistic and yawpy that I quiver at the thought of their existence, and entreat you, in mere kindness to me, to burn them" (LHA 3:567). On March 5, 1900, he would renew his instruction that she destroy his letters.[54]

Elmira, N.Y. July 28/83

(It is easily forgiv-
able, madam, anyway!)
It is the French _chute_ (fall,) applied in the sense of "short-cut."
To go up or down the narrow passage (or _chute_) behind an island
is generally a much briefer
road than to follow the ^wide^ main
river around the _other_ side of it—just
as it's shorter to shoot past London on the
Thames than it is to travel _around_ the city.

Truly Yours
Mark Twain

Samuel Clemens to Franke Carpenter Culp, July 28, 1883.

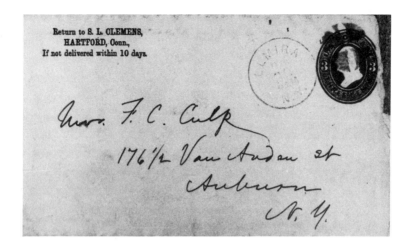

Then, in November 1915, Adams proposes to Cameron that she
produce a volume of correspondence that might serve as a memorial
of their old social set; "I suggest this—supposing you to have preserved the letters,—as much because it would occupy and amuse you
for years, as to immortalise you or us" (LHA 6:704). Was ever a proposition to publish a portion of a major epistolary achievement ever put in
such an offhand manner? However urgently Adams may have felt
about such a project, what might strike us most about this statement is
its subordinate clause: "supposing you to have preserved the letters."
Insofar as he has more than once instructed her to destroy his, it may
surprise us that he can suppose her to have preserved them, but even if
he did mean to be taken at his word, he (a keeper of letters) had reason
to doubt that Cameron could destroy the evidence of his personal
attention to her. But surely it must the more astonish us that so ambitious a letter writer does not even know whether a vast part of his
epistolary opus still exists—until Cameron writes back to tell him that,
although she has destroyed many of her personal documents relating
to their old Washington life, she has "kept every scrap you have ever
written me" and that "they are all in a chest at Stepleton" (LHA 6:704).
Unsorted, uncatalogued, preserved on their sentimental more than on
their literary merit, letters are typically kept in a chest somewhere.
Elizabeth Cameron's practice of selectively ridding and keeping such
papers is common.

Even so, they continue to lead an imperiled existence: not until the
chest is opened, the manuscripts photographed and transcribed, and
the text preserved between book covers or on disk, is this writing

exempt from the material hazards of a private correspondence. And yet a transformation has then occurred, for the tensions that called the correspondence into being no longer exist, the writers having been released from what their letters register as spatiotemporal isolation, the incessant urgencies of the inscribed present tense. The holograph that implores a response, that bears the entreaty "Burn when read," engages in a rhetoric that cannot be duplicated when the transcription appears in print for a readership that stands outside the protocol and options of the live reciprocating exchange. In reading transcribed letters, we are at some level perhaps always aware of such sedimentary reference: the text articulating its confinement to mortal letter sheet and envelope, to the interval of time in which a live voice may speak to a contemporaneous ear. Again and again throughout this book, in the letters of the unknown as of the well-known writer, of the unlettered as of the professionally literate, we will perceive references to a time, a place, and the utterance that aspires to venture beyond. It is by virtue of such confinement, of a piece with the mortality of letter writers, that epistolary voices achieve their distinctive resonance.

2

I Have Taken This Opportunity of Writing You a Few Lines
A Genre as Popularly Practiced

. . . .

As a chapter of Western epistolary history, letter writing in America begins with the communications that early explorers and settlers sent to their sponsors and families in Europe. As European settlement proceeded, correspondence among colonies flourished alongside an increasingly regular transatlantic exchange. The regularization of dispatch over vast land and ocean distances has less to do with the increased reliability of the exchange (although relatively speaking, exchanges did become more reliable) than with the letter writers' accommodation of the uncertainties of corresponding over boundless geographic space. A habituation to the doubtful fate of the transoceanic missive enters into the expression of writers on both sides of the Atlantic. From Leyden, in 1625, Roger White, an expatriate Separatist who has remained in the Netherlands, begins a letter to William Bradford and William Brewster at Plymouth Colony announcing the death of their pastor, John Robinson, as follows: "I know not whether this will ever come to your hands or miscarry, as other my letters have done." Against such discouragement, the need to affirm bonds of community in this as in other letters prevails: "I have had a great desire to write unto you. Knowing your desire to bear a part with us, both in our joys and sorrows, as we do with you."[1]

Correspondents would face similar discouragement for some time to come. From the fifteenth through the eighteenth centuries, and to a considerable extent in the nineteenth as well, letters directed from, to, and within America were not conveyed by anything resembling an organized, efficient, confidence-inspiring postal system. Generally they proceeded by courtesy of overland travelers or ship captains who happened to be going in the direction of the addressee; such unofficial carriers might upon arrival at their destinations leave the letter at a designated drop point, turn it over to a local post, or deliver the letter personally. The stock phrase "I embrace this opportunity to write you a letter" arises in reference to the imminent departure of a person by whom a letter may be sent. The chances of a letter arriving or miscarrying absorb letter writers regardless of the means by which the letter is conveyed. A postal system is not necessarily more reliable than a private arrangement, and until the advent of widely accessible telegraph and long-distance phone systems, confirmation of successful conveyance depended on a single means of communication exchange subject at many points to breakdown. Even after a federal postal system had been created, irregularity in the movement of mail from and within the United States persisted until after the Civil War.[2] From the age of exploration forward, the chance afforded by circumstance to send a letter with some expectation of its arrival in the hands of the intended recipient weighs importantly among the thematic concerns of the epistolary text, as does the experience of letters "miscarrying," the term commonly used in speaking of a letter's loss or delay.

Letter writers who lack reliable postal service learn to make allowance for mischance; they proceed in the assumption that letters are answered as they get through and consent to write five letters on the chance that one might reach the addressee. "I apprehend that this will never reach you yet this apprehension shall not prevent my writing by every opportunity," Abigail Adams assures John Adams in 1778 (AFC 3:109). "I have very little reason to believe in the probability of your receiving my many letters, yet I continue to write with the bare possibility that they may some of them reach you," writes the mother of a Civil War soldier in 1862.[3] However desperate for a reply, however despairing of the post's capacity to convey it, a letter writer must resist questioning the partner's will to requite epistolary attentions, for the exchange economy of the correspondence is founded on a transcendent belief in the mutuality of the will to correspond. One must credit the letter that almost certainly was written but that has not yet and now probably never will arrive. To question the partner's commitment is to bring about a crisis in the correspondence, one that admits of difficult resolution if the flow of letters is obstructed.

The internal exchange economy of a given correspondence, although largely self-sustaining, is tied to and complicated by the social economics of postal systems, and the relation is frequently a matter of implicit and occasionally one of explicit comment. Letters whose delivery was charged to the recipient at a fixed rate per sheet tend to be very full, with sentences winding into margins and script shrinking to fit cramped space. Uninscribed paper is poor economy. "Every line of yours is invaluable to me," Abigail Adams reproves John Adams in 1783, "yet blank paper is not so, and the double covers pay as large postage, as if they were wholy written. . . . I payd 3 dollors the other day for what one sheet of paper would have contain" (AFC 5:260). If the would-be recipient of a letter is poor, one might think twice before sending a letter that would require payment upon delivery; in 1764 Benjamin Franklin discourages his wife from sending a condolence to his sister, Jane Mecom, after she has lost a daughter.[4] A rare indictment of the practices that support an efficient mail occurs in *The Journal of John Woolman*. Appalled by a British system that sacrificed postboys, pedestrians, and horses to rapidity, Woolman, who maintained a prolific personal and pastoral correspondence as a recorded Quaker minister, was willing to forgo communication with his family during his 1772 travel in England rather than have recourse to a grossly exploitative service.[5] Woolman's scruple draws attention to the fact that, although communication between relatives and friends provided assurance and consolation, there was nothing necessarily benign about the labor-intensive industry by which letters were exchanged.

Changes in material conditions often have an inappreciable effect on what it means to send or to receive a letter. Throughout the nineteenth century, the increasing volume of brief communications within American cities and villages indicates the establishment of an efficient local post; after the Civil War, letters were sent and received more rapidly across regions. By the 1860s, the old practice of folding a letter sheet in threes and sealing it with wax gave way to enclosing the sheet in a sealable envelope; in the 1870s, the postcard came into use, and although this created an opportunity for messages to be intercepted by unauthorized readers who would never have thought to break a seal, it gave letter writers who did not wish to engage in banalities fresh opportunities to produce cryptic text.[6] Even with the advent of the telegraph and telephone and the transforming effect such communication technology had on human conceptions of time and space, it is arguable that letter writing exhibits little in the way of a progressive history as a form of discourse. As the examples in this and other chapters show, when it comes to such matters as spatiotemporal isolation, separation from family and friends, the invocation of a transcendental principle of enduring presence, dread of change in the intended recipient, anxiety over the miscarriage of incoming and outgoing mail, longing for reunion, and fear of death, much letter writing of the seventeenth and eighteenth centuries resembles much letter writing of the nineteenth and twentieth.

Even a consideration of who, over the course of several centuries, wrote letters contributes little to a demonstrably progressive history of the genre. With the establishment in America of common schools, an increasing portion of the populace attained the basic literacy that letter writing requires, although with assistance fully illiterate persons could also dictate and receive letters.[7] Politically, the letter as a popularly accessible genre had a distinct role in a representative democracy, and post offices and post roads were mandated by the Constitution for the stated purpose of creating the means by which the public could communicate with elected officials.[8] One measure of how widely practiced the genre had become by the second half of the nineteenth century is the abundance of surviving Civil War correspondence at every level of literary accomplishment and from every region, and the fact that so many exchanges between soldiers and their families were preserved and in some cases printed indicates a readiness to recognize in such documents writing of historical and moral value.[9] Although members of the middle and upper classes enjoyed special privileges in their command of literary fluency and the means to purchase paper, postage, and leisure to write, there was never a time in American history when people without material advantages did not also write letters. In addition to the incentive offered by representative government to acquire the ability to inscribe a political voice, advice books and letter-writers encouraged those aspiring to middle-class status to cultivate an epistolary mastery of the varied occasions of business and domestic life.[10]

My purpose in this chapter is to explore the conditions of letter writing in America through the first decades of the twentieth century and to sample the diversity of those who had occasion to correspond.

The central preoccupation of this book—what over the course of the past five hundred years it has meant to be absent, and what it has meant to be present, to another—will serve as a constant point of reference. As the epistolary practices under discussion are those of a decidedly migrant people, this inquiry assumes a more specific form: How did writers commonly inscribe themselves at the distance their letters were intended to traverse, and what effect did such distance have on their self-representations and the relationships that their letters were intended to confirm or transform? What in the rhetoric of the epistolary text serves to mitigate or exaggerate the effects of geographic separation, and what manner of generational, class, gender, and racial difference do these texts articulate and address? Finally, in anticipation of the lengthy discussions of Emerson, Dickinson, and Adams, in whose letter writing the genre not only becomes highly cultivated but fully theorized, I ask: What evidence of self-conscious practice do letter writers in general manifest, what efforts toward achievement of literary form do they demonstrate, and what theoretical insight into the epistolary genre do they themselves articulate?

MAILINGS FROM EARLY AMERICA

The earliest record of an epistolary communication originating in the New World derives from the log book that would become known as *The Journal of Christopher Columbus*. In an entry of February 14, 1493, following the description of a tempest encountered west of the Azores on the return voyage, "which caused him to fear that Our Lord willed that he should perish there," Columbus, representing himself in the third person, gives this account of writing and mailing a letter to Ferdinand and Isabella: "he took a parchment and wrote on it all that he could about all the things he had found, earnestly begging whomsoever might find it to carry it to the Sovereigns. This parchment he enclosed in a waxed cloth, very carefully fastened, and he commanded a large wooden barrel to be brought, and placed it in it, without any one knowing what it was, for they thought that it was some act of devotion, and he ordered it thrown into the sea."[11] It would be difficult to imagine a more dramatic illustration of the relationship of letter writing to extreme human experience than this desperate attempt to convey the intelligence of newly discovered lands. Momentous as it appears as an episode in the mythology of Columbus and the history his explorations inaugurated, however, the epistolary occasion herein depicted exemplifies a motive commonly associated with letter writing in which vast distance and mortal boundaries figure prominently. The letter written to the Spanish sovereigns and the material conditions of its mailing articulate what other writers in other extremities likewise articulate: *I will compose and dispatch this message if it is the last thing I do*; what at the time is understood by the writer as possibly the final act of life is the production of writing that anticipates a posthumous reading. The consignment of the parchment to the sea, with a barrel to serve as envelope, marks a degree rather than a kind of desperation to communicate.

Another feature of the story is also in keeping with common epistolary rituals: although Columbus intends this communication to become the public proclamation of his discoveries, vindicating his reputation and securing the fortune of his sons for whom he expresses solicitude in the journal entry of February 14, the writing and sending of the letter are pursued in secret. He intends that the conspicuous dispatch of the barrel should pass as "some act of devotion," which he must nonetheless have actually considered it to have been, inasmuch as he looks upon his accomplishment as providential and himself as the personal object of divine favor. From such a viewpoint, providence might well be counted upon to direct the barrel to safe arrival on a receptive shore.

Ironically, the entry of February 14 not only provides an account of the earliest letter from the New World but also registers the first instance of a transatlantic letter lost in transit; as the storm abated, the writer himself survived to pen missives that we may assume to be variations of what the waves failed to deliver. "That eternal God who has given Your Highnesses so many victories now gave you the greatest one that to this day He has ever given any prince." So opens the letter of March 4, 1493; in both that and the well-known letter of February 15 Columbus writes of the fabulous yet materially accessible opportunities that lie across the western horizon—"the trees and fruits and grasses" that he finds both "extremely beautiful and very different from ours," the "marvelous meadows and fields incomparable to those of Castile," the "gold and mines and spicery and innumerable peoples"—a world that, in its manifold difference, "was unknown nor did anyone" in former times "speak of it except in fables."[12] The phrasing betrays the consciousness that the writer himself might be taken as speaking in a fable; as though to discourage such a hearing, Columbus not only itemizes the commodities these islands offer but goes so far as to propose the exchange value of his information: a cardinalate for a son, a royal appointment for a friend, in addition to the generous subsidy of further excursions should he survive. In an effort to assign the occasion of writing to a higher, more compelling authority, from first to last Columbus invokes the God they commonly serve and whose presence extends to the European explorer in all the lands of unlikeness.

In meeting the task of representing his accomplishments before his arrival in Barcelona, Columbus addresses questions that much epistolary writing from the New World to the Old implicitly or explicitly addresses: How does one speak credibly of the new and unknown while conveying the impression that conditions in that world are scarcely to be believed? How does one account for such transformations of the self as success or failure in the venture has effected, and how does one maintain or revise one's European identity, which, in the case of Columbus and many other explorers and colonists, is socially very fluid and heavily invested in projects calculated to elevate class standing? Laden with the Old World language (in which the clichés "marvel" and "fable" signal the inexpressibility of an extreme novelty) and driven by ambitions defined by European religious, philosophical, and political paradigms, how, given the restricted and ever unreliable means of sending and receiving communications, may one presume to present oneself to Europe at the always potentially annihilating distance that the written word must bridge?

To affirm, as Columbus does, that he is in process of returning from the Indies and the coasts of Cathay, to whose islands he has given Spanish names and on whose promontories he has planted the cross, is to proclaim the degree to which the European signifier abrogates what the explorer apprehends as the alien presence of the new lands as well as his absence from the Castilian home scene. He can never (to himself) feel absent from that scene given his engagement in ambitions that exist wholly in reference to it; but his language continually registers the threat of difference, both in its account of the native people whose aspect is comely but whose reputed cannibalism constitutes an underlying menace, and in its evident anxiety over whether the sovereigns will credit the report and duly recognize the magnitude of the accomplishment. In response to circumstances that simultaneously excite sensations of danger and good fortune, Columbus, in writing to Ferdinand and Isabella, constructs a presence that collapses distance: a description of the Indies that stereotypes its otherness and that subjugates the New World, far removed from the Old, to the political will of the sovereigns. Indeed, Columbus expresses even headier ambitions for the conquering of vast space and the difference that renders space dangerous. In the letter of March 4, personal ambition and Euro-centric geography come together in Columbus's proposition that gold mined in the Indies should finance his conquest of Jerusalem, for which he will require "five thousand cavalry and fifty thousand foot soldiers."[13] To conquer the Levant, Columbus asserts, was always the ultimate purpose in opening the western passage to India.

Reflecting a multitude of conditions, letter writers in the New World approached in different ways the task of affirming one's presence far from home while endeavoring to effect a virtual presence in Europe. The common burden of all such communications is to register a self-presence that persuasively asserts a continued relevance to those from whom the writer is absent. In much letter writing from the New World, the European second person is addressed as one who dispenses favor, promotion, supplies, rescue; it is of utmost importance to colonists that European correspondents recognize their existence and accede to their arguments that, by virtue of their enterprising absence from Europe, the New World is materially, politically, and spiritually contiguous with the Old. To the degree that writers can make their absence felt, they perpetuate at a distance their presence in the place of European origin; it is when they are not missed, when their absence has no perceived relevance, that they are in trouble. In their letters home, colonists exhibit a broad range of confidence, but few communications are entirely free of the anxiety that one's being has been absorbed by a world that can have no compelling existence for Europe. Even writers who write with self-assurance and who have little fear of being forgotten insert their often mundane communications between reflex invocations of God, as though nothing could be said without first affirming an ontology that comprehends the writing self and the far-off European addressee.

Inasmuch as the proposition of their corresponding at all is an anxious one, the anxiety betrayed by those who write at a distance from the European sources of being, meaning, and exchange value takes as many forms as there are occasions to correspond. In one of three letters dated August 12, 1585, which together constitute the earliest correspondence from the first North American English settlement, Ralph Lane, a lieutenant-general in the second Roanoke voyage who has been left in charge of the company on Roanoke Island, characterizes his situation in the following terms in a letter to Sir

Francis Walsingham, a prospective patron in the unstable world of colonial sponsorship:

> My selfe haue vndertaken with ye fauoure of God, and in hys feare, with a good compagnye moore aswell of gentlemen as others, to remayene here, ye returne of a newe supply. As resolute rather to loose our lyfes then to deferre a possessione to her Maieste, our Countrey, and that our moost Noble Patrone Sir Water Rawelley.... for myne owne parte [I] doo finde my selfe better contented to lyue with fysshe for my dayely foode, and water for my dayelye dryncke, in ye prosecucione of suche one Accione, then oute of ye same to lyue in ye greateste plenty yt ye Courte coolde gyue mee.[14]

The letter is thick with the rhetoric of doughty resourcefulness and noble self-sacrifice; yet few situations could be more precarious than Lane's on Roanoke Island, where he and his men must increasingly subsist on what the island has to offer while awaiting supplies from England. Not only must the ship reach England, it has also to find its way back, successfully navigating the shoals that surround the island and that very nearly wrecked the flagship at their initial landing. Aware of his utter dependence on the return of English ships, Lane affects a preference for the perilous course and crude fare of the overseas settler in his service to God, Country, Queen, and Raleigh, for whose glory he is willing to lay down his life, yet the letter in every line constitutes a plea that Lane's capacity for sacrifice and accomplishment be recognized and that he not be abandoned in a far corner of the world. Lane moreover has an additional agenda in the letters of August 12. Having become disenchanted with Sir Richard Grenville, the commanding officer of the voyage, he wishes to promote himself to Walsingham and his son-in-law, Sir Philip Sydney, who with Sir Francis Drake have discussed plans to establish a settlement on the coast of North America from which to conduct raids on Spanish possessions in the West Indies. Having arrived in "Verginia" by way of Saint John's and Hispaniola, he has information that renders his proffered services as commanding officer particularly valuable. In another letter of August 12, Lane—whose situation, again, was extremely perilous—characterizes himself to Sydney as the master of formidable and competing exigencies: "My Moost Noble Generalle. Albeyt in ye myddest of infynytt busynesses, As hauing, emungst sauuages, ye chardege of wylde menn of myne owene nacione, Whose vnrulynes ys suche as not to gyue leasure to ye goouernour to bee all most at eny tyme from them.

Neuerthelesse I wolde not omytte, to wryte thes fewe lynes of dewety, and affeccione vnto you."[15] Lane himself is the "governor" referred to in this passage, an unofficial title that he adopts in order to exalt his true office of lieutenant-general. Carefully constructing the image of his own impromptu authority over a situation in which he is obliged to rule over two distinct varieties of "wylde" men, he addresses Sydney as one who undoubtedly has had similar experiences with underlings, and whose sympathy with Lane's position is therefore to be assumed; the self-assured and confidential tone, the characterization of circumstances that require Lane's constant attention to preserve order, seem calculated to produce a text fully able to abridge space and eliminate the uncertainties of a professional relationship by virtue of its compelling vividness. The hard-pressed but capable man in charge has seized the occasion to author a letter in which he aggressively fulfills his "duty" as a subordinate. In his attempt to elect an authority and win favor, Lane elaborately fashions the impression that he, a loyal and resourceful subaltern, has established control of his circumstances: he thereby illustrates one response to a situation in which a European is left to deal with the unknown and dangerous conditions of an un-mapped country, mercurial fellowship, and the absolute exigency of waiting for a supply ship that may or may not arrive.

Other colonists confess their indigence more openly. Writing to his parents in 1623, Richard Frethorne, an indentured servant in the Jamestown Colony, creates the image of an existence hedged all about by deprivation and peril: "I have nothing to comfort me, nor there is nothing to be gotten here but sickness and death, except that one had money to lay out in some things for profit. But I have nothing at all— no, not a shirt to my back but two rags (2), nor no clothes but one poor suit." In three letters dated March 20, April 2, and April 3, Frethorne cites instance after instance of disease, unsatisfiable hunger, thievery among fellow English, and ambush by natives; nearly half his sentences begin with the word "and." A parataxis of febrile and panic-stricken utterance, Frethorne's epistles recurrently implore his father to dispatch money or goods by which he might purchase his freedom. "Any eating meat will yield great profit. Oil and vinegar is very good; but, father, there is great loss in leaking. But for God's sake send beef and cheese and butter, or the more of one sort and none of another." "I entreat you not to forget me, but by any means redeem me; for this day we hear that there is 26 of Englishmen slain by the Indians." "Good father," Frethorne pleads, rhetorically engaging his conviction that his written expression cannot adequately convey the depth of his emergency, "do not forget me, but have mercy and pity my miserable case. I know if you did but see me, you would weep to see me; for I have but one suit."[16]

If you did but see me. The problem, as Frethorne conceives it, is that he exists at present invisibly to his father, and is therefore in no position to convince him by the spectacle of his material and social reduction (signified by his possession of only one suit), his disease and malnutrition (his emaciation), and his sorrow (his tears); if the father were to see the son, he would read the signs of duress, grief, and imminent starvation and be moved to such compassion as the son in turn would read in the father's tears ("you would weep to see me"). It is thus that Frethorne returns to the theme of having to make a case for himself in the absence of his body, which serves in its involuntary responses as the primary articulation of his state of distress. "Oh, that you did see my daily and hourly sighs, groans, and tears, and thumps that I afford mine own breast, and rue and curse the time of my birth, with holy Job. I thought no head had been able to hold so much water as hath and doth daily flow from mine eyes."[17] Letters composed under such circumstances are, from the perspective of the writer, weightier than the addressee can ever suspect. Consistent with his determination to state his peril exactly, Frethorne, in closing the letter of March 20, identifies what is at stake in much immigrant correspondence: "the answer of this letter will be life or death to me."[18] As with many incomplete narratives offered by fragmentary correspondence, nothing is known of the sequel, and the three letters with their desperate appeal constitute Frethorne's sole impress upon the historical record.

For Frethorne, not to be seen in person by his father threatens all relationship between them; as he has identified that relationship as his one link to a continuable existence, he equates its dissolution with death. Similar anxieties are likewise represented in an unsigned letter written in March 1631 by a young Massachusetts Bay colonist probably named John Pond to his father William Pond, "a seemingly illiterate workman" on John Winthrop's estate in Suffolk.[19] As does Frethorne, Pond pleads for commodities that might well make the difference between life and death; like Frethorne, Pond cannot make his plea without addressing the nature of a relationship mediated by letter sheet over distances that have left him disoriented. "I know, loving Father," Pond states in his opening paragraph, "and do confess that I was an undutiful child unto you when I lived with you and by you, for the which I am much sorrowful and grieved for it, trusting in God that He will so guide me that I will never offend you so any more, and I trust in God that you will forgive me for it, and my writing unto you is to let you understand what a country this new Eingland is where we live."[20] There follows a rambling account of the land and its climate and the similarities and differences between Old and New England: the differences amount to a harsh cold and a susceptibility to disease that renders the colonists acutely dependent on continued supplies. Pond specifics items especially needed even as he reflects upon the strangeness of pleading at a great distance: "I pray, father, send me four or five yards of cloth to make us some apparel, and, loving Father, *though I be far distant from you, yet I pray you remember me as your child,* and we do not know how long we may subsist, for we cannot live here without provisions from ould eingland" (italics added).[21] The fact that he depends on his father (and that New England depends on Old) is compelling to the one who suffers from want, but Pond expresses doubt that he can represent that fact to those for whom the leagues of ocean have conceivably dissolved the bond of relation.

Like Frethorne, Pond registers a fear of being forgotten: from his perspective, survival requires that he adequately (if redundantly) remind his father of his existence and state the details of his distress; the father, should he receive the letter, will need to be compelled by what he reads to hold the writer sufficiently in mind to undertake the measures the writer importunes. Pond, like Frethorne given to digressive and repetitive discourse, again like Frethorne is also able to state precisely what is at stake in his letter's safe arrival at its intended destination and its subsequent success as a piece of argument: "So, Father, I pray consider of my cause, for here will be but a very poor being and no being without, loving Father, your help with provisions from ould eingland."[22] Frethorne and Pond seem equally intent to overcome an anticipated skepticism on the part of fathers whose pathetic dependents they would show themselves to be.

The image of abject dependence that we find in the Frethorne and Pond letters should not, however, obscure from us what both men, in the extremity of their need and the chaos of their condition, comprehend as the appointed structure of human relations, which at once encourages them to petition for aid and preserves their dignity as they do so. Both men plead within an economy of reciprocal duties and attentions; their letters open with nearly identical expressions of filial respect:

My most humble duty remembered to you, hoping in God of your good health, as I myself am at the making hereof. (Frethorne)[23]

My humble duty remembered unto you, trusting in God you are in good health. (Pond)[24]

Pond, who goes on to make amends for real or imagined lapses of duty prior to entering into the substance of his petition, closes his letter on the same note: "My wife remembers her humble duty unto you and to my mother and my love to my brother Joseife. . . . Thus I leave you to the protection of almighty God."[25] Asking for remembrance and protection—the fulfillment of paternal duties—Frethorne and Pond for their part profess a remembrance of parental obligations previously fulfilled and commend their fathers to the care of a father protector God. If in much letter writing the formulaic phrase seems to verge on meaninglessness, here it articulates the sanctified communal relations to which the letter writer legitimately appeals for relief.

The same ship that carried Pond's letter to his father also bore one of several extant letters written by the colony's governor, John Winthrop, to his son, John Winthrop Jr., as well as one of numerous surviving letters that he wrote to his wife, Margaret Tyndale Winthrop. The contrasts between the single letter Pond is known to have written to his father and the many letters Winthrop wrote to his son, wife, associates, and backers are instructive if to some extent predictable. Pond, in the position of a grown child, addresses his father in tones of supplication; a member of his society's lower order, he is a minimally educated and unpracticed writer (his handwriting is uncultivated and his spelling, as we have seen, is nonstandard in such common terms as "eingland"), and his father may well have been obliged to find someone to read the letter to him. No wonder, then, that Pond's text exhibits doubt that he can adequately represent himself and his case at such removes from old England. Winthrop writes as a father, the patriarch not only of a family but of a colony; as the product of an educated man, a practiced and skillful writer, his text accordingly demonstrates the confidence of one who regards himself as able to state his meaning exactly and expect to see his intentions fulfilled. Facing the same hardships as the rest of the colony, his requests for provisions assume the tone of commands rather than petitions. Nevertheless, in writing family members, Winthrop like Pond adverts to the sanctity of relationships, routinely framing them sub specie aeternitatis:

My good son:

The blessing of the Almighty be upon thy soul and life forever.
Among many the sweet mercies of my God towards me in this
strange land, where we have met many troubles and adversities, this
is not the least, and that which affords much comfort to my heart,
that he hath given me a loving and dutiful son. God all-sufficient
reward thee abundantly for all thy care and pains in my affairs and
for all that love and duty thou hast showed to thy good mother.[26]

Thus Winthrop commences on March 28, 1631, a letter that spec-
ifies the last-minute preparations his son must see to before taking ship
to New England. Not only does Winthrop write with a social and
familial authority absent from the letters of Pond and Frethorne, but
he writes as well with a political self-assurance absent from those of
Lane. Although materially dependent on the continued attentions of
his "loving and dutiful son," Winthrop's tone reflects his status as the
unquestioned head of his family; and although dependent on the continued indulgence of the British Crown, Winthrop and company in
their own minds reject the spiritual and hence political authority of the
King and the Anglican Church. Having come to New England to stay,
Winthrop does not, like Columbus, Lane, and many other European
adventurers in the New World, engage the epistolary medium to ad-
vance an ambition centered in Europe and dependent on European
figures of authority. Winthrop is aware that the success of his colony requires the maintenance of cordial relations with Parliament and
Crown; his company is by no means avowedly Separatist. As a Con-
gregationalist who has effectively separated from the Anglican Church,
however, he has vested ultimate authority in a divinity abstracted from
that geopolitically grounded compound, God-and-King. God, for
Winthrop and like-minded dissenters, encourages the exodus of his
people; New England, although an alien and hostile country, entangled
politically in the vicissitudes of England, can serve as a divinely appointed geographic center of activity.

As a consequence, Winthrop does not write as one displaced from
the frame of reference that defines his presence and absence. As one
absent from his addressee, he represents himself in his letters as self-
present before an ever-present God, and reconciles himself to the
absence of his addressee by imaging the addressee's presence before
God as a faithful fellow servant and participant in the great exodus.
The lines written to his son illustrate this strategy; a more forceful
imaging of this mutual presence before God occurs in the closing lines

of the letter Winthrop wrote to his wife, Margaret Winthrop, soon after his June 1630 arrival: "I kiss and embrace thee, my dear wife and all my children and leave thee in His arms who is able to preserve you all and to fulfill our joy in our happy meeting in His good time, Amen."[27] The writer of such lines feels acutely the absence of his wife, as is indicated by his claim to kiss and embrace her in what the act of letter writing acknowledges as the absence of her body to his, an absence moreover registered in his consignment of his family to the metaphorical arms of a God who is bodiless and therefore ever present. The affirmation of a God who is present in (and by virtue of) bodily absence permits Winthrop to affirm their abiding presence to one another: rather than figuring his wife and himself as mutually absent, he conceives of them as incompletely present. Their reunion in "His good time"—in heaven if not in New England—is ordained. He hopes that they will meet in New England, but they are together already in eternity.

Winthrop develops this motif—absence that is not really absence but rather an incomplete presence—more dramatically in a letter to his wife that crossed on the same ship that carried the March 28, 1631, letter to his son as well as Pond's letter to his father. Winthrop knows that his wife and family are preparing to sail for New England; because the departure of the ship bound for England is delayed, he doubts that his communications can reach them before they have left for New England. Nevertheless, he feels compelled to write. From its first lines the letter must confront the possibility that the intended reader may never see this writing; moreover, as the intended reader in crossing the Atlantic is subject to shipwreck and the diseases that ravaged passengers, it is possible that she may already be beyond reach of all earthly communication. The text contemplates the likelihood of its futility as writing addressed to another: beneath an evident resolution to bear an anxiety hopefully, the letter comprehensively images Margaret's absence: her absence in New England (the primary occasion for writing), in England (if the ship has sailed), and in the world generally (if she has died or is soon to perish in the process of emigrating). Although Winthrop does not completely dismiss the chance that the letter will get through, he creates a text that develops other reasons for existing and that takes shape as a prayer-meditation addressing a solitude deepened by the uncertain status of the one missed; it is a text that may thus speak finally only to himself and God. Implicitly affirming that in any event they shall reunite in God beyond death (and that all of God's dispensa-

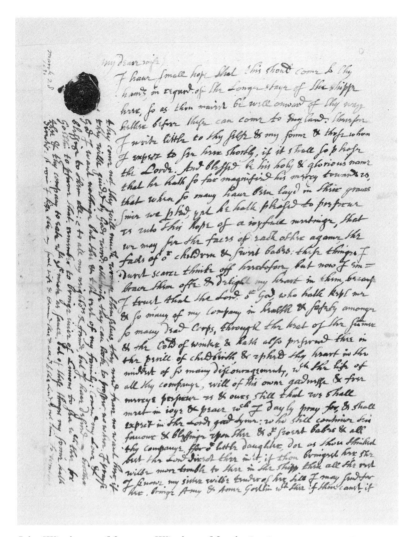

John Winthrop to Margaret Winthrop, March 28, 1631.
Courtesy of the Massachusetts Historical Society, Boston.

tions are equally just), the letter still dares to visualize his family's safe
arrival and his joyous reunion with them in New England.

My dear wife:

I have small hope that this should come to thy hands, in regard of
the long stay of the ship here, so as thou mayest be well onward of
thy way hither before these can come to England. Therefore I write
little to thyself and my son and those whom I expect to see here
shortly, if it shall so please the Lord. And blessed be His holy and

glorious name that he hath so far magnified His mercy towards us that when so many have been laid in their graves since we parted, yet He hath pleased to preserve us unto this hope of a joyful meeting, that we may see the faces of each other again, the faces of our children and sweet babes. These things I durst scarce think of heretofore, but now I embrace them oft and delight my heart in them, because I trust that the Lord our God, who hath kept me and so many of my company in health and safety among so many dead corpses, through the heat of the summer and the cold of winter, and hath also preserved thee in the peril of childbirth, and upheld thy heart in the midst of so many discouragements, with the life of all thy company, will of His own goodness and free mercy preserve us and ours still that we shall meet in joy and peace, which I daily pray for and shall expect in the Lord's good time, who still continues His favor and blessing upon thee and our sweet babes and all thy company.[28]

It is remarkable that a letter for which the writer can express only a "small hope" that it will not miss its intended recipient should go to such lengths, such elaborately clausal affirmation, to project an image of presence regained. All possible discouragement, from the probable futility of addressing his wife, to the casualties of the voyage and early settlement ("so many dead corpses") and the contemplation of Margaret's peril as childbearer and now transoceanic traveler, do not prevent Winthrop from celebrating their prospects of reunion in New England. Nevertheless, the detailed elaboration of disasters passed and yet always inherent in their mortal condition renders this letter as much a meditation of thwarted effort, death, and absence as a vision of the (restored) presence that compensates for the anguish the letter writer chooses to face down. In writing and dispatching such a text against so many uncertainties, Winthrop takes the measure of the world's ability to requite his efforts and his faithfulness to the vision that has thus far led and sustained him.

MORE PROBABLE TO UNITE SOULS THAN BODIES
Although any Christian letter writer addressing a fellow Christian may make more or less conventionalized reference to the unity of the correspondents in God and Christ, letters written among members of dissenting English sects for whom emigration was politically expedient invest great emotional intensity in the trope of the Lord's encom-

passing presence. Whether of a familiar or officially clerical nature, Puritan and Quaker correspondence has particular occasion to allude to and be loosely modeled on the Pauline epistles. Letters meant to admonish and encourage were regularly dispatched to settlements in the New World; as the eastern seaboard became settled, correspondence affirming a religious social identity flowed among scattered communities. Authors of religious epistles readily assumed Paul's rhetorical position of being "absent in body, but present in spirit" (1 Corinthians 5:3). "Loving and Christian Friends," John Robinson, pastor of the Leyden community, begins a lengthy letter of July 1620 addressing the company about to cross on the *Mayflower*, "I do heartily and in the Lord salute you all as being they with whom I am present in my best affection, and most earnest longings after you. Though I be constrained for a while to be bodily absent from you."[29] According to Paul, to be present with one's friends "in the Lord" was to achieve a truer unity with fellow believers than could ever be attained in the mutual pursuits of an earthly existence: "whilst we are at home in the body, we are absent from the Lord" (2 Corinthians 5:6). Certainly it would have been comforting to friends and family separated from one another and bereaved of loved ones who had succumbed to the hazards of emigration to know that they had "a building of God, an house not made with hands, eternal in the heavens" (2 Corinthians 5:1), the site of ultimate reunions. Yet, as Winthrop's July 1631 letter to his wife makes clear, those whose hands were engaged in the building of earthly habitations in the New World wished to be joined with the embodied presence of those taking part in the exodus from England.

Familiar correspondence in early America was frequently occasioned by circumstances that prompted religious reflection and commentary. In addition to the obvious situations in which a correspondent reports an affliction, a blessing, or a concern, there is the condition in which one person longs for another's company or word, and wishes against the possibility of the addressee's death or disappearance to be reunited. For some writers, the posting or receipt of a letter was so closely associated with transcending the separations inherent to mortal life that the epistolary exchange intrinsically constituted a religious experience. The following letter, written by Elizabeth Woolman to her brother John, conflates the experience of human contact with that of an encompassing divine presence, and offers itself as a metonym of God's persevering care. "Beloved Brother, John Woolman," the letter of November 1, 1743, begins,

In that love which desires the welfare of all men I write unto thee. I received thine, dated 2nd day, 10th month last, with which I was comforted. My spirit is bowed with thankfulness that I should be remembered, who am unworthy, but the Lord is full of mercy and his goodness is extended to the meanest of his creation. Therefore, in his infinite love he hath pitied and spared and showed mercy, that I have not been cut off nor quite lost. But at times I am refreshed and comforted as with the glimpse of his presence, which is more to the immortal part than all which this world can afford. So with desires for thy preservation with my own, I remain thy affectionate sister, Elizabeth Woolman, Jr.[30]

This letter is noteworthy for the concision with which it identifies the receipt of a letter and the comfort that it bestows with the extension of divine mercy; the communication Elizabeth has received indicates that she is "cut off" from neither her brother nor God. Having registered this testimony to "that love which desires the welfare of all men," Elizabeth expresses desire for John's "preservation with my own," and ends without reference to anything remotely quotidian. Indeed, there is no reference made to past or future visits, no desire expressed that she should like to see John in person. The text exclusively concerns the divine love that establishes Elizabeth and John in eternal union despite the phenomenal experience of separate existence that has induced an exchange of letters. Woolman printed the letter in the *Journal* as a memorandum of his sister, who died at age thirty-seven of smallpox after a life of spiritual disquietude; having preserved the document beyond the occasion of its initial reception, he now posthumously receives and readdresses the letter as a testimony of one who in life may have often felt herself lost, but who has henceforth died into full presence.

The Pauline trope is not restricted to overtly religious or meta-physical expressions. Toward the end of a facetiously performative letter seasoned with biblical and classical reference, nineteen-year-old Thomas Jefferson enjoins his boyhood friend John Page: "Remember me affectionately to all the young ladies of my acquaintance, particu-larly the Miss Burwells and Miss Potters, and tell them that though that heavy earthly part of me, my body, be absent, the better half of me, my soul, is ever with them, and that my best wishes shall ever attend them."[31] Andrew Burstein has argued that Jefferson's mature letter writing, along with that of his fellow "genteel Revolutionaries," man-ifests a specifically "Ciceronian Ethos": shaped by a curriculum that included Cicero's *Epistles to Atticus* and *Letters of Pliny the Consul*, the elite set of colonial lawyers who assumed the lead in the early republic forged epistolary relationships that proceeded in the belief that civic virtue arises in such personal integrity, private friendship, and learned disquisition as their correspondences purported to evince. Cultivating a degree of philosophical detachment, these correspondences explored issues pertaining to political authority, citizenship, and representative government in view of ancient and current events as well as classical and contemporary commentary.[32] The celebrated exchange between the retired Thomas Jefferson and John Adams—successor to an earlier, largely diplomatic correspondence that had terminated in 1801 with their political and personal rupture—undoubtedly represents the furthest extension and highest achievement of such colloquy.

Yet the neoclassical republican culture that Jefferson and Adams share is informed by the non-Ciceronian metaphors of presence and absence that are expressed in the 1763 letter to Page and that are conventionally invoked in an effort to close the geographic and temperamental space between correspondents. Freethinkers both, their letters advert to a generic theological frame: "Whether in the body or out of the body I shall always be your friend," Adams concludes a letter of 1821. And in his condolence of November 13, 1818, on the occasion of Abigail Adams's death, Jefferson articulates the vision of a transcendent presence (as metaphor and desire if not as belief, and perhaps more as an appeal to Adams's susceptibilities than to his own) in these phrases: "it is of some comfort to us both that the term is not very distant at which we are to deposit, in the same cerement, our sorrows and suffering bodies, and to ascend in essence to an ecstatic meeting with the friends we have loved and lost and whom we shall still love and never lose again."[33]

Unity in God is very commonly cited as a consolation for what correspondents knew to be the uncertainty of earthly convergences. Reunion in this world may fail for a host of reasons, not least of which is an ambivalence on the part of correspondents to appear in person to one another. An exchange that negotiates intriguingly with the notion of reunion is the sixty-three-year correspondence between Benjamin Franklin and his youngest sister, Jane Franklin Mecom (1712–94), whom Franklin counseled and financially supported throughout much of their lives. The one sibling with whom Franklin maintained affectionate relations, Mecom was married at an early age to an improvident saddler; she herself kept a boarding house in Hanover Street, Boston, and led a life of toil and hardship in which there was never any chance of venturing beyond the family's lower-middle-class origins. The letters Mecom and Franklin exchanged are a decided study in contrast. Mecom's are those of an articulate but incorrect writer whose text abounds with phonetic spellings and whose sentences lack defined borders. Her penmanship is clear but her words are irregularly sized; the sentences waver in their horizontal rank. Franklin's letters are written in the polished conversational style that his autobiography depicts him as studiously cultivating in his youth; the sentences are strictly defined and the penmanship is in all respects perfect. His success as deputy postmaster-general of the colonies no doubt contributes to the self-assured tone of his epistolary expression. In addition to the distances between Boston and Philadelphia, Boston and London, and Boston and Passy that their correspondence was obliged to bridge, there is the ever evident class distance that Franklin has established between himself and his social origins.

Given his ability and willingness as a man of means to address his sister's need, the difference in class works to perpetuate their relation. Yet it is not simply a sense of responsibility that induces Franklin to keep up the exchange but also an affection rooted in childhood and the connectedness with kin that their relation permits; in later life, after they had survived their respective spouses and their many Franklin siblings, they share a sense of having only each other for the soul's true companion. This is particularly so for Mecom, although in a letter she writes to Franklin in 1779, when he is serving as a commissioner in France, she makes reference to a passage in one of his letters in which he has expressed a decided longing for her company.

> I have after a long year recved yr kind leter of Nov 26—1778 wherin you like yr self do all for me that the most Affectionat Brother can be desiered or Expected to do, & tho I feel my self full of gratitude for yr Generousity, the conclusion of yr leter Affectes me more; where you say you wish we may spend our last days together o my Dear Brother if this could be Accomplished it would give me more Joy than any thing on this side Heaven could posally do; I feel the want of suitable conversation I have but litle hear, I think I could Asume more freedom with you now & convence you of my affection for you[.][34]

Although Mecom is sixty-seven and Franklin is seventy-four, she imagines fresh developments in their relationship, and believes herself ready to conquer the diffidence that has hampered her in her relationships and that she has particularly felt in her brother's eminent presence.

The thought of reuniting with her brother receives further expression in a letter of March 1781 in which she visualizes the pleasures of what at the same time she concedes to be their probably unattainable mutual company ("what nither of us have much grounds to hope for"): "I often contemplate the Happines it would afford me to have you settled in a Country Seat in New England & I have premition to Reside with you that we might End our Days to gather Retiered from all but a few choice wons that would give & recive Mutual Injoyment & make us forgit any litle disagreable Incidents that would Unavoidably happen while we Remane in the boddy[.]"[35] A deeply cherished notion, this theme was repeated in other letters with longing if not with hope; during this period of their correspondence letters miscarried, and between 1780 and 1783 she read newspaper accounts of Franklin's activities but did not hear directly from him. In a letter of September 1783, evidently the second of two letters that he wrote his sister in that year, Franklin lays to rest any hope that they might actually join together in a private domestic arrangement: "Your Project of taking a House for us to spend the Remainder of our Days in, is a pleasing one; but it is a Project of the Heart rather than of the Head. You forget, as I sometimes do, that we are grown old, and that before we can have furnish'd our House, & put things in order, we shall probably be call'd away from it, to a Home more lasting, and I hope more agreable than any this World can afford us."[36]

Franklin perhaps misjudged his sister's recognition of the extreme unlikelihood that they should ever retire together in New England; he heard the cry of a heart that unabashedly confessed its loneliness ("I have many Lonely Hours to bewail the Distance betwen us which makes it so difficult to hear from Each other") and answered her with what appears to be a genial if condescending and undoubtedly deflating urbanity.[37] In July 1784, a year before Franklin's return to the United States, Mecom, expecting an earlier homecoming, wrote with mixed emotions: "I shall never see you, traveling will be so Incomodous to you that when you are got home you will not Prevail with your self to see New England but If you come hear first you can go mostly if not Altogather by water. . . . God grant I may see you again hear but if not that we may Spend an happy Eternity to gather In His Presence[.]"[38] She never did see him again, although from the time of Franklin's return to Philadelphia in September 1785 to his death in April 1790, they corresponded with gratifying frequency.

Contemporary with the Mecom-Franklin correspondence and crossing nearly identical geographical distances (between Braintree, Massachusetts, and Philadelphia, and afterward between Braintree and Paris, Amsterdam, and The Hague), the letters exchanged by Abigail and John Adams are among the best known of American correspondence. Because John Adams's side of the exchange affords a detailed perspective on the proceedings of the Continental Congress and the negotiations that culminated in the Treaty of Paris, and because Abigail Adams's side documents life in and around Boston in the first years of the War of Independence and articulates an intellectually gifted woman's critical views of the principle of equality as set forth in the Constitution, political and cultural historians have justly valued their letters as primary sources. And given the inherent drama of the letters, the heroic qualities both partners abundantly manifest, as well as the appeal of a personal and romantic narrative unfolding behind the scenes of monumental public events, the correspondence has lent itself to readers' editions aimed at general audiences. Aside from the circumstances that give the contents of their writing an unusual public interest, however, the letters of Abigail and John Adams face the common conditions of much letter writing of the era. The correspondents are separated for long periods without prospect of reunion or certain knowledge of where the other may be. Each writes with a heightened sense of the other's mortality. And because the war disrupts an already unreliable post, they must write with the expectation that their letters will miscarry.

John and Abigail Adams are both gifted letter writers with an extraordinary sensitivity to the spatial and temporal distances that separate the one from the other and an acute awareness of both the capacity and incapacity of the letter to mitigate that distance. What is fascinating about their letters is the spectacle not simply of history "come to life" but of the epistolary form engaged in the articulation of a dimension of that history, a substratum consisting of unrelieved and unappeasable private agony. Because the familiar letter lends itself to the confidential inscription of private, inward, individual experience, the conjunction of private and public worlds is particularly felt in this correspondence; this conjunction foregrounds the discursive peculiarities and thematic repertoire of the epistolary genre. In addition to the information concerning public affairs that, depending upon the likelihood of their letters' interception, they are more or less free to relate, John and especially Abigail record the experience of separation, longing, and anxiety for the other, in moments that look ahead to an interminable succession of more such moments. Although they avow a patriotic willingness to undertake hardship, their letters document an agony potentially unredeemed by historical conclusions, an agony whose relief is not so much the successful issue of a war as the reunion of correspondents in domestic peace. Against the public demands of their times, their letters construct a utopian image of private life that the correspondents themselves suspect to be unattainable.

Before Abigail Smith and John Adams were married and Adams's career as a statesman required the lengthy absences from home that provided an incentive to correspond, the two carried on a lively exchange as an engaged couple. To read their courtship letters is to view the verbal rituals of lovers kept apart by a conventional period of waiting rather than by public duties, to observe the privations of a couple separated by several rather than hundreds or thousands of miles. The letters written between 1762 and 1764, the year they were married, express a sexual tension that their later letters also express among the complications of politics, household economy, and child rearing; they allow us to see that their whole correspondence unfolds as an exchange of love letters. The theme of seeking their own private world, recurrent throughout their correspondence, is consistent with the amatory expressions they wrote to one another in the first months of their relationship. Those expressions are characterized by features common to courtship letters: a proliferation of metaphors that trope absence and the activity of letter writing; an inscription of what are represented to be dreams of sleep or wakefulness that stand as metaphors of erotic longing; a tendency to write the "I" and the "you" as third persons, especially when reference is made to their capacity as loving subjects and loved objects. Representation of self and other as third persons often proceeds by an assumption of alter egos, the personae of mythological, historical, or dramatic figures, signifiers in the coauthorship of an intimate and confidential code. In the early phases of their correspondence John is Lysander, Abigail is Diana (later she signs herself Portia).

Among the distances negotiated in their courtship letters, then, are those the writers rhetorically create between inscribing selves and a set of third persons who serve as proxies invested in a love relationship that may be promising but remains unproven. What must be particularly subjected to proof is the veracity of the lover's word, and incoming mail that speaks to the heart must be read at a distance from its focus of appeal. Thus Abigail Smith deliberates: "You was pleas'd to say that the receipt of a letter from your Diana always gave you pleasure. Whether this was designed for a complement, (a commodity I acknowledg that you very seldom deal in) or as a real truth, you best know. Yet if I was to judge of a certain persons Heart, by what upon the like occasion passess through a cabinet of my own, I should be apt to suspect it as a truth" (AFC 1:8). Her deliberation betrays a readiness to collapse such distances, to know his heart by the promptings of her own, and to admit him unreservedly to her confidence. Seven months later she begins a letter to John with frank coquetry: "Here am I all alone, in my Chamber, a mere Nun I assure you, after professing myself thus will it not be out of Character to confess that my thoughts are often employ'd about Lysander, 'out of the abundance of the Heart, the mouth speaketh,' and why Not the Mind thinketh" (AFC 1:25). At that moment John was under the quarantine of a voluntary smallpox inoculation, eagerly anticipating "the soft Ligaments of Matrimony" that awaited the couple later that year, and producing for her in his enforced idleness "a Nest of Letters" (AFC 1:24, 22).

Ten years later, Adams would leave for Philadelphia to represent Massachusetts at the First Continental Congress and begin the first of several protracted absences from home that would renew this otherwise inseparable couple's impassioned engagement of the epistolary form. In letters written during brief absences at relatively short distances, Abigail had already exhibited a compulsion to imagine the formidable nature of the space that separated her from her correspondent; during a December 1773 visit to her mother in Weymouth, Massachusetts, she begins a letter to her husband and children in Boston (fewer than twenty miles distant) thus: "Alass! How many snow banks devide thee and me and my warmest wishes to see thee will not melt one of them" (AFC 1:90). Regarding herself as by nature a stationary and anchored object—exactly what we might expect of someone who ran a household and was primarily responsible for three small children—she conceives of geographic space as resistant to being crossed. John's months in Philadelphia exaggerated Abigail's sense of fixity in Boston and Braintree as it intensified her perception of her husband's inaccessibility. From the beginning of this absence she registers the temporal dimension of her separation from John. Nine days after his departure she writes: "The great distance between us, makes the time appear very long to me. It seems already a month since you left me" (AFC 1:142). And after a month of separation: "Five Weeks have past and not one line have I received. I had rather give a dollar for a letter by the post, tho the consequence should be that I Eat but one meal a day for these 3 weeks to come" (AFC 1:151).

Increasingly, with emotions alternating between guilt and anger, she becomes preoccupied with her private claim on his attention. "I dare not express to you at 300 hundred miles distance how ardently I long for your return," she writes in a letter of October 1774. "I have some very miserly Wishes; and cannot consent to your spending one hour in Town till at least I have had you 12." As a warrant of her statement's urgency, she adverts to the physiological effects (impressed upon and therefore present in the letter sheet) of her efforts to inscribe a half-formed indignation: "The Idea plays about my Heart, unnerves my hand whilst I write, awakens all the tender sentiments that years have encreased and matured, and which when with me were every day dispensing to you." A self-reflexive letter writer, Abigail writes with a consciousness that the distance separating her from John compels language whose forcefulness may transgress canons of acceptable speech, but that she must write that language to affirm their bond. "The whole collected stock of ten weeks absence knows not how to brook any longer restraint, but will break forth and flow thro my pen. May the like sensations enter thy breast, and (in spite of all the weighty cares of State) Mingle themselves with those I wish to communicate, for in giving them utterance I have felt more sincere pleasure than I have known since the 10 of August" (AFC 1:172). The remainder of the letter is more temperate, although it concerns preparations in Boston for a state of siege; amid the public unrest, Abigail has indulged the "sincere pleasure" of voicing the heart's pain.

Given the probability of war and the dissolution of the public stability necessary for the enjoyment of domestic relations, Abigail recognizes that space for privacy may not exist and that she must be prepared for all manner of sacrifice. As this letter proceeds she resigns herself to the public claim, invoking the common epistolary trope of ultimate reunion with those whose geographic separation serves as prophecy of a separation by death. "You cannot be, I know, nor do I wish to see you an inactive Spectator, but if the Sword be drawn I bid adieu to all domestick felicity, and look forward to that Country where there is neither wars nor rumors of War in a firm belief that thro the mercy of its King we shall both rejoice there together" (AFC 1:172). For his part, John, more consistently resigned than Abigail, has his own moments of panic. In September of 1774, hearing a rumor that Boston was in a state of siege, he begins a letter to Abigail with the observation that he cannot confidently envision the circumstances under which she will receive his communication: "When or where this Letter will find you, I know not. In what Scenes of Distress and Terror, I cannot foresee. —We have received a confused Account from Boston, of a dreadfull Catastrophy." Yet by the end of the letter, which briefly reports his activities in Philadelphia, he writes with a restored ability to visualize the normality of his family's world: "My Love to all my dear Children—tell them to be good, and to mind their Books. I shall come home and see them, I hope, the latter End of next Month" (AFC 1:150).

Additional communications penned in expectation of the collapse of civil order would follow. Writing just before the Battle of Bunker Hill, Abigail speculated that "the very next Letter I write will inform you that I am driven away from our, yet quiet cottage" (AFC 1:217). But as the theater of war shifts from New England and as John's absence, first in Philadelphia and later in Europe, becomes the continuous and defining feature of their married life, the Adamses grudgingly inure themselves to a relation by letter sheet, conversing of war and the formation of a government and nation, conversing ever of domestic life in matters ranging from farm income and the education of the older children to the ravages of a dysentery epidemic and the stillbirth of a daughter, all the while anxiously regarding (in Abigail's words) "these seperations as preparatory to a still more painfull one" (AFC 2:258). The straining of a relationship so dependent on writing takes the form of complaints about the character and quantity of the writing. Answering John's suggestion that she has done too little to encourage his Boston friends to write him, Abigail counters, "May not I in my turn make complaints? All the Letters I receive from you seem to be wrote in so much haste, that they scarcely leave room for a social feeling. . . . I want some sentimental Effusions of the Heart. I am sure you are not destitute of them or are they all absorbed in the great publick" (AFC 1:247). After a four-month lapse occasioned by John's passage to France, "the sight of his well known hand" alone is enough to fill the reader's eyes with "tears of joy," yet Abigail also admits to having felt "mortified at so Short a Letter" (AFC 3:51, 52).

She would have indeed the fullest possible account of his life away from her: "I must request you always to be minute and to write me by every conveyance." Yet no volume of writing can possibly compensate for his absence, and although she affirms his essential presence with her—"The whole Heart of my Friend is in the Bosom of his partner"

(AFC 3:52)—in the first months of John's residence in France, Abigail, distressed over his short and infrequent communications, questions what remains for him of the adhesive force of the marital bond. Well aware as she must have been that letters were lost in transit and that the dangers of interception necessarily limited what he could represent of his business and even his personal condition, her unsatisfied (and unsatisfiable) desire to be copiously addressed generates what she herself acknowledges to be harsh accusations. "Could you after a thousand fears and anxieties," she asks,

> long expectation and painfull suspences be satisfied with my telling you that I was well, that I wished you were with me, that my daughter sent her duty, that I had ordered some articles for you which I hoped would arrive &c. &c. —By Heaven if you could you have changed hearts with some frozen Laplander or made a voyage to a region that has chilld every Drop of your Blood. —But I will restrain a pen already I fear too rash, nor shall it tell you how much I have sufferd from this appearance of—— inattention. (AFC 3:110–11)

Although willing to admit the rashness of her utterance, she does not offer to retract the statement, and her suggestion that his heart has changed—that she may no longer assume she knows his heart as she knows her own, that his heart no longer beats in her bosom—is left as the expression of an indignantly unrestrained pen.

This letter, along with at least two others, represents the nadir of the Adamses' epistolary relationship, as Abigail generates text of an exorbitance that John cannot adequately answer. Having attempted to address her complaints directly, he writes of the breakdown of his ability to do so and thus maintain his side of the correspondence. Speaking of two previous letters "in this complaining style," he writes that he "had Endeavour'd to answer them. —I have wrote several answers, but upon a review, they appear'd to be such I could not send. One was angry, another was full of Greif, and the third with Melancholy, so that I burnt them all. —if you write me in this style I shall leave of writing intirely, it kills me." Representing himself to be at a loss in marshaling the language adequate to her need, and claiming that her suspicion of his esteem, affection, and remembrance "sickens" him, he resorts to simple formulas: "Be assured that no time nor place, can change my heart" (AFC 3:138). Whether Abigail in the interim received letters of reassurance that John had previously dispatched or had intuited that her letters of reproach imposed an insupportable strain on their already tenuous communications, she abandoned her "complaining style" even before she read this reassurance, and was prepared to repeat a formula of her own: "How insupportable the Idea that 3000 leigues, and the vast ocean now devide us—but devide only our persons for the Heart of my Friend is in the Bosom of his partner" (AFC 3:140). And so they passed this difficult turn in their correspondence.

As John Adams's already protracted and tedious service abroad became ever more complicated by emerging factions in the nascent federal government, and as Abigail Adams's loneliness and anxiety increasingly fostered her resentment of what she perceived to be the country's ingratitude of her family's sacrifices, the theme of retirement from a turbulent and corrupt public realm to a life of pastoral calm and private virtue arises on both sides of their correspondence. Images of private retirement and utopian domesticity, as we have seen, arise in the late phase of the Franklin-Mecom correspondence: they constitute the dream of reunion that their epistolary exchange picks up and lays aside but never takes steps to making a realizable goal despite Jane Mecom's intense desire that they set up house while still in the body. For John and Abigail Adams, the prospect of once again becoming partners in domesticity is very real: in John's absence Abigail endeavors to acquire property in Vermont for the purpose of securing a reclusive sylvan retreat. Even so, private retirement in this as in the Franklin-Mecom correspondence exists as a theme that reflects the privacy of the relationship and the privacy of the genre that has served to maintain the relationship; the idealized dream of renewed contact, reunion, and reconciliation, apart from the rest of the world or in the clarified space of an afterlife, figures among the recurrent motifs of correspondences between friends, lovers, spouses, and family members. In the later correspondence of John and Abigail Adams, the motif of retirement and insistence on privacy become increasingly obsessive.

Ironically, private life emerges in their exchange not only as the refuge from an unappreciative public but also as the refuge of republican civic virtue. Thus Abigail writes in March 1782 to a beleaguered John that he may be "assured at least of finding one Friend in the Bosom of *Portia*, who is sick, sick of a world in which selfishness predominates" and who unites with him "in the wish of a sequestered Life, the shades of Virmont, the uncultivated Heath are preferable in her mind to the servility of a court" (AFC 4:293). "You can scarcely imagine a more beautifull Place than the Hague," John writes home in June 1782. "Yet no Place has any Charms for me but the Blue Hills. My

Heart will have in it forever, an acking Void, in any other Place" (AFC 4:324). "My Ambition, my happiness centers in him," Abigail writes in April 1783, "who sighs for domestick enjoyments, amidst all the world calls happiness—who partakes not in the jovial Feast; or joins the Luxurious table, without turning his mind to the plain unadulterated food which covers his own frugal Board, and sighs for the Feast of reason and the flow of soul" (AFC 5:116). And in June 1783: "This little Cottage has more Heart felt Satisfaction for you than the most Brilliant Court can afford, the pure and undiminished tenderness of weded Love, the filial affection of a daughter who will never act contrary to the advise of a Father, or give pain to the Maternal Heart" (AFC 5:181). On these points the correspondents agree. The conclusion to their separation is thus ironic: Abigail joins her husband in Europe; upon their return, John serves first as vice president and then, to his misery, as president. Retirement from public life was still a long way off. The images of futurity that a correspondence projects do not necessarily anticipate the life that the partners actually elect.

In the end, the reunions that epistolary texts dream may or may not have much to do with what is possible for correspondents who once again become physically present to one another. As Emily Dickinson so brilliantly perceived, such dreams are composed of nostalgia, idealization, compensation, wish fulfillment; their satisfaction exceeds anything that could realistically present itself to actual human life. This is not to underestimate the joy felt by the reuniting Adamses. Yet there are moments in which Abigail, as a theorist of epistolary relations, seems close to articulating what Dickinson understood so well. In November 1780, Abigail writes: "I fancy the pains of absence increase in proportion to distance, as the power of attraction encreases as the distance diminishes. Magnets are said to have the same motion tho in different places. Why may not we have the same sensations tho the wide Atlantick roll between us? I recollect your story to Madam Le Trexel upon the Nature and power of Attraction and think it much more probable to unite Souls than Bodies" (AFC 4:14). This may be true even after bodies resume a familiar physical proximity.

Abigail Adams's observation that the pains of absence increase in proportion to the distance between separated parties proceeds from her having a basis of comparison: John in Amsterdam seems much less accessible than John in Philadelphia, although his distance from Abigail of four hundred miles at the time seemed insuperable. Perhaps the true measure of distance in pre-electronic communication is the degree to which correspondents reflect upon the fact that they are far enough away from one another that one might die without the other knowing about it for some time; such reflection has a way of making all intervening space and time appear as so much annihilation of human connection. The distance between Lowell, Massachusetts, and Rochester, New Hampshire, is a mere fifty miles, but in a June 1830 letter written by Wealthy Page, a woman who worked in the Lowell mills, to former neighbors in Rochester, the space that in fair weather could easily be traversed by a one-day journey appears as a vale of death: "When you feel to pour out your soul to God . . . dont forget us who are far distant from you." A family illness no doubt exaggerates her consciousness of death, but the state of separation induces her to view her whole home circle as so many mortal beings disunited in this life. "When I think of home and the sufferings of my dear Brother it oft causes a heaving sigh and a falling tear and then I retire and breathe a prayer to Almi[ghty] Father . . . methinks if I continue to pray and faint not and hold out to the end watch and be sober do the commands of God I hope one day to meet you all with my Dear Brother to part no more is the sincere prayer and desire of your unworthy friend."[39] The distance from family and friends is thus measured by the journey through life that lies ahead of her and that must be lived correctly for her to arrive at the ultimate reunion.

In 1858 the Reverend Charles Colcock Jones's plantation in rural Liberty County, Georgia, stood about fifteen miles from Savannah. Yet for Abream Scriven, an African American abruptly sold by his master, any geographic distance is in principle unnegotiable, and his separation from family is mitigated only by such mailings as his new owners permit him to send and that his family in turn is permitted to receive. The letter that he wrote and sent to his wife as he awaited departure for New Orleans in the company of a slave trader represents a distance from his family that can only increase; in his desperation Scriven is left to emplot a reunion beyond the grave. Few letters can surpass the intensity of grief Scriven inscribes in this hastily written statement:

Savannah Sept the 19. 1858
Dinah Jones
  My Dear Wife
  I take the pleasure of writing you these few with much regret to inform you that I am Sold to a man by the name of Peterson atreader and Stays in New orleans. I am here yet But I expect to go

before long but when I get there I will write and let you know where I am. My Dear I want to Send you Some things but I donot know who to Send them By but I will thry to get them to you and my children. give my love to my father & mother and tell them good Bye for me. and if we Shall not meet in this world I hope to meet in heaven. My Dear wif for you and my Children my pen cannot Express the griffe I feel to be parted from you all I remain your truly husband until Death

Abream Scriven.

The text indicates a familiarity with the conventions of beginning and closing letters, while the holograph exhibits a practiced hand. This suggests that Scriven had been educated by his master (indeed, his name is curiously close to "scrivener," although the surname probably derives from a local planter family). If much of the pathos of this letter arises from the fact that separation from his family in life may well constitute, as Scriven recognizes, separation for life, that pathos is deepened by our knowledge that he was exceptional in being able to inscribe his condition—that the grief he felt would have been experienced by a multitude of slaves whose voices have not survived. The reverse of this letter, folded in thirds in the conventional manner, bears the notation: "Abram's Letter to his Wife Dinah / Dated Sept. 19. 58 / Answered for her by her mistress." Nothing is known of the ghost-written reply or of the subsequent fate of Abream Scriven.[40]

Throughout the nineteenth century, migration across the North American continent compelled many people to become letter writers, challenging them to image the genuinely vast physical distances traveled and to affirm—through a space and time that annihilated fellow travelers—connection with those they hoped their letters would reach. Such communications are more or less self-reflexive, yet even the most ostensibly naïve letter writing demonstrates complex strategies of relating experience and preserving bonds. Writing her cousin from eastern Wyoming, thirteen-year-old Virginia Reed, a member of the Donner party who traveled from Springfield, Illinois, to Napa Valley, California, in 1846, provides the following synopsis of the trip across the plains; the care given to the account of the grandmother's death is belied by the extreme parataxis of the style:

My Dear Couzin I take this opper tuny to Write to you to let you know that I am Well at present and hope that you are well. We have all had good helth—We came to the blue—the Water was so hye we had to stay thare 4 days—in the mean time gramma died. she be came spechless the day before she died. We buried her verry decent We made a nete coffin and buried her under a tree we had a head stone and had her name cutonit, and the date and yere verry nice, and at the head of the grave was a tree we cut some letters on it the young men soded it all ofer and put Flores on it We miss her verry much evry time we come in the wagon we look up at the bed for her We have came throw several tribs of indians the Caw Indians the saw the shawnees. . . .

In death the grandmother, speechless in her final hours and thereafter, becomes the occasion of a redundancy of writing, and Reed's letter focuses long enough to tell how the deceased is attested to by the headstone and tree, even as the letter attests to the grandmother's conspicuous absence ("evry time we come in the wagon we look up at the bed for her"). Returning after nine short sentences to the theme of remembering the absent, her letter details a rite by which her father and former associates have arranged to remember and acknowledge the existence of one another while pausing in remembrance of the origin of an omnipresent national identity. "We selabrated the 4 of July on plat at Bever criek several of the Gentemen in Springfield gave paw a botel of licker and said it shoulden be opend tell the 4 day of July and paw was to look to the east and drink it and thay was to look to the West an drink it at 12 oclock[.]" The letter itself formulaically ends in concentrated remembrance of the addressee: "maw and pau is well and sends there best love to you all. I send my best love to you all. . . . You are for ever my affectionate couzen[.]"[41]

The recurrent affirmation that the family is well and the repeated hope that the addressee is equally well characterizes a letter that Reed wrote to her cousin from Napa Valley after surviving a series of snowstorms in the Sierra Nevada Mountains that others of their company also survived only by cannibalizing those who died. "I take this oppertunity to write to you to let you now that we are all Well at presant and hope this letter may find you all well to," the letter begins conventionally before going on at great lengths to detail "our trubels geting to Callifornia."[42] In a breathless rush of short declarative sentences punctuated by occasional exclamations, Reed proceeds to tell a story harsh even by the standards of Oregon Trail experience, and for a while she avoids but then comes around to relate something of the horror of the ordeal: "Thare was 3 died and the rest eat them thay was ten days without any thing to eat but the Dead[.]"[43] The burden of the letter, written to bridge the geographical distance between California and Illinois, is to identify this moment as the furthest point in Reed's experience from any affirmable normality, and to assert a measure of normality regained that encompasses both Reed and her Cousin Mary: "I hav Wrote you anuf to let you now that you dont now whattruble is but thank the Good god we have all got throw and the onely family that did not eat human flesh[.]" And again: "we have got through but Dont let this letter dishaten anybody and never take no cutofs and hury along as fast as you can[.]"[44] Reed meant for this letter to present her as one unclaimed by the moral darkness of this experience, and to clear her of any imputations of barbarity that should render her per- haps more absent than death itself could render her: "Mary take this letter to uncle Gurshon and to all tha i know to all of our neighbors . . . and let them read it Mary kiss little Sue and Maryann for me and give my best love to all i know[.]"[45]

Despite the extremity of experience that Virginia Reed has been through, her letter speaks with a voluble if sober directness expressing a confidence that her communication will find its way to her addressee and represent her as she wishes to be represented. Letters written by pioneers more typically speak from what they conceive to be a geo- graphic and spiritual remoteness, as when in 1862 Nancy Glenn, on reaching Oregon, prefaces a letter to her family in Iowa by acknowl- edging the uncertainty with which her family must regard her in her lengthy absence: "after so long a silence I am again permitted to write a few lines to you to let you know that we are all yet upon the land among the liveing I doubt not but you have had many fears concerning our safety crossing the plains." The letter proceeds to narrate the journey west, although not without a significant digression that develops the anxiety voiced in the opening line with respect to maintaining one's status in the land of the living. The digression begins when Glenn remarks how the beauty of the Black Hills of eastern Wyoming recalled for her the beauty of her first home in Ohio:

> they were the most beautiful of any thing I had seen on the road. They reminded me of the dear old home of my childhood and soon the unbidden tear was finding its way down my cheek. yes I do often think of that place and some dear ones there. But not so often as I do of my once happy home in Iowa and the dear ones there that such a short time ago could sooth and cheer my heart by their presence. but now what a change No father nor Mother sister nor brother to cheer my home. Think of me when you enjoy each others

society and think also what a blessing it is to be where you can see each other often but I do not despair I hope to meet you all again this side of the grave if the Lord will but if not I hope we may be able to say his will be done[.][46]

Glenn writes as though her family, who live among daily visual evidence of one another's existence, enjoy a much fuller self-presence than can she, who, in moving across the continent, exists even in her own mind as a memory to those she has left behind; they are not so much absent to her as she is absent to them. Life, in this passage, is imaged as a series of removals, absentings, and departures from origins, and only ambivalently can Glenn affirm the guarantees of restored presence that come with the acceptance of the will of God. In closing, Glenn does her best to invoke and affirm family connection:

give my best respects to Uncle Edwin and aunt Paulina and family and all the rest of our relatives there it is of no use to name them all for I should be glad to see or hear from any of them I want you to write as soon as you get this write a long letter Farewell
Nancy C Glenn to Wm and Mary A Beckwith
brothers and sisters one and all[47]

A letter that dwells so emphatically on her separation from the family thus ends in dismissing the essential reality of the distance that separates them.

A letter composed under strikingly different circumstances that nevertheless bears remarkable similarities in phrasing to the letter of Nancy Glenn is that written in March 1848 by Washington W. McDonough, an African American colonist and missionary in Settra Kroo, Liberia, to John McDonough, his former master in New Orleans. As in the Glenn letter, vast distance attenuates the bond that people who are in constant contact routinely if unconsciously affirm; like Glenn, McDonough writes from a position sufficiently remote that he imagines his absence as a kind of death and represents himself as one who commands a clear view of the borders that mark off one world from another. Yet the complicated relations between slave and former master (one who felt divinely led to "free" his slaves by educating them for the religious and political colonization of West Africa) inevitably come out. Washington McDonough, although wishing to preserve relations with his former master, writes as though the distance between them has effected a leveling of the human field in which he is free to fashion himself as John McDonough's political equal. At the same time, the distance assumes form as a difference in moral geography that bestows on the writer superior spiritual status.

> Hon. Sir.
>
> I have taken this opportunity of addressing you a few lines to inform you that I am still in the land of the liveing and injoying the rightes of man for although I am in a land of darkness I have nothing to fear My wants are few and of course easily supplycd, Not like you who are liveing in a land of milk & honey and yet never satisfied. I have lived in the same land myself and had the pleasure of enjoying all that the heart could wish for or that would make one happy and yet I was not willing to denie myself of the lease things. but alas, what a change has since taken place. Things that seemed to have been of so much value to me in those times are no more to me now than idle dreams. when compared to my present views of them, all that I now wish for is just enough to make me comfortable and happy while I live in this world, for we are told in scripture that we can carry nothing out of it when we go hence.[48]

In this miniature conversion narrative, it is difficult to determine whether the commonplaces of evangelical witnessing are intended as a pointed challenge to the former master's moral complacency. (Does "Not like you" refer specifically to John McDonough or to any "you" who has not undergone the transformation of the author?) Yet it is evident that Washington McDonough distinguishes a world of milk and honey (the promised land it has been his privilege to escape) from "a land of darkness" in which he has overcome his temptation to become enamored of the things of "this world": although still "in the land of the liveing," he is in a purer state of readiness to go on to the next than is his addressee. As neither he nor his materially privileged former master can carry anything out of "this world" "when we go hence," and as both must equally go hence, he assumes a moral ground implicitly higher than that occupied by his addressee.

Yet the relationship is further complicated by the fact that, like the colonists in the Americas, the colonist in Africa is dependent materially on the mother country even if he means to lead a severely self-denying life that will distinguish him from the citizens of the land he has left. In the sentences immediately following the passage quoted above, Washington McDonough announces that he has become engaged to a woman of good family from Cincinnati who is worthy to share his fortunes; this news is followed by a plea that the former

Washington W. McDonough to John McDonough, February 18, 1846.
Courtesy of the Howard-Tilton Memorial Library, Tulane University.

master assist him materially in establishing a household: "I hope that you will be so kind as to send me out some thing to start on in the way of makeing a liveing or to live on for you know that my time is all spent in the Lords Service and not in worldly gains or speculations." This letter expresses the needs of its writer to declare himself radically apart from and yet united, however tenuously, in a divinely appointed purpose with his addressee. From the former slave's point of view, their common destiny as souls in God's presence obliges John McDonough to continue to support his conversion of the heathen in Africa.

Although Abigail Adams's observation that it is "more probable to unite Souls than Bodies" makes reference to the forbidding expanses of geographic space, it is also true that the smallest measure of geographic space may still be invested with insuperable barriers and that persons whose bodies occupy the same locale may well unite more readily through a steady paper converse. This, as we will have occasion to explore, is certainly the case with Emily Dickinson. But doubtless too it was true of many correspondences that took place in urban areas where, if the partners in the exchange did not choose to place bodies in proximity to one another, they could take advantage of the multiple daily mail deliveries to keep up alternate orders of intimate contact. In an essay that examines differences between communication by letter and communication by telephone, Vivian Gornick writes of a married man named Levinson, a resident of the Bronx, who in the 1920s addressed a constant stream of meditative, descriptive, philosophical letters to Gornick's mother when the latter was a young unmarried woman living on the Lower East Side. As coworkers in the same wholesale bakery, they did not choose to cultivate a significant face-to-face contact. Yet because a letter Levinson might write at 8 P.M. could reach the young woman the next morning, a density of conversation was easily maintained.[49]

SELF-CONSCIOUSNESS

As we turn to an examination of the letter writing of those who are authors by vocation, we do not enter a world of practice that differs formally and thematically from the correspondence of nonliterary writers of letters. What distinguishes the letters of an Emerson, a Dickinson, or a Henry Adams from those produced by correspondents who are not authors by vocation has largely to do with the self-conscious use of language that the vocational writer brings to the task and the ability of the writer to see the epistolary exchange as exemplary of the destiny of language in general. For these authors as for others of comparable sophistication, the sending and receiving of letters becomes a trope for the linguistic act. This does not mean that such self-consciousness is present in all the letters that Emerson, Dickinson, or Adams ever wrote, as scores of letters produced by these three are indistinguishable in many respects from the letters written by their nonvocational counterparts or by the less gifted letter writers with whom all three maintained passionate correspondences. Nor does it mean that nonprofessional writers lack self-consciousness, are devoid of a feeling for literary form, or are incapable of making theoretical insights into the nature of the epistolary exchange.

It cannot have escaped notice that letters written by men and women of vastly different circumstances resemble one another in certain predictable ways. In example after example we have seen writers incorporate in their salutations references to the distance that separates them from their addressees, the lapse of time since the last communication or face-to-face contact, and the means by which the present communication will be conveyed; in letter after letter closure is made with reference to the writer's abiding memory of the addressee, the hope that they will be reunited, and the transcendental principle of presence that upholds them and that renders their physical separation a transitory or illusory state. Such resemblances may be attributed to the fact that writers modeled the letters they wrote on those they received; the authority of letter-writing manuals and conduct books would have played a secondary role in encouraging an unquestioning acceptance of certain structures and phrasings. One of the first places one might look for evidence of self-consciousness, then, is in the handling of the genre's stock gestures; and yet it is surprising that, outside of the practice of vocational writers, ironic play rarely attaches to such gestures. The most extraordinary communications are frequently prefaced, and thus made possible, by the most commonplace beginnings. When Abream Scriven begins the letter to his wife with the phrase, "I take the pleasure of writing you these few with much regret to inform you that I am Sold," the first nine words create the impression of a conventional opening grasped hurriedly (and fragmentarily, as "these few" are an obvious truncation of the phrase "these few lines") to deliver a message in which no pleasure can be taken, yet the line serves Scriven as a way to commence the writing of his experience.

For many letter writers, the clichés of the genre are part of its condition and are instrumental in articulating epistolary relationships.

Two correspondents quoted in the foregoing discussion who differ in regional origin and ethnic identity begin letters in nearly identical ways: "I have taken this opportunity of addressing you a few lines to inform you that I am still in the land of the lieving," writes Washington McDonough in 1848 from Settra Kroo, Liberia; "after so long a silence I am again permitted to write a few lines to let you know that we are all yet upon the land among the lieving," writes Nancy Glenn in 1862 from Oregon. In 1863, on the banks of the Yazoo River, Henry Clay Bear, a private in the 116th Illinois Volunteer Army taking part in Sherman's unsuccessful siege of Vicksburg, opens a letter to his wife as follows: "I can still say I am in the land amongst the living; something that I hardly expected a few days ago."[50] In all three the writers proclaim what is not only far from self-evident to addressees but even somewhat improbable to themselves; in each case the recipient must have read the statement with the consciousness that the writer might well have perished in the interval between the time the letter was written and the moment that it is read. The formulaic affirmation that one is "still in the land of the living" serves to articulate a condition that language perhaps does not easily reduce to triteness. The authors are not aware of such reduction, and the phrase by no means detracts from what is compelling about what they have to relate.

Persons previously lacking experience in letter writing or exposure to the correspondence of others could find models for many of life's situations in one of scores of cheaply produced letter-writing manuals, all descendants, in one way or another, of Richardson's *Familiar Letters on Important Occasions*. A husband beginning an overseas journey might consult the following example from *The Ladies' and Gentlemen's Model Letter-Writer* in framing a dispatch to his wife:

> I take the opportunity of the pilot's return to send you a hurried and last farewell. Oh, my dearest, what but duty could reconcile me to leaving you? What but the certainty that we are both protected by our Heavenly Father could support me through the weary days and nights which I am destined to spend far from you? Ah! the waves that are now washing the sides of our vessel will soon cease to beat upon that shore where my wife, where my friends are all thinking of me.[51]

Like much authentic correspondence we have examined, the sample invokes an enduring principle of spiritual presence ("our Heavenly Father") and like much authentic correspondence it reflects (in the figure of the waves) upon the disrupted physical contiguity of correspondents. These thoughts come equipped with the emotional inflection of an interrogatory structure ("What but the certainty that...?") and an ostensibly involuntary exclamation ("Ah!"). The sample also articulates the absolute importance attached to the idea that a correspondent's continued existence is supported by the active remembrance of those who remain at home ("where my wife, where my friends are all thinking of me"). Contrived as it is, the sample reflects themes that occur commonly in actual letter exchanges.

As does the following sample, offered by *A New Letter-Writer, for the Use of Gentlemen* as an appropriate utterance in a letter "From a Brother to his married Sister in a Foreign Country":

> The distance which now separates us invests all that concerns you with a peculiar interest, and our anxiety on the subject of your welfare can only be allayed by as full and particular a recital as you can possibly write. Believe me, it is no mere curiosity that elicits this wish on our part to be better informed of all that befalls you; as, since we have but too much reason to conclude that our meetings together are perhaps now forever closed, we are the more anxious to hear from you as often as possible, and I am sure you will not withhold from us this pleasure.[52]

The sample inscribes the absence of the addressee as prophetic of a mortal separation and emphasizes the importance of a regular exchange by which the correspondents can maintain a mutual presence-at-a-distance. But this sample, like the one before it, is composed in ways that even the productions of gifted letter writers rarely are: not only is the structure excessively hypotactic while the components remain utterly clichéd, but beyond the generic occasion announced by the title there is nothing to suggest the specific contingencies that prompt even the most predictable epistolary expression.

A formula sometimes surfaces in unexpected contexts. A model condolence "On a Child's Death" appearing in *A New Letter-Writer, for the Use of Ladies* offers the following consolation:

> If anything could have caused me especial pain, it was the news of your sad bereavement. How I remember your dear child! Affectionate, lively, and intelligent, ever displaying a thoughtfulness beyond his years, and holding forth hopes of happiness in after times which will scarcely bear reflection.

donable. You are aware that the handwriting is considered one of the talismans of character. Whether this test may be depended on or not, the fact that letters travel farther than the sound of the voice, or the sight of the countenance can follow, renders it desirable that they should convey no incorrect or unfavourable impression. The lesser niceties of folding, sealing, and superscription, are not beneath the notice of a lady. Mrs. Farrar, in her excellent little work on Letter-writing, remarks, that it is " well to find out the best way of doing every thing, since there is a pleasure in doing things in the *best way*, which those miss, who think *any way* will do." Do not indulge in a careless style of writing, and excuse yourself on the plea of haste. This nourishes a habit which will be detrimental to excellence. Our sex have been complimented as the possessors of a natural taste for epistolary composition. It is an appropriate attainment, for it admits the language of the heart which we understand, and rejects the elaborate and profound sciences in which we are usually deficient. Ease and truth to nature, are its highest ornaments, and Cicero proved himself to be no less a master of its excellences, than of his more sublime art of eloquence, when he said: " Whatever may be the subject of my letters, they still speak the language of conversation."

To a finished female education, the acquisition of languages is generally deemed essential. The patient research which they require is a good dis-

Page from A New Letter-Writer, for the Use of Ladies *(1860)*.

It has, indeed, been a heavy blow, and I scarcely know how to talk of consolation under so bitter an affliction. But think, my dear ——, of One who "careth for all," who loves little children beyond others, and think of the bright and never-ending future life of that dear child, whose spirit has passed away but for a brief period, whose soul only waits in heaven to hail the mother from whom he has been parted.[53]

Although this model appears in a volume commended to "the use of ladies," men were free to employ such language, the typical expressions of grieving commonly inscribed in poems and letters and uttered aloud. In a letter written from Antelope Springs, Wyoming Territory, on June 24, 1876, Lieutenant Thaddeus Capron writes as follows to his wife, Cynthia, at Fort Laramie on receiving word of their two-and-a-half-year-old's death: "he has gone from us to that bright and better home—where Jesus calls and says Suffer the little children to come to me for of such is the Kingdom of heaven—I have faith that our little pet who has been taken from us is now among the number and that 'he is not lost but gone before' and will want to welcome his Papa and Mama to that bright and happy home where life's trials and troubles are o'er—."[54] In Capron's letter as in the model condolence, Jesus is represented as receiving the child's soul and the parents are asked to find consolation in the thought that the lost child will be restored to them at their own decease.

Yet the cliché condolence prepares for an utterance in which Capron's absence from his dying child, and his need of assurances of a particular sort, are registered with specifically articulated anguish: "[I] as yet do not know that he asked for papa," Capron writes, "—but hope that he did it will be a consolation to me to know that he thought of his absent papa—while he was in his death sickness even though I could not come to him he could feel that were papa there all would be done that papa could—[.]" More or less consciously, Capron hereby instructs his wife to write that he was indeed remembered by the deceased child and that a connection was made, an understanding was reached, that might redeem the permanent separation of the now absent son from the then absent father. True consolation for Capron thus lies in the epistolary future and will take the form of such affirmation as his wife cannot possibly withhold. Turning toward the end of his letter from domestic tragedy to an account of battlefield activities— and death in a different context—Capron assumes a soldier's characteristically laconic tone: "We found Indians in force—gave them a fight—lost 9 killed & 21 wounded. Indian loss heavy but not known."[55]

Nonliterary correspondents no doubt mined letter-writing manuals for language and suggestions, but the recurrence of phrases and rhetorical positions chiefly derives from the tendency of correspondents to imitate what they read in letters received. In irreverent mood, even unsophisticated writers are sometimes moved to parody the formulaic phrase. In July 1860, Mary Trussell, a New Hampshire farm girl of about thirteen, begins a letter to her foster sister, Delia Page, with this self-reflexive paragraph: " 'I now take my pen in hand to let you know I am well, and hope you are the same.' Oh did you ever in all your life see a letter commenced so. I know in 'old times' they always did begin so, and a good many begin so now. I always hated it. Well, Father recieved your kind letter of Tuesday night; I am very sorry I must wate 3 long weeks for a letter. But patients!"[56] Despite the ironic opening, however, the rest of this letter is thoroughly conventional; again, it is generally to the more gifted correspondent that we must look for the meta-commentary on epistolary discourse.

If ironic commentary on the stock features and phrases of the epistolary genre is unusual, self-consciousness that takes the form of a cultivated literary style or an embedded essay or extended narrative is not, and American letter writing abounds in examples of amateur literary effusions. The stylistic touch may be fleeting, as when Thaddeus Capron affects verse in what can only be the deliberate rhyming of "o'er" with "before." Some effusions are developed at length and possess a genuine uniqueness, like the two flirtatious letters Benjamin Hawkins (1754–1816) wrote as an Indian agent on the southeastern frontier to Elizabeth House Trist, a Philadelphian who married into a Virginia family and was early widowed.[57] Hawkins, a former Confederation congressman and U.S. senator from North Carolina who would have met Trist while representing his state during congressional meetings in Philadelphia, postures in two letters written to her in 1797 as a backwoods bachelor conversant with the Creek ladies yet wishing whimsically that Trist herself might one day "be Queen of Tookaubatche." In the second of the two letters, Hawkins rather boldly writes Trist into his mock-erotic fantasy. "I was some few days past, sorely afflicted with the gout or rheumatism. I could not turn in my blankets, and the arrival of the Queen of Tuckabatche was announced to me . . . I was so sure that it was you, that the gout left me for a moment and I rose up, but alass!"—it was not his addressee. Hawkins goes on to report that the young Creek widow offered her cattle and prestige as queen in exchange for the protection he could provide as her consort. "I immediately rose up in my bed and took her in my arms and huged her," Hawkins continues, "my hands wandered to certain parts the most attractive and she resisted not."[58] Perhaps the distance between Hawkins and Trist alone permitted the freedom with which he writes of a woman's body that she might well have read as the narrative proxy of her own.

Other examples of epistolary literariness are more conventional. "On this island, dear Mother, there are secret, hidden, insidious foes which undermine one's happiness," writes William Thompson Lusk (1838–97), an officer in the New York State Militia, afterward a prominent New York City obstetrician, from Battery Island, South Carolina, in June 1862:

> Flies march over one in heavy Battalions—whole pounds of them at a time. Mosquitoes go skirmishing about and strike at every exposed position. Sandflies make the blood flow copiously. Fleas form in Squadrons which go careering over one's body leaving all havoc behind. Ticks get into one's hair. Ants creep into one's stocking. Grasshoppers jump over one's face. You turn and brush your face. You writhe in agony. You quit a couch peopled with living horrors. You cry for mercy!—In vain. These critters are "Secesh."[59]

In addition to excelling in such commonplace satire, Lusk also distinguishes himself as a critic of letter writing, occasioned by the interception of a package of Confederate letters. "Of course we had to read them to glean as far as possible the state of political feeling in the South," Lusk explains, "and I blush to say we read with special interest the tender epistles which fair South Carolina maidens penned for the eye alone of South Carolina heroes." Among "the peculiarities of the Aborigines" learned from such perusals are "that the ladies are so modest that they write of themselves with a little i" and "that all Southern babies send their papas 'Howdy' "; but "above all, penmanship, spelling and composition showed that the greatest need of the South, is an army of Northern Schoolmasters."[60]

Lusk was not in the position to observe that Northern correspondence was as likely to be incorrect as Southern. "I rote you yesday but have not maile it we are Order to be ready to march a 10 O clock to nite with 3 days Provishion in our Haversacks," George H. Ewing of Company K, the 20th Michigan Infantry, begins a letter to his parents from

Fredericksburg in December 1862; "Last night we throwed up brest works to protect the artillerist from fire of the Sharp shooters," writes Henry Clay Bear from the banks of the Yazoo. "We can see that they war not Idle either. They was pounding all night."[61] In matters of style, war letters tend to be laconic, a diarist treatment of a succession of days, although it is not unusual to see such writing adopt the sentimental style of contemporary popular literature and domestic language generally—a discourse of professional military facts alternating with a discourse of familial feeling, such as we see in Thaddeus Capron's letter written in the decade following the Civil War. Given Lusk's evident literary and social pretenses, he perhaps could never easily have been compelled by such unschooled writing.

Finally, there is the cultivated letter writing of authors like Celia Thaxter, a writer of children's books who lived as a recluse on an island off the coast of Maine; Mary Abigail Dodge, the essayist and biographer who wrote under the pseudonym "Gail Hamilton"; and Susan Hale, the younger sister of Lucretia and Edward Everett Hale, who spent much of her life in study and travel; as well as others whose letters, prized sentimentally by their recipients, and deemed to possess at least a secondary literary merit, were gathered for publication after their authors' deaths.[62] Such belletristic writing is "professional" in ways that most of the writing considered in this chapter is not, but it reflects nonetheless a popular practice and taste; letters of this sort tend to be witty, opinionated, heavily descriptive, and occasionally pious, and showcase a sensibility of everyday appreciation as expressed in word pictures and the registry of fugitive sensations. Yet beneath the impression they often give of a life of leisured aesthetic pursuit, these letters often contain allegories of deeper psychological and social resonance. In contrast to the insistent jauntiness and surface optimism of such letters, the unsentimental, ironic, darkly sophisticated letters of Alice James and Marian Hooper Adams manifestly record the marginalization of socially privileged, highly intelligent, ultimately debilitated women who might well have written professionally.[63]

In the early letters of Emerson, Dickinson, and Adams we meet with much writing that deserves to be called amateur literary effusion. Yet their productions are accompanied by an ironic self-reflexivity and a capacity for experimentation that presses for an understanding of the epistolary genre as a literary form in which much may be learned about the nature of language and human discourse generally. This self-reflexivity and capacity for play are not always obvious, however, and much of their letter writing will impress us as consistent with the common practice and recurrent themes this chapter has reviewed. Where their distinction as letter writers becomes particularly evident, we are often struck less by their difference than by their ability to foreground common epistolary conditions, what the letter genre exacts of all who would practice it.

3

I Cannot Write This Letter

Ralph Waldo Emerson

· ·

Like children in other literate households across New England and the United States, Emerson was accustomed to writing letters from the time he could hold a pen. The first evidence of his activity as a correspondent dates from his fourth year; the sophistication of his earliest surviving letter, written when he was nearly ten, suggests an already inveterate practice.[1] Given the residence of relatives in Concord and Kennebunk, Maine, Emerson and his brothers would have had many opportunities to contribute to family epistles. After the death in 1811 of Emerson's father, the household (six children and the widow, Ruth Haskins Emerson) became financially dependent on family, moving to various Boston addresses as opportunity offered, and residing for a while in Concord; epistolary contacts in these years would no doubt have been assiduously maintained. As the Emerson brothers in turn left home to pursue studies and take temporary positions as schoolmasters, there arose a rich and complicated sibling correspondence. Reading, health, and family finances constitute the staples of discussion, and the fraternal exchanges accrue to the narrative of their ongoing efforts to complete schooling and choose professions consistent with the upper-middle-class station of Ruth Haskins Emerson, daughter of a prominent Boston merchant, and William Emerson, late minister of the First Church.

The narratives that Emerson, his brothers, and their paternal aunt, Mary Moody Emerson, constructed in their correspondences established models of friendship and patterns of coherence that Emerson would draw on throughout his life. Efforts to keep poverty at bay would soon be accompanied by a struggle with ill health brought on by overwork and depression; tuberculosis, the disease that would claim the lives of Edward and Charles, threatened Waldo and carried off his first wife, Ellen Louisa Tucker Emerson, whose own narrative of chronic illness made her as much a member of the family as the fact of her marriage to Waldo. For a large portion of his life, Emerson's letters would tell the story of isolated and afflicted individuals or groups of disaffected scholars attempting to realize spiritual possibilities while negotiating a variety of social and physical burdens. The marginalization that his early circumstances imposed on him reinforced the solitude to which he would perhaps in any event have been predisposed, a solitude that remains central to his life's ongoing narratives. Emerson's early circumstances profoundly shape his career as a writer of letters, his literary and social experiments with the epistolary form. His career as a writer of letters in turn shapes his course as an author who came of age in antebellum America. Yet, extreme as the uses to which he put the letter may appear, they exhibit what less ambitious and less self-conscious letter writing of the period also invests in the genre: a desire to construct an alternative, utopian domain of social relation.

Although the central plot of the brothers' correspondence consists in their constant struggle against penury, it is a narrative largely present by implication. The foreground is occupied by accounts of recent events and—especially in Ralph Waldo Emerson's case—intellectual and verbal play. Examining the first several years of his surviving letters, we see Emerson experimenting with a wide range of expression, constructing a self that is already identified with facility in verbal art. We see him take a productively ironic approach to the letter genre and make free use of its relaxed constraints. And we observe him cultivate in the letter occasions to fashion an at once private and social persona, alternately signing himself *Ralph* and *Waldo* until the former is dropped altogether when he turns eighteen. The circumstances of Emerson's early letter writing are by no means unique: the dispersion of siblings is a common inducement of nineteenth-century family correspondence, and the special situation of the Emersons, for whom a death has necessitated long-term material and psychological adjustments, is matched in the narratives told by other family correspondences.[2] Although an ironic handling of epistolary formulas is unusual outside the practices of those who go on to pursue literary interests, the working out of self-identity in letter sheet occurs in the correspondence of most young adults. Emerson's correspondents were perhaps little struck with the inventiveness of his early letters. Yet his lifework begins in the astonishing if largely conventional epistolary practice of his adolescence.

An interest in form distinguishes Emerson's early letters. Among the most impressive of his youthful performances is a rebus that Emerson at age eleven sent to his brother William (a facsimile of this communication appears as the frontispiece of the first volume of *The Letters of Ralph Waldo Emerson*): interspersed with the childishly tall and well-formed cursive script are finely drawn ink images that combine with the script to make coherent if uniformly banal sentences. Of images, eyes and yew trees predominate, representing the first and second persons of epistolary address; haystacks, top hats, scrolls inscribed "last will and testament," and inns also recur as visual puns and phonemes. Even without the famous caricature of Christopher Cranch in mind, it might be hard to observe the eyes without recalling the famous passage in *Nature* (1836) in which the ocular organ figures so prominently, yet a more than casual connection can be made between the effort in both to render the familiar strange, the commonplace transcendent: "Crossing a bare common, in snow puddles, at twilight, under a clouded sky, without having in my thoughts any occurrence of special good fortune, I have enjoyed a perfect exhilaration. . . . Standing on the bare ground . . . all mean egotism vanishes. I become a transparent eye-ball. I am nothing. I see all" (CW 1:10). Decoding the rebus, William read sentences like the following: "I hope you will not be offended if I attempt a letter in hieroglyphics . . . I like Concord very much. I go to school here and I like it more and more every day . . . Aunt and Charles send love Charles more than he can express. . . . Hieroglyphics take up too much time and paper; so pray excuse my shortness" (LRWE 1:7). Yet even after the reader arrives at the pedestrian message, the pictures remain, and with them an artifact that exhibits a strong if not yet self-conscious desire to bespeak the mysterious aspect of common experience.

Emerson is not known to have ever again written a letter by means of pictorial hieroglyphics, although the principle, articulated in *Nature*, that "every man's condition is a solution in hieroglyphic to those inquiries he would put" (CW 1:7), reveals a lasting fascination with a self and world that exist to be read and whose initial resistance to reading gives way to euphoric, clairvoyant recognition on the part of the knowing subject. As author, Emerson would come to approach experience as an emblem whose interpretation is mediated by the poet's language. It is therefore noteworthy that Emerson should present himself in the early letters as poet (if also, self-deprecatingly, poetaster): two of the earliest survivors are letters in verse to Sarah Alden Bradford, who appears to have encouraged Emerson to translate portions of the *Aeneid*. Although he is far from conceiving, much less assuming, the hierophantic role that he would later ascribe to the poet, even in his self-satiric heroic couplets he employs language to transform the deathly ordinary conditions that regular correspondents characteristically register in an effort to sustain what they agree to be the necessary frequency of the exchange. "Again, dear brother, I have commenced a letter," Ralph (as he then mostly signs himself) writes to William,

> It is now after 2 and Mother is at dinner, Edward & Charles are gone of an errand; all is quiet, or in dialect Poetice—
>> Here Silence holds her reign & all is quiet
>> Save where the wintry wind howls hoarse without
>> And enters at the chink—
> But I forgot you do not like My Lisping Muse why then should she be called from her slumbers to give entertainment to one who will only answer her with reproofs and say "Ralph don't make poetry till you have gone through Algebra." (LRWE 1:15)

This excerpt is interesting for the way that it exerts counterpressure on the quotidian present that Emerson is obliged to record, refracted in the mock-somber observations that take their tone from Gray's "Elegy," and it is noteworthy for the way that it also exerts counterpressure on the older brother to whom the letter is addressed, who would hold Ralph to a more serious-minded progression through the secondary curriculum. Emerson proceeds to give an account of his current studies and to report what was preached on Sunday from the pulpit of First Church. Toward the letter's close he returns to his Lisping Muse:

> Barren of all information or news I am obliged to
>> Leave, dear William in unfinish'd state
>> This sorry letter to its dreaded fate (LRWE 1:16)

—that fate being William's indulgent if decided disapproval.

Long before Emerson is ready to assert that "Idealism acquaints us with the total disparity between the evidence of our own being, and the evidence of the world's being" (CW 1:37), he proceeds in the conviction that one can exert imaginative pressure against the barren facts of a despotic present—can construct language that at once represents and redeems those facts. The letter genre and the correspondent's obligation to employ its forms figure for Emerson among those facts; although he wrote letters throughout his life, finding in the genre an outlet for what he claimed to be unable to state in any other, he often betrays an impatience with the epistolary occasion: "I was not born under epistolary stars," he would write to Elizabeth Peabody in 1838 (LRWE 2:176). Emerson's awareness of the letter as a potentially oppressive fact—a fact of stock gestures and set boundaries—takes the form, as one would expect with an intellectually restless youth, of a parody of its clichés: "I cannot begin with that sublime expression 'I now take this opportunity' because I do not know of any," Emerson opens a letter of November 1816 to Edward Bliss Emerson; "All send love for that is very cheap," he remarks in closing to Edward in July 1817 (LRWE 1:26, 38). "I have nothing to interest you, no news to tell, no business to transact, no sentiment or poetry to communicate, no important questions to ask," he addresses William in 1819, measuring the obligation to write against his capacity to produce something more than the rote confirmation that he lives and breathes, "& yet with all these negatives I am presumptuous enough to put so much trust in the workings of my own barren brain as to sit down with the intention of writing a letter of respectable length to your most serene sobriety" (LRWE 1:83).

The trust that Emerson was willing to invest "in the workings of my own barren brain" (itself a fact requiring applications of self-trust and will) is the motive resource of his early letters. The literary intention of this writing is able to draw all passing thought into its avowedly subsistence economy, and for that it can thank the letter's paratactic structure, which does not privilege the overall unity of the composition so much as the local effect of the momentary utterance. Unable to resist parodying the conventional phrases of epistolary address, Emerson glories nonetheless in the license that derives from the letter's attenuation of compositional constraints, behavior we see repeated in the early letter writing of Dickinson and Adams. "My letters in general you see are a strange medley of every thing and any thing," he writes to Edward in 1816, "—Whatever comes first I put in, if I think it will interest or amuse you at all" (LRWE 1:27).[3]

Such medley had a transformative effect on the often gloomy present of Emerson's childhood and adolescence. In a letter of October 15, 1816, to Edward Bliss Emerson, a younger brother more receptive to poetic flights than William, Ralph brilliantly compensates for a change in circumstances in which Edward anxiously leaves home for preparatory school in Andover while Ralph and other members move into depressing quarters in Boston. Twice in the letter Emerson resorts to his Lisping Muse, in the first instance celebrating Edward's arrival at Andover ("And now arrives the chariot of state / That bears with regal pomp Ned, Bliss the great"), and in the second matching the evidence of his own being against that of the world's as the latter appears through the window of his basement lodging. "The wide unbounded prospect lies before me," he begins, echoing the conclusion to *Paradise Lost*,

Imprimis then, a dirty yard
By boards and dirt and rubbish marr'd
Pil'd up aloft a mountain steep
Of broken Chairs and beams a heap
But rising higher you explore
In this fair prospect wonders more
Upon the right a wicket grate
The left appears a jail of State
Before the view all boundless spreads
And 5 tall Chimnies lift their lofty heads— (LRWE 1:19)

This is a poetry of satire and psychic subsistence, creating prospects of language where the eye meets only confinement, asserting the power of word and eye. "Every spirit builds itself a house; and beyond its house, a world; and beyond its world, a heaven," Emerson would write in "Prospects," the concluding section of *Nature* (CW 1:44). The work of building the house required a familiarization with tools and a preliminary clearing of space. In such lines as appear in the ungoverned discursive spaces of Ralph's correspondence with Edward, tools are tried out and preliminary acts of clearing proceed.

As Emerson attains young manhood his letters mature accordingly: his pen is less freely given to paratactic urgings, poetic fancy no longer parades across the sheet, and his prose is able to sustain argumentative focus. Increasingly his journals and notebooks provide space for such verbal experiment as appears in his earliest letters. His epistolary communication continues to be flexible and improvisational but in ways that are more engagingly interlocutory. Beyond serving purposes of self-expression and affirmation of family bonds, Emerson's letters strive now to build an intellectual basis of friendship. Sibling politics continue to figure in the correspondences with his brothers, but discussion of religious, philosophical, and political issues as well as questions relating to professional vocation constitute an increasingly adult exchange. The intellectual friendship that Emerson and his brothers establish with one another owes a great deal to the active mentoring—most of it conducted through the mails—of their paternal aunt, Mary Moody Emerson, with whom Emerson corresponded from boyhood and whose role in the formation of Emerson's thought and literary style is well documented.[4] In epistolary conversation with Mary, Ralph Waldo Emerson was encouraged to consider religious and philosophical matters with grave earnestness and portentous mood. In discussions that centered on innate depravity, divine immanence, and the irreducible mystery of God and existence, as well as the divine and demonic powers of poetry, he was able to claim philosophical and religious inquiry as his vocation.

If in his earliest surviving letters Emerson exhibits an understanding of the ways in which language restructures the reality it is called on to represent, in the letters that he writes as a young man, and particularly in his correspondence with Mary Moody Emerson, he begins to identify philosophical inquiry as a transformative exercise of human power and freedom. The lengthy missives he wrote to Mary throughout his young manhood and especially while he was preparing to be approbated for the ministry confess a singular dependence on her critical readership, and although doctrinally they have already gone their separate ways, in writing to his aunt Emerson has the attention of one with whom he shares emotional and visionary intensity. "I need small persuasion to send you pretty long letters," Emerson writes her from Cambridge on September 23, 1826. ". . . I am so pleased to get rid of my mean cares a little & sculk into the lobbies that lead into the heaven of philosophy and listen when the door is open if perchance some fragment some word of power from the colloquy sublime may fall on mine ear—Such words purify poor humanity. They clear my perceptions for my duties" (LRWE 1:174). The "colloquy sublime" that Emerson seeks through his exchange with Mary is a notion that contains the seed of later thought, inasmuch as by it Emerson refers less to a conversation between two historical people than to the immemorial process of philosophical inquiry ("the heaven of philosophy"), which people join as their preparation and circumstances permit. As we saw

in chapter 1, Emerson invokes conversation on the order of a "colloquy sublime" in his early correspondence with Thomas Carlyle; he
does so with various others, most remarkably, as we shall see, with
Caroline Sturgis.

Having attained in the letter of September 23, 1826, a sense of
intellectual and intersubjective sanctuary, Emerson proceeds to articulate what would become one of the foundational tenets of his mature
thought: "it is one of the *feelings* of modern philosophy, that it is wrong
to regard ourselves so much in a *historical* light as we do, putting Time
between God & us; and that it were fitter to account every moment of
the existence of the Universe as a new Creation, and *all* as a revelation
proceeding each moment from the Divinity to the mind of the observer" (LRWE 1:174). In such sentences we may perceive anticipation
of the "Divinity School Address" and the call, in the prologue of
Nature, for "an original relation to the universe" (CW 1:7). But we also
see Emerson merging the idea of conversation with the notion of an
ongoing revelation that occurs to the human mind sufficiently observant of its infinite connection. In a journal entry of September 1838
that later appears in "The Over-Soul," Emerson remarks that "in all
conversation between two persons tacit reference is made, as to a third
party, to a common nature. That third party or common nature is not
social; is impersonal; is God" (JMN 7:67; CW 2:164). Here as in many
other passages Emerson argues that truth is experienced or arrived at
through an interlocutory process: that what humans know of truth
proceeds from divine sources within if also beyond them, and that
awareness of the true arises from such "sublime" colloquy as human
conversation, open to visionary susceptibilities, is able to reflect.[5]

Early in his mature correspondence, Emerson distinguishes a written conversation, in which he might excel, from a spoken conversation, in which he felt himself deficient. When he alludes in his journals
and essays to the satisfactions of conversing he draws on an experience
that for him was largely conducted by letter sheet. His adult discussions with Mary Moody Emerson, who could be abrupt and abrasive
in person, were by mutual agreement almost entirely epistolary; her
preference of written to spoken conversation no doubt did much to
instill his.[6] The distinction between oral and inscribed colloquy is important not only to an explanation of his epistolary practice but to any
examination of how he saw himself as an author whose social and
political existence must be mediated by texts prepared in private. What
he would reiterate at various points in his life as his preference of the

written to the spoken utterance receives its fullest treatment in a letter of February 23, 1827, to his brother Charles, dispatched from Saint Augustine, Florida, where Emerson had gone for his health in the weeks following his approbation. Encouraging Charles to join him in a copious correspondence as a way to promote intellectual growth, Emerson registers his conviction that the activity of writing permits the highest communication between souls. In letters, Emerson affirms, the writer finds the most favorable conditions of philosophic discourse, the purest opportunities for language to serve Truth. "Write. write," Emerson exhorts his brother.

> I have heard men say (heaven help their poor wits,) they had rather have ten words viva voce from a man than volumes of letters for getting at his opinion. —I had rather converse with them by the interpreter. Politeness ruins conversation. You get nothing but the scum & surface of opinions when men are afraid of being unintelligible in their metaphysical distinctions, or that the subtlety & gravity of what they want to say will draw too largely on the extemporaneous attention of their company. Men's spoken notions are thus nothing but outlines & generally uninviting outlines of a subject, & so general, as to have no traits appropriate & peculiar to the individual. But when a man writes, he divests himself of his manners & all physical imperfections & it is the pure intellect that speaks. There can be no deception here. You get the measure of his soul. Instead of the old verse, "Speak that I may know thee," I write "Speak, that I may suspect thee; write, that I may *know* thee." (LRWE 1:191)

Emerson represents spoken conversation as so corrupted by canons of politeness as to constitute nothing of the self-presence that speech in Western metaphysics traditionally invokes; instead of serving as the "dangerous supplement" that it does for Rousseau, writing for Emerson rescues the very possibility of truth and consensus in language.[7] Elsewhere Emerson does affirm the power of speech to reveal being and suggests that his privileging of the written word derives alternately from a personal weakness as a conversationalist and from a historical condition in which face-to-face dialogue is obstructed by social forms or callused by the aggressive manner of political disputation.[8] Hence his departure in this matter from the Judeo-Christian and Platonic traditions that generally inform his thought is one decidedly qualified: in his preference of the written utterance, Emerson nevertheless glorifies the voice that speaks by way of the inscription (in writing, as he states above, "it is the pure intellect that *speaks*"), and his work as poet, essayist, and letter writer always attempts to image a voice. In his public work, voice is performatively monologic. In the letters he writes to his circle of epistolary intimates, Emerson speaks as though utterance finally might put off disguise, and the voice as written performs as a dialogic and intimate intellection. Although he does not designate the letter as the exclusive genre of ideal conversation, in the act of epistolary inscription Emerson frequently identifies what he sets down on the page as his word's freest and fullest pronouncement.

As Emerson wrote in praise of writing at the age of twenty-one, he had before him a long career of speaking from pulpit and lyceum lectern. Much of his thought about what he wished to accomplish as an author, as we might expect of someone who would give years of his life to public speaking, concerns what he may effect as one who speaks (or reads a prepared text) before a roomful of auditors. What he expects of his oratorical performances is true to the curriculum of the age and to the civic and religious rituals that readings in Demosthenes, Cicero, and Hugh Blair supported: the orator was to command, move, and transform those who listened.[9] "I anticipated a flaming excitement in mine & in the popular mind," he writes his brother William in October 1827, critiquing their brother Edward's commencement oration. ". . . As it was, people were pleased & called it the finest of orations . . . but I meant they should be electrified. *and too* much astounded to be complimentary" (LRWE 1:210–11). Even in an age that asked much of its public speakers, Emerson's standards were sternly Olympian. As a young man about to enter the ministry, he might well contemplate the spectacle of an Edward Everett or a Daniel Webster and regard himself as "the meek ambassador of the Highest." Daunted by the prospect of public tasks, he applies to the familiar, private sources of his intellectual and spiritual life. "Can you not suggest the secret oracles which such a commission needs," he writes Aunt Mary in September 1826. ". . . Can you not awaken a sympathetic activity in torpid faculties? Whatever heaven has given me or withheld, my feelings or the expression of them is very cold, my understanding & my tongue slow & unaffecting. It may be each excitement administered from within may impel a swifter circulation in the outer channels of manner & power. The letters I get from the Vale," Emerson concludes, referring to his Aunt Mary's dispatches, "prove this purpose better than any other compositions" (LRWE 1:171).

Emerson's recourse to an "excitement administered from within" reflects what would become his lifelong cultivation of a solitude open to the interlocutory stimulus of an inner circle as well as his habitual conversion of private utterance to public statement, visible in the innumerable sentences and paragraphs first set down in journals and letters that subsequently appear in his lectures and essays. But the passage quoted from the letter to Mary Moody Emerson suggests a fundamental ambivalence with which his authorship would long contend. Although journal and letter writings precede and prepare for the composition of lectures and essays, there is a marked discontinuity between private and public discourse—between writing directed to a known reciprocating audience and writing that is not. The discourse of the private exchange possesses a facility and affords satisfactions not to be found in the discourse crafted for public address. The private life of the mind and soul as lived out in the pages of journals and letters assumes a familiarity of readership that the public word cannot assume. Emerson would sustain a long career as a public speaker, but the aversion that he confesses to Mary Moody Emerson as he is about to enter the ministry would never entirely leave him.

Emerson transcribed large extracts of his correspondence with Aunt Mary to his journals. Under the anagram "Tanmurya" he records both sides of the exchange, his own often boldly speculative expatiations and his aunt's disputatious, frequently tart, consistently severe, yet highly valued responses. Many of the ideas that form the nucleus of *Nature*, "The Divinity School Address," and *Essays: First Series* receive an early or initial statement in the letters of 1826–27 to Aunt Mary: his objection to the historical claims of religious authority and to the exclusive validity of Christianity, his skeptical stance toward personal deity, and his affirmation of an in-dwelling God, continuing revelation, and self-trust. The letters serve the purpose of allowing Emerson to articulate such religious leadings as are stimulated by his readings in Hume and his growing knowledge of German biblical criticism; addressing his conservative if similarly visionary, his ever trustworthy if disagreeable aunt, he is able to gauge the heresy of his emerging convictions as well as explore themes and rehearse phrasings for the supply of sermons that will constitute his stock-in-trade. Although at this point in his life Emerson is making extensive use of journals and notebooks to record and reflect upon his reading and experience, it is significant that many of his fundamental ideas receive early articulation in the overtly dialogic letters from which the journal repository is thereafter established. Passages from letters to his brothers and other correspondents likewise appear in his journals; the practice of transcribing extracts of correspondence, both outgoing and incoming, would continue for many years.

The letters transcribed to the journals comport well with Emerson's other journal entries in which he observes and meditates with an impromptu, conversational voice. The voice of the letters and journals makes its way into the language of the lectures and essays, the conversationality of which Emerson cultivates in an effort to speak familiarly to the public ear, avoiding the formulaic oratory generally fostered by his neoclassical education.[10] In *Nature*, Emerson identifies conversation with picturesque, idiomatic, spontaneous utterance, metaphor and poetry—locution that confesses the "immediate dependence of language upon nature" (CW 1:20). Objecting in a journal entry of June 1839 to the nonidiomatic triteness of much conventional writing, Emerson observes that "whosoever draws on the language of conversation ... will speak as the stream flows" (JMN 7:208). We may trace the emergence of Emerson's conversational public style to his conversational private style (such as appears in his letters to Mary Moody Emerson) and our ability to do so suggests that his celebration of colloquial language only partly derives from what, following the Wordsworth of *Lyrical Ballads*, he supposes to be its closeness to Nature (God, Truth, originary meaning). Emerson's deficiency as a conversationalist coexisted with a vast need to participate in philosophical dialogue as well as to form and sustain a variety of relationships. To the extent that satisfactory interchange was unavailable to him in social situations—"All conversation among literary men is muddy," he complains in September 1839 (JMN 7:242)—he pursued an idealized version in the written medium. The letter became his chief means for the fashioning of personal contacts.

Not all of Emerson's personal contacts were based in philosophical dialogue, and even those so founded were not exclusively philosophical in their orientation. The exchange with Thomas Carlyle, for instance, is in large measure a business correspondence in which Emerson, as Carlyle's de facto American literary agent, reports on matters of book contracts, sales, royalties, and piracies.[11] Emerson's extensive correspondence with publishers, lyceum directors, aspiring authors, and submitters of manuscripts to the *Dial* demonstrates that the letter existed for him as a pragmatic medium of negotiation permitting him to maintain a masterfully aloof self-representation more or less invested in the issue at hand. The rhetoric of congeniality and sincerity is a standard feature of Emerson's epistolary style, a style that often seems intent on minimizing conflict, ambivalence, and hostility, as the troubled Emerson-Carlyle and Emerson-Fuller correspondences particularly illustrate. In examining the philosophically self-conscious correspondences, we do not find a first person disjunct from that inscribed in more mundane letters, much less a "truer" Emerson, but we do find a voice elaborately constructed as the true, ideal, supremely sincere self, set off at a salubrious distance from the business of the world and the embodied selfhood of others, and because of that distance superlatively eligible (in Emerson's view) for friendship and conversation. It is these correspondences that are the most genre-reflexive of the many Emerson maintained.

Epistolary exchange not only promised access to the "colloquy sublime" but provided what Emerson theorized in journal entry, essay, and letter as the one true occasion of friendship. Friendship, in exalted form, alone made sincere language and philosophical inquiry possible. For Emerson, friendship, letter writing, and authorship would remain inextricably bound.

THE POETICS OF EPISTOLARY FRIENDSHIP

Early and late, friendship and writing converge for Emerson in what he regards as frank and spontaneous utterance, discourse that achieves a transparency unrivaled by other forms of expression. The correspondences with his brothers and aunt were self-consciously consecrated to philosophic truth, yet Mary's impress is not the only one that his letters register and other exchanges bring out significantly different personae and nuances. His correspondence with first wife Ellen Louisa Tucker Emerson, judging by the letters she wrote to him (his letters to her have disappeared), must also have been formative in that it allowed Emerson to participate in colloquy at once philosophic, poetic, and erotic—a melding of motives that reappears later in his correspondence with Caroline Sturgis.

"I am resolved to night to let you peep into the deep well of my heart which is bubbling up with a crowd of newly arrived thoughts," Ellen begins a letter in 1828, inscribing an intimacy that dissolves the binary oppositions of head to heart, body to soul—the copious language of the missive endeavoring to project the absent lover as a pellucid and idealized presence. "Your letter was better than all the empty parting kisses in the world," she writes the following spring, "and though some did wonder why I did not poke my hand out the window to give a parting shake you I well know did not—What a blessed thing is this silent mutual understanding!" Articulating a theme that Emerson must certainly have developed in his letters to her, Ellen at once celebrates the occasion of a letter's arrival and the wordless accord that makes letter writing strictly redundant. Yet it is just such redundancy that Ellen and Waldo (with countless other epistolary lovers) prize. "I tell you Waldo Emerson you must not leave off writing me when we live together," Ellen remarks in September 1829, after their wedding but before they have set up their household. "I love such long lived lines of affection—and your last letter gave me such a hopeful peaceful, happy, joyous hour as I never find anything else can produce."[12] Ellen's letters reflect the passionate bond between the newly united husband and wife still ascertaining the ways in which they may be present (and absent) to one another, yet avowals of intense response to letters received is common in Emerson's circles of correspondence.

In "Friendship" (1840), an essay that at once sets austere standards for friendship and that implicitly grieves the deaths of Ellen in 1831, Edward in 1834, and Charles in 1836, Emerson not only conflates the human bond with letter writing but also letter writing with authorship generally. Indeed, he opens the essay by identifying the conditions of the epistolary exchange as those most conducive to his aims as author. "Our intellectual and active powers increase with our affection," begins the third paragraph. "The scholar sits down to write, and all his years of meditation do not furnish him with one good thought or happy expression; but it is necessary to write a letter to a friend,—and, forthwith, troops of gentle thoughts invest themselves, on every hand, with chosen words" (CW 2:113). Letter writing is represented as fluent and nonepistolary writing as halting, and this in the context of a volume of essays that comes as the culmination of "years of meditation" for the scholar Emerson.[13] Although the colloquial tone and metaphoric invention that characterize *Essays: First Series* hardly support this view of his prose, the process by which he commodified his work for public consumption—first as lectures, later as essays—clearly wore at Emerson. His literary wares lacked the unbounded and interlocutory character of such epistolary communion as he had enjoyed in his youthful correspondences with his brothers, Mary Moody Emerson, and Ellen, and as he sought in the late 1830s to establish with a new circle. In letters written in the years preceding the book's publication, Emerson registers the strain of economic enterprise and looks on his gainful production as so much alienated intellectual labor.[14]

In friendship, by contrast, his authorship seeks as recompense the letter written in reply: an exchange in kind that levels distinctions between writing and reading, author and audience, and that exists materially as a metonym of the social bond. Although Emerson never explicitly identifies it as such, friendship, as theorized in the essay, is from first to last a *written* relationship, one that unfolds, more or less coauthored, as an intellectual and spiritual narrative. Given its inscribed nature, friendship requires an exchange of texts to bridge a distance that always separates individuals and that physical proximity and face-to-face conversation do nothing to diminish. Consistently in "Friendship," Emerson represents the epistolary medium as the exclusive channel of intercourse, the site of a friendship's success as well as its failure. "Dear Friend," he gives as an example of a letter that a person in all candor might write "to each new candidate for his love": "If I was sure of thee, sure of thy capacity, sure to match my mood with thine, I should never think again of trifles, in relation to thy comings and goings. I am not very wise: my moods are quite attainable: and I respect thy genius: it is to me as yet unfathomed; yet dare I not presume in thee a perfect intelligence of me, and so thou art to me a delicious torment. Thine ever, or never" (CW 2:117). In the essay's severe argumentation, failure always seems more probable than success, "never" the more probable term of friendship than "ever."[15] Yet Emerson's actual correspondence during the years that "Friendship" was written tells a different story. Far from perpetrating an impossible elevation of thresholds, his letters of this period proceed in the assumption that supreme moments of interpersonal consensus are being or are always about to be realized in the abundant flow of epistles for which he serves as node. Rather than discouraging what might uniformly be written off as a mere pretense to friendship, the ideal terms of human bonding serve, in his letters, to locate friendship in the facile expression of like-minded aspiration.

Beginning in the late 1830s, after the deaths of Ellen, Edward, and Charles and the crisis of vocation that culminated in his resignation from the Second Church, and after Mary Moody Emerson had receded as his major intellectual interlocutor, Emerson came into what may be distinguished as a second community of correspondents. Finding himself among a set of people who constituted a following, Emerson discovered in the companionship of a private circle fresh and at times euphoric occasions for conversation and friendship. The principal figures of this group were Samuel Gray Ward, Anna Barker Ward, Caroline

Sturgis, and Margaret Fuller, through whom Emerson had become acquainted with the others. Letters and appended journals, circulated among friends, served as the media of a loosely formed society of individuals who subscribed to such views as Emerson had articulated in *Nature* and who looked for inspiration to such European luminaries as Carlyle, Kant, and Goethe, as well as Bettina von Arnim, whose *Gunderode* and *Goethe's Correspondence with a Child*, for all of their drawn-out Sturm und Drang, were prized by Emerson and his friends.[16] Whereas in his correspondence with his brothers and Mary Moody Emerson the letter had been the vehicle of experiments in idea and expression, in his correspondence with these friends the letter becomes an experimental medium—text and metonym of an ongoing exploration of friendship and community. These experiments developed in opposition to Emerson's efforts as lecturer and essayist; they may be said to represent an epistolary privatization of the idea of community.

A good share of the interest of Emerson's letter writing lies in the respite from the public realm that his epistolary practice reflects and facilitates. His desire for alternatives to the society of the lecture hall is evinced in his conception of the audience as the paying consumers of culture and in his appropriation of the ideals of spiritual community to the sphere of private fellowship. His respite never culminated in withdrawal: as long as he made his living as a lyceum speaker Emerson found ways to "look upon the Lecture room as the true church of today & as the home of a richer eloquence than Faneuil Hall or the Capitol ever knew" (October 23, 1839; JMN 7:277–78). But despite the pleasure he took in performance, Emerson seldom approached the lectern without ambivalence. A side of him was ever disposed to abhor public gatherings and to scorn the topical discussions that often provided their focus; he inveterately shrank from open debate and was averse to the venting of popular passions. Against the public occasion he asserted the unconditional priority of a private expression of truth. "I do not gladly utter any deep conviction of the soul in any company where I think it will be contested," Emerson writes in October 1838. ". . . Truth has already ceased to be itself, if polemically said; & if the soul would utter oracles, as every soul should, it must live for itself . . . observe with such awe its own law as to concern itself very little with the engrossing topics of the hour, unless they be its own" (LRWE 7:320–21).[17] Only where private study coincided with public interest was he prepared to instruct his contemporary audience.

The demand for his lectures indicates that the terms he set were well-received by his audiences, many of whom were no doubt happy enough not to attend topically polemical lectures. Perhaps because he resolutely elected his opportunities, he preserved his capacity to rise to the public occasion. Sufficiently roused, he engaged his contemporary audience in all of its agonizing dissensus, and some of his best-known works are written to utter his deepest convictions in company where he knows they will face contestation.[18] Yet even when Emerson read lectures that did not particularly court religious or political controversy—lectures in which he could dwell serenely on a philosophical plane and assume a more or less consensual reception on the part of his audience—his oracular vocation was complicated by the necessity to make a living. Unrelenting economic pressure existed as a more serious if comparatively low-level source of alienation for Emerson than the religious and political controversies of the antebellum forum. As early as 1838 his vocation was obscured by the business of lecturing, and the discourse that should liberate the world was reduced to parcels that Emerson could view with irony in a garrulous letter to William. "The suds toss furiously in our washbowl . . . Do you know that Walker refused my paper on Carlyle sent to the Examiner all but two paragraphs the first & last which now stand a critical notice in that Magazine. . . . Then there is a new edition of the oration printing this week. . . . And now it is 13 Feb. & I have to flee to Roxbury on a sudden call to pour out these decanters or demijohns of popular wisdom" (LRWE 2:108–9). In the same vein Emerson would describe his enterprise in an 1839 letter to Margaret Fuller as "Human Life in Ten Lectures or the Soul of man neatly done up in ten pinboxes exactly ten" (LRWE 2:179). And in a letter to William two and a half years later, the thought of a new lecture series moves him to elaborate, against the commerce of the lyceum engagement, a vision of what he would accomplish by his orations:

I believe I shall lecture in Boston this season: but on what topics? Shall it be The Times; or Books; or Ethics; or Manners; or Philosophy? I have a dream sometimes of an eloquence that is still possible that drawing its resources from neither politics nor commerce but from thought, from the moral & intellectual life & duties of each man, shall startle and melt & exalt the ear that heareth, as never the orators of the caucus or the parliament or the forum can. I think these "lectures" capable of a variety of style & matter which no other form of composition admits. We can laugh & cry, curse & pray, tell stories & crack jokes, spin a web of transcendentalism a

thousand times finer than spiderthread or insist on the beauties &
utilities of banks, railroads, india rubber shoes & the Cunard line,
nay, do all this in one discourse. Well, when the true man is born
who shall do what we dream, we shall then have an end to the fame
of Demosthenes & Cicero. As it is, they seem yet to have a reprieve
for the current year. (LRWE 2:460)

The facetious tone cushions somewhat the admission of defeat. Yet
not only does Emerson continue to imagine an eloquence that should
"startle and melt & exalt the ear that heareth," far surpassing classical
example, he envisions also a curious form of public address in which
the "I" of the speaker becomes the "we" of the speaker and auditors
united in something approximating mutual conversational discourse:
"*We* can laugh & cry, curse & pray, tell stories & crack jokes, spin a web
of transcendentalism a thousand times finer than spiderthread." Such
perhaps would mitigate certain consequences of living in a time that he
elsewhere enthusiastically identifies as the "age of the first person
singular."[19] Assuredly this *we* is not the image of the genteel middle-
class lecture in which an esteemed authority monologues, but of an
occasion in which an orator speaks the pervasive, common language
that he assumes to underlie the spiritual and material dimensions of
reality. Nothing like that occurs in the lyceum hall, however, and Emerson's lecture, as he well knows, figures in the world not as the poesis of
such phenomena as railroads, rubber shoes, and Cunard steamers but
as an economic product that enters the public world on equally commercial terms. These terms oblige Emerson to consider carefully
whether this season he shall hawk his commodity as discourse on The
Times, Books, Manners, Ethics, or Philosophy. The need to gain a
livelihood from lecturing necessarily curbed Emerson's ironic view of
his enterprise.

Had Emerson possessed the spontaneous verbal facility of Bronson
Alcott or Margaret Fuller, he might have tried to engage his audience
in the lecture-and-discussion format of his friends' so-called conversations, but even then, given the eloquence and intimacy he desired, he
may well have been disappointed. What he projects as a form of address in which the "I" of the speaker becomes the "we" of participants
in one large conversation reflects the informality and dialogicity he was
pursuing in his private correspondence in the years leading up to the
publication of *Essays: First Series*. Letter writing, in the distinctly non-
Walpolian mode that Emerson pursued it, constituted an alternative
form of literary expression; although in German the possibilities of

lyric correspondence had been suggested by Bettina von Arnim's letters to Goethe, no such published and canonized instance existed in English. A more exact and expressive form of writing than was commonly met with in print, such letters as Emerson would write and receive could exist in America only in manuscript, or so he and certain of his correspondents believed. A glorification of the letter as an introspective lyric record of an individual soul's search for the infinite is evident not only in the kind of letter written by Emerson's circle and the frequency with which it was written, but also in the way such text was valued as confession, spiritual testimony, or embodiment of "noble" character. From such privacies sprang the grand transpersonal philosophical conversation.

A passage from a letter Emerson wrote to Fuller in February 1840 serves as an example of what might be called the art of the transcendentalist epistle:

> These spring winds are magical in their operation on our attuned frames. These are the days of passion when the air is full of cupids & devils for eyes that are still young; and every pool of water & every dry leaf & refuse straw seems to flatter, provoke, mock, or pique us. I who am not young have not yet forgot the enchantment, & still occasionally see dead leaves & wizards that peep & mutter. Let us surrender ourselves for fifteen minutes to the slightest of these nameless influences—these nymphs or imps of wood & flood of pasture & roadside, and we shall quickly find out what an ignorant pretending old Dummy is Literature who has quite omitted all that we care to know—all that we have not said ourselves. (LRWE 2:255)

We may observe in this passage a distinctly genre-reflexive aesthetic. As a dated text, the passage presents its reflections as those of a particular time and place, connected with the reality of the passing moment, which is in turn integrated within a large pattern of recurrence. In such premonitions of spring the writer observes both a volatile "passion" and an enduring "enchantment." Noting that he is no longer young, Emerson represents this recurrence with a properly sober (verging on somber) enthusiasm, his recognitions shaped by the sense of mortal time that the letter genre with its dated statements formally articulates. In the paradoxical proposition that the eternal is ever to be grasped in the common quotidian detail typically recorded in letters, the genre argumentatively asserts its presence: to "surrender ourselves for fifteen minutes" to the slightest influence is to come into relation with a permanent reality that "Literature," but not the letter—inasmuch as this letter offers itself as evidence—tends to ignore. Although the passage is indebted to the rhetoric of the homily ("Let us surrender"), and although we may easily imagine a refinement of such sentences finding a place in one of Emerson's essays, the passage itself makes the argument that such perceptions are peculiarly enabled by the quick, improvisational, ampersand-studded registry of the epistolary form.

Letters bearing such passages were commonly shared.[20] Those Emerson writes to Margaret Fuller were apt to be forwarded to Caroline Sturgis, whose own letters to Fuller might in turn be read by Emerson. Carlyle's letters to Emerson routinely made the rounds. An unknown person worthy of attention was sometimes announced by a letter received that seemed to exhibit character or genius. Fuller's letters in particular are filled with commentary—critical, admiring—on letters received. Letters written under such circumstances had to anticipate extended readership; they constituted performances that were less than fully public but more than merely private. Among the transcendentalist literati, letters contributed to the cult of personality, the preparation to greet some evidence of genius in its phenomenal human form. Much cultural work was accomplished by their correspondence; Fuller's promotion of the literature of contemporary Germany might stand as an example, or the innumerable critical readings that such letters bear of manuscript essays and poems. Beyond inscribing and encouraging the intellectual and literary life of the time, however, these artifacts constituted a kind of metaliterature: tokens of inspired personalities, fetishes by which a more intimate contact—a higher genius, a more absolute relation—might be invoked. For Emerson in particular, such texts compensated for the awkwardness that often frustrated social contacts with friends as well as for what he had come to regard as the predictable disappointment of a public literary life.

So engrossing were Emerson's exchanges with his friends that he reports to have found it difficult at times to concentrate on more conventional literary pursuits. "I am trying now to get my essays ready for print," he reports to William in October 1840, "but the writing in them I find very hard & mechanical compared with my writing romances of letters which I have done all this idle happy summer" (LRWE 2:348). In the epistolary sharing of texts with friends, which elicited a warm and palpable if not uncritical response, Emerson sought different orders of fulfillment; although he would toil alongside Fuller in an effort to launch and sustain the *Dial*, their circle's aspiring and ever troubled public organ, the voluminous circulation of letters and journals served friendship and conversation in ways that publication and face-to-face contact could not. Conceiving friendship as an inscribed relation existing between solitary individuals, Emerson considers the writing thus generated as the most fluent, boundless, spiritual colloquy vouchsafed to human conditions, compared to which his lectures and essays seem "hard & cold" (JMN 7:405) and his spoken conversation handicapped. "Strange that there is almost no attempt to realize a fine & poetic intercourse but that always there should be such vast allowance made for friction," he remarks in a letter to Fuller in 1841, lamenting the absence of a public literary life in which personalities do not obstruct the possibilities of exchange. "I think if you should read the letters & diaries of people you would infer a better conversation than we ever find" (LRWE 2:441).

The collaboration of Emerson and Fuller in editing the *Dial* has made their correspondence well-known. But although both looked upon the letter exchange as an occasion of spiritual and emotional intimacy as well as the channel of collective effort, their exchange is a study of correspondents whose attempts to arrive at a personal and professional rapport produced miscommunication and quarrels, if finally also mutual accommodation. Both regarded epistolary discourse as one in which two souls might achieve intimacy, but they could never agree as to what forms of intimacy were possible between them: Fuller repeatedly complains of Emerson's aloofness, Emerson claims in response that he is not cold but constitutionally reticent. Beginning a letter in March 1838, Fuller expresses her frustration with their relationship through the trope of blocked epistolary impulse: "Many a Zelterian epistle have I mentally addressed to you full of sprightly scraps about the books I have read, the spectacles I have seen, and the attempts at men and women with whom I have come in contact. But I have not been able to put them on paper, for even when I have attempted it, you have seemed so busy and noble, and I so poor and dissipated that I have not felt worthy to address you." Fuller's letters to Emerson often bristle with the implied reproach. In the fall of 1840, her accusations of his supposed frigidity become explicit to the point of threatening a rupture in their relations. "How often have I left you despairing and forlorn. How often have I said, this light will never understand my fire; this clear eye will never discern the law by which I am filling my circle; this simple force will never interpret my need of manifold being."²¹ Emerson became the focus of Fuller's pathological sense of abandonment, but her letters of this period brim generally with accusations directed to long-time correspondents.

In response to a subsequent but no longer extant letter from Fuller, Emerson represents what had been his view of their relations and establishes what henceforth must remain the protocol of their friendship and discourse.

> I was content & happy to meet on a human footing a woman of sense & sentiment with whom one could exchange reasonable words & go away assured that wherever she went there was light & force & honour. That is to me a solid good; it gives value to thought & the day; it redeems society from that foggy & misty aspect it wears so often seen from our retirements; it is the foundation of everlasting friendship. Touch it not—speak not of it—and this most welcome natural alliance becomes from month to month, —& the slower & with the more intervals the better, —our air & diet. A robust & total understanding grows up resembling nothing so much as the relation of brothers who are intimate & perfect friends without having ever spoken of the fact. But tell me that I am cold or unkind, and in my most flowing state I become a cake of ice. I can feel the crystals shoot & the drops solidify. It may do for others but it is not for me to bring the relation to speech. Instantly I find myself a solitary unrelated person, destitute not only of all social faculty but of all private substance. (LRWE 2:352)

Given the frequency with which Fuller accused Emerson of failure in his friendship to her and of incapacity for friendship in general, it is not surprising that he should take refuge in the argument that for him friendship lies in implicit trust, that "it is not for me to bring the relation to speech." And to illustrate his expectations, Emerson makes reference to "the relation of brothers who are intimate & perfect friends without having ever spoken of the fact." The illustration is revealing on two counts. First, it suggests that, for Emerson, the relationships with William, Edward, and Charles, constituted by ongoing epistolary narratives, represent a model of social relations—even though such a model offers little guidance in dealing with the social and political complexities of antebellum America or in negotiating conflicts in which sexual tension is a factor. Second, in citing brotherly rapport as a model for how he would relate to Fuller—in expressing the wish that he could relate to Fuller as a brother to a brother—

Emerson attempts to deny the sexual difference that he himself suspected was at the root of their difficulties.[22] Emerson liked to think of his friendship with Fuller as one founded on an ideal plane, but the limited if genuine sympathy that Emerson bore to Fuller becomes evident when we compare their relationship to the friendship between Emerson and Caroline Sturgis, who presented for Emerson a more engaging if also troubling form of sexual tension. To his extension of brotherly affection, Sturgis existed as "sister." And in the course of their friendship Emerson constantly brought the relation to speech.

With Sturgis, Emerson was to form his most emotionally intense epistolary relationship in the years between 1838 and 1842. More than any other correspondence to which he was party his exchange with Sturgis freely adopts the heightened rhetoric of the essay "Friendship," in which the soul is represented as undergoing a crisis in its election of a brother or sister soul. Such rhetoric diminishes after 1842 as their friendship enters new phases: the exaltation of the human bond that dominates the first years of their correspondence cannot abrogate the world of conflict, death, and commonplace events that characterize human life and that letters have as much of a generic predisposition to register as utopian aspiration. If much of the interest of Emerson's letter writing lies in the respite from the public realm that his epistolary practice facilitates, much of it also lies in his adaptation of the ideals of friendship to the practical matter of making and keeping friends: his having to adjust expectations to the conditions under which particular friendships flourish, evolve, fluctuate, and decline. Emerson's correspondence with Carlyle is noteworthy for its disappointments and adjustments, its preservation of the forms of friendship after mutual antipathy had reduced it to a staggered exchange of nostalgic reference and abiding good wishes.[23] With Sturgis, there were personal frictions but never a philosophical breach, and in their exchange Emerson would furthest pursue the idealities of friendship as well as the realizable terms of enduring affection.

Friendship, in the correspondence of Emerson and Sturgis, is self-consciously a form of discourse, and relations between them may be gauged by the varying protocols they articulate to define their contact by letter sheet. The letters exhibit an infatuation alternately cultivated by Sturgis and Emerson over a period of some ten years, an infatuation that Emerson's designation of himself as "brother" to the sometime *Dial* contributor sixteen years his junior may have been in part intended to neutralize.[24] The eros of the friendship lent it an urgency for

Emerson that other associations lacked, and its sublimated sexuality took the form of an open-ended conversation, an intellectual and spiritual dialogue that Emerson sustained when other discussions failed to hold his interest. "I cannot write to you *with others*," he addresses Sturgis in a letter of August 1840, "any more than I can talk with you at a round table. From you I hear my own mother tongue, & not a patois of that, or a foreign language" (LRWE 7:402). Theirs is an interchange that Emerson would define as requiring peculiar privacy: withdrawal from the scenes of social life, from the immediate scrutiny of others of their circle (in "Friendship" he writes: "I find this law of *one to one*, peremptory for conversation, which is the practice and consummation of friendship"; CW 2:121). Such privacy for Emerson recalls speech to an original transparency and inclusiveness unruled by the genres of the literary marketplace or conventions of polite and politic conversation: "to you I can speak coldly and austerely," he continues, "as well as gently & poetically—and always truly" (LRWE 7:402).

Perhaps because of the sexual undercurrent of their relationship, Emerson is careful to define an intellectual basis of sympathy that can extend across what for him must remain a permanent distance. To Sturgis he represents "the great event" of his "social life" as the meeting "of a strong mind by a strong mind," which to his thinking all but obviates protocol: "they understand each other so fast, so surely, & so dearly, yet so passionless withal, that not possibly henceforth can they ever be unrelated, but must occasionally beckon to each other across forests, seas, or ranks in society" (LRWE 7:402). Emerson's insistence on the passionlessness of the contact would at once seem to confess his passion and to declare his determination to found the friendship in the absence of emotion, eros, body. For Emerson, physical absence figures strongly in his theorizing of the conditions of the highest friendship, and the conception of friendship as an intimate meeting mediated by occasional beckoning is decidedly epistolary. It is conversation between isolated individuals who in their physical absence to one another are not after all really two, but one. "Between eternal souls," Emerson writes, "or, yet more strictly speaking, in that eternal soul which we, at last, are, is an unity impossible to be broken" (LRWE 7:403). "Now I will identify you with the Ideal Friend, & live with you on imperial terms," he addresses Sturgis in September 1840. "Present, you shall be present only as an Angel might be, and absent you shall not be absent from me"—for absence is not possible for those who live consciously among "these tides of the Infinite wherein love truth

127

& power blend & are one, roll unchecked for me for thee their everlasting circles" (LRWE 7:407).

Between himself and certain correspondents (Caroline Sturgis, Elizabeth Hoar, Samuel Gray Ward, Thomas Carlyle, John Sterling), Emerson affirms the existence of a platonic bond, a kinship that manifests itself in nearly telepathic intimations: "In whatsoever thought of God I live," he writes Sturgis, "I must find the inhabitants of that thought" (LRWE 7:411).[25] The insistence that friendship consists in thought is in keeping with the disembodied character of relations Emerson proposes at this time; indeed, he was able to dismiss with contempt any notion of the friend as a physical entity to be possessed in time and space. "Why go to his house," he asks in "Friendship," or "be visited by him at your own? Are these things material to our covenant? Leave this touching and clawing. Let him be to me a spirit." Toward the close of the paragraph, Emerson adverts to the all-important text of friendship. "To my friend I write a letter, and from him I receive a letter. That seems to you a little. It suffices me. It is a spiritual gift. . . . It profanes nobody. In these warm lines the heart will trust itself, as it will not to the tongue, and pour out the prophecy of a godlier existence than all the annals of heroism have yet made good" (CW 2:123–24). As for the body, it is sufficiently present in the "warm lines" in which the heart can "trust itself."

Consistent with this argument, in a letter of September 1840 to Elizabeth Hoar, Emerson affirms a sympathy that, strictly speaking, renders letter writing superfluous: "Do not complain that I have written you a letter & said no good word. What I think & feel, you think & feel also—Why should I sit down to write it out?" (LRWE 2:331). Yet in this same letter he speaks of the pleasures taken in what for the first time exists for him as a circle of nonfamily intimates: "Have I been always a hermit, and unable to approach my fellow men, & do the Social Divinities suddenly offer me a *roomfull* of friends? . . . So consider me as now quite friendsick & lovesick, a writer of letters & sonnets" (LRWE 2:330). The roomful of friends and the letters exchanged in their absence clearly satisfy a need for something other than an imagined telepathy proceeding from a presumed unity in the spirit. And of Caroline Sturgis in particular Emerson asked more than a tacit mutual sympathy. In December 1840 he vehemently encourages her to continue sending him "mail after mail whole sheets of confessions & fancies & fairylands" (LRWE 7:439). The call for intimacy is unmistakable—an intimacy that would suspend formal and generic constraints,

Ralph Waldo Emerson to Caroline Sturgis, September 6, 1840. Used by permission of the Ralph Waldo Emerson Memorial Association and of Houghton Library, Harvard University.

and that identifies letter writing as the medium of frank, transparent, and copious personal communication. There is nothing ascetic about Emerson's appetite for letters, and in his correspondence with Sturgis the sacred and erotic join for him as they perhaps previously had only in his correspondence with Ellen Louisa Tucker Emerson: "The wild & untameable word of God—who is likely to speak that, but he that loveth much?" (LRWE 7:440). And where, Emerson might also have asked, speak that word more intimately and safely than in the familiar letter?

Emerson's letters to Sturgis count as some of the most improvisational and inventive writing that he was ever to produce. Friendship for Emerson was always associated with confession, although a confession of philosophical mood rather than autobiographical reference. Within certain constraints he felt free to allow the pen to define its own course in writing to Sturgis, yet his attention often seems taken up less by the substance than by the process and pleasure of communication. In his letters to her a portion of his consciousness is absorbed in the potentialities of the genre: by the question of what might be expressed under the epistolary condition of discourse. Between 1839 and 1842, Emerson sometimes seems to have little actually of a personal nature to say to Sturgis, although much to expound on the subject of friendship and much to voice in celebration of the discourse friendship makes possible. This often takes the form of a dilation upon the affection one soul feels in the presence of another soul's utterance:

> My true sister
>   dwells in the clear upper sky and is haunted by no "quality of darkness." Your letter rings with so pure a tone that I have been happier ever since it came, with the wish to invite the universe to our confidence saying, see by what means the soul is raised in the worlds. (September 6, 1840; LRWE 7:403)

> You are my summer harp, and in these amber days let me hear the notes. When the world is so warm, green, & sweet-scented as now, perhaps there is not much to be thought, but a letter has carried how oft! the cheeringest words of kindness, and renewed the face of the world to the reader. (June 24, 1841; LRWE 7:457)

Whatever foundation it may have in a specific interpersonal rapport, the regard expressed in such passages is very much an affection literarily rendered. It is rendered very deliberately so, as it is Emerson's purpose to redeem the friendship from anything like historical circumstance (the first passage, in fact, addresses with characteristic aloofness and unspecificity the question of what would happen to their friendship were Sturgis to marry). In these years Emerson steadfastly writes to an idealized notion of Caroline Sturgis whose life in the material world exists only as a kind of implication.

The abstract expression of affection in the letters to Sturgis contrasts tellingly with the agenda of news, endearments, anecdotes, and humor that characterizes his correspondence with Lidian Emerson when either of them is absent from the home. Lidian's physical absence is represented as a phenomenal fact rather than a philosophical condition, and the letter exchange between husband and wife makes insistent reference to the temporal and familiar things of this world. To Lidian in Boston, Emerson writes from Concord on November 8, 1840:

> Dear Lidian,
> The babes are well. Mother returned duly yesterday noon. Dr Francis arrived last evening with Mrs Ripley, drank tea with us, & Dr F. spent the night & Mrs R. was here again today. . . . Nothing has occurred of any interest Ellen was delighted to see Dr F. smoke his cigar & shouted Fire Fire to the wreaths of smoke . . . She affirms to all inquirers that Mamma is "gone Bonson" and Waldo especially desires that you will finish your errands & come home quickly. Do not fail to get what you want for your own wardrobe—whatever it was you were considering to do—and for carpets—when we see the good floor through the present, will it not be time enough to buy more?
> Yours affectionately,
> Waldo E. (LRWE 2:355–56)

And in writing to Lidian from Nantasket on July 15, 1841, Emerson portrays himself as one sorely deprived of news regarding his household's vital ephemera:

> what is the reason that my wife never writes to me. I have written her three letters already since I have been here & not had so much as a message requesting me not to jump overboard. Well I have no such intention but am always glad to hear from you, being neither an oak nor a rock. But I can never persuade you to make my distinctions . . . I too who read the Transcript & listen to all the gossip of bar rooms: Surely I am no philosopher: send me word of the very peas & beans: I have got into a pretty good way of reading & writing at last, and so rather grudge to write letters. (LRWE 2:427)

This is not the Emerson who in theorizing ideal friendship abjures the mundane. Lacking the intensity of his correspondence with Sturgis, his exchange with Lidian, tenacious of detail, confesses a dependence on the continuing narratives of domestic life.[26] In such a world there is little room for the idealistic assertion and disembodied eros that characterize his letters to Sturgis.

As singular as the Emerson-Sturgis correspondence is, it arose within a shared philosophical frame of reference and system of manuscript circulation and exchange. Again, it is important to emphasize that letters exchanged between Emerson and Sturgis were not as confidential as their obvious (if sublimated) sexuality might lead us to suppose. Thus Emerson writes to Sturgis (September 6, 1840): "I showed your letter to Lidian & to Elizabeth. Lidian reads it with solemn joy, and Elizabeth gave it many tears & called it 'a diamond letter'" (LRWE 7:404). "Tuesday Cary spent with me, and we read all Mr. E's letters to both of us this summer," Margaret Fuller writes William H. Channing in November 1840. "They make a volume, and passages are finer than any thing he has published."[27] Emerson's pursuit of literary prophecy in the comparatively private discourses of journal and letter had distinctly communal support. The community that contributed to the *Dial* is in many respects a loosely cohering one, but to the extent that it circulated inscribed artifacts and gained from that practice a sense of community, it existed in its own view as an alternative to the political and commercial mainstream culture of the day. Through the exchange of lengthy dispatches with Sturgis and others and through the circulation among his elect of transcriptions from his journal, Emerson secured a relationship with an audience that, however epistolary, was more immediately responsive than what he experienced as a lecturer. On the following terms Sturgis affirms such manner of "private" publication:

> [It] is much more childlike & beautiful in you to write a little journal for those who love you, to plant your acorn in the secret dell where it shall spring up & become a wide-spreading oak, than to collect your thoughts in a great book, then select, combine & recombine until the flowers are all well-arranged in a fine public garden. Not but that the garden also is good, but the gushing spring has a sweeter voice than the octagon marble fountain. (LRWE 7:412)

The disjunction of the private and public worlds was not a problem Emerson faced alone. It was collectively met in the difficulty that Emerson and his friends experienced in sustaining the *Dial* as a publication that reached beyond a small audience predisposed to visionary aspiration—that could figure in the world not as the embarrassed bearer of Alcott's "Orphic Sayings" but as an agent of spiritual redemption.[28]

Although not especially confidential, Emerson's correspondence with Sturgis drew upon what he represented as his most intimate reserves of hope, and the course of their exchange is critical to Emerson's further development both as letter writer and as author generally. Significantly, it is difficult to discern a self-defining narrative (such as we find in his exchanges with his brothers, Aunt Mary, and Lidian) in the Emerson-Sturgis correspondence; after he has identified her with the "ideal friend," much of their epistolary relationship seems invested in sustaining and refining the ideality of their friendship. Yet in his letters to Sturgis a point is reached at which Emerson seems to perceive limits not only with respect to what he can say to her but to what he can say under any circumstance in any genre; such thought as he cannot write in what he has designated as the infinitely flexible latitude of their correspondence loses its occasion for utterance. The "confession" that Emerson records in a letter of September 7, 1841, is no doubt prompted by Sturgis's distance (geographic but also personal) as an addressee, and his recognitions are enabled by the epistolary genre with its special capacity for reflecting upon the minutiae of commonplace events and the time that passes in bland mortal increments. This letter articulates the predicament of an undeveloping friendship and an ostensibly stalled authorship, and depicts a life that in its "proper" (phenomenal) forms watches its opportunities vanish. "I wonder why no line comes to me from the Merrimack," he opens, adverting to the mail that has not come, referring as ever to Sturgis as the friend from whom a letter is due or has just arrived.

> Life seems not long enough that we can afford to go a month without a letter from a dear friend. I have nothing that I can spare,— certainly not the right to receive a letter. Thus I am always poor. Yet I believe that a man should be always rich. Will the theory & the experience ever approximate? I entertain myself all day & (I think) all night in my dreams with pictures of tranquility & erectness of mind; and all my days are hurried & referred. Thence I infer that in my proper life as Waldo Emerson, none of my questions will be answered but only in a series of lives the tendency will inscribe itself on the fair sky. (LRWE 7:470)

Such all-encompassing lament proceeds from the seemingly simple observation that mail is overdue. Tacitly, by means of the paratactic, telescoping progression of sentences, the unreceived letter becomes a trope of unfulfilled, unanswered, unaddressed life, in which "experience" must perennially disappoint "theory." Written four months before the death of his son Waldo, the letter anticipates transitions that the loss of Waldo would dramatically precipitate and that would find statement in the *Second Series* essay "Experience." "Only in a series of lives," not in a life that is as hurried and impoverished as his is turning out to be, will the redemptive tendency "inscribe itself on the fair sky" in utter clarity and plain view. It is at this point that Emerson significantly chooses not to go on, to close the meditation with the suggestion of where it might lead and an expression of his less than committed ambition to follow it: "I will not begin to confess myself lest my shrift should have no end. Yet I think if I were once set to recount my history every day for some weeks I should be better known to myself as well as to my confessor, & should receive absolution that would do me much good. Dark untold turbid inaccessible is the thought of the most serene & uneventful day. There need be no fear of want of originality if it were laid bare" (LRWE 7:470–71). "To recount my history every day" had been the purpose of his journal keeping for many years, but the journals, however much they circulated among a private readership, were not oriented toward the horizon of a specific addressee in the way that letters generally were.

This passage signals an end to Emerson's experiments with the unbounded potential of the letter. Nine months earlier (December 25, 1840) he had blithely asserted, "if my friend is wont to write, then let me have the writing, for the spirit of all wisdom & beauty writeth through friends" (LRWE 7:440), but such confidence has run its course. Although he would continue to write eloquent letters, letters that distinguish themselves by their ability to draw the form of the genre into the theme of their utterance, the letter has ceased to exist for him as a form of writing that could elude constraints and elevate the basis of personal relationships. Thwarted on the lecture circuit in his attempts to realize the dream "of an eloquence that is still possible"—that should derive "its resources from neither politics nor commerce but from thought"—he was no longer moved to pursue such eloquence in letters addressed to friends, no longer impelled to cultivate the semblance of ideal friendship in the flux of epistolary text. He was henceforth to represent experience in ways that increasingly acknowledge the "dark untold turbid inaccessible" dimensions of daily life and that concede limits to the transformative power of the word.

This transition may be traced in his progressive abandonment of references to the "prophecy" of friendship: the "godlier existence" to which the human bond, platonically conceived, serves as a ladder. In this view, as Emerson rather coldly renders it in "Friendship," the ideal friend was ultimately released from any obligation to requite love or answer mail; even the most beloved companion constituted an always diminishing presence, a beguiling absence who yet conduces to eternal being. "It has seemed to me lately more possible than I knew," Emerson begins the last paragraph of "Friendship," "to carry a friendship greatly, on one side, without due correspondence on the other." Given the volume of mail that sustained his friendships at this time, "due correspondence" in this context might well have possessed an epistolary connotation for Emerson, even though, as may be seen from his frequent pleas to Sturgis to write, he actually held exorbitant notions of the mail due him. Indeed, "Friendship" sounds a note of suspicion that an ongoing letter exchange can hardly tolerate. What he gives as an example of a letter to be written to a potential friend is, we have seen, more admonitory than inviting and bears little resemblance to any letter that he ever actually sent. More discouraging still is the affirmation that he comes to in the final paragraph: "True love transcends the unworthy object, and dwells and broods on the eternal, and when the poor, interposed mask crumbles, it is not sad, but feels rid of so much earth, and feels its independency the surer." The essay does not end before Emerson admits that such remarks betray "a sort of treachery to the relation" (CW 2:127).

One can readily perceive a biographical reference in the phrase "when the poor interposed mask crumbles, it is not sad," for by this time Ellen, Edward, and Charles had all died, leaving him with love that had to seek alternative terms of requital. The treachery that he names in "Friendship" reflects a renunciation of sorrow that was required of Emerson to move from the debilitating exactions of bereavement; in practice it has nothing to do with those friendships that he currently maintained through the mails. Yet in the aftermath of his son Waldo's sudden death in 1842 (Ellen's death, in contrast, had been long anticipated and deeply meditated), the proposition of ideal relations no longer figures in Emerson's thought about human bonds. The void left by his five-year-old's death is not irradiated by a compensatory light: "Dear Boy," he writes in his bereavement to Sturgis, "too precious & unique a creation to be huddled aside into the waste & prodigality of things!" (LRWE 7:485). Such, perhaps, reveals his undistilled sentiment about all of his loved ones' deaths as well as his dismay at the prospect of further loss. In the years ahead, although he maintains a distance between himself and Sturgis, he wishes no longer "to dissipate" his friendship with her "into any universalities" (LRWE 8:37), and the ground of the relationship consists alternately of philosophical observations and a regard for her as one with whom he shares a past, their bond defined less by "the prophecy of a godlier existence" than the retrospective consideration of a specific human attachment.

THAT UNWRITTEN LETTER ALWAYS DUE

From the mid-1840s on, Emerson's letters are notable for their abandonment of the ideal expectation as a failed or unsatisfactory ground of friendship as well as by what he comes to recognize as a steady acquiescence to a silence that constitutes a prophecy of death. His isolation may be outwardly reckoned by the death of Fuller in 1850, his estrangement from Thoreau after 1848, and his disaffection from Carlyle dating from the visit to England of 1847–48, but it is also told by the loss from within of the epistolary motive. On the surface he maintained a busy social calendar and circulated increasingly as a club- and committeeman; his letters, however, speak insistently of solitude. During his most prolific period as a correspondent, Emerson remarks that the exchange of letter sheet is redundant for friends who sustain spiritual contact. In his later practice, as he drops references to the ineffable unity of friends in the eternal mind, he nonetheless relies increasingly on the conceit of the absent friend's abiding presence, on relations unmediated by written or spoken conversation, on friendship that rests on faith when material contacts lapse. "You must always thank me for silence," Emerson writes to Carlyle in July 1851, "be it never so long, & must put on it the most generous interpretations" (CEC 469).[29] His self-awareness as a correspondent is particularly visible in such letters: taking stock of disappointments, he breaks what he feels to be an enveloping epistolary silence to speak with a resignation informed by an ironic engagement of the genre's peculiar discursive conditions: its origin in spatiotemporal isolation, its wish to fashion language that transcends a present fixed in time and space.

His dispatch of July 22, 1853, to Caroline Sturgis Tappan (she had married William Tappan in 1846) is one such letter. In it Emerson addresses a friendship that has accumulated much by way of a shared particular past; at no point does he identify his addressee as "the Ideal Friend." Written in the month following the suicide of Caroline's sister, Susan Sturgis Bigelow, the letter posits bereavement as an experience that has come to constitute the common ground of their relationship. "You say truly & wisely, we must learn from our losses not to let our friends go," Emerson opens, quoting his correspondent in his bid to converse,

. . . and yet when we do not speak or write, it is out of a confidence that we know our party, & are known for our own quality, once for all. I believe, my slowness to write letters has grown from the experience, that some of my friends have been very impatient of my generalizings, as we weary of any trick, whilst theirs are still sweet to me. So I hesitate to write, except to the assessors, or to the man that is to slate my house. And my friends are an ever narrowing troop. Yet I am incurable, &, to this day, only rightly feel myself when I meet somebody whose habit of *thought*, at least, holds the world in solution, if I cannot find one whose will does. Friends are few, thoughts are few, facts few—only one: one only fact, now tragically, now tenderly, now exultingly illustrated in sky, in earth, in men & women, Fate, Fate. The universe is all chemistry, with a certain hint of a magnificent *Whence* or *Whereto* gilding or opalizing every angle of the old salt-&-acid acid-&-salt, endlessly reiterated & masqueraded through all time & space & form. The addition of that hint everywhere, saves things. (LRWE 8:374)

The letter continues in this strain, affirming that meditation of the "*Whence* & *Whither*" alone redeems a world of commerce, crowds, mechanical laws, a world in which his "generalizings" (in all their "infinite diffuseness") have lost their old hearers and his sense of isolation has returned with force: "Heavy & loathsome is the bounded world, bounded everywhere." As if to underscore the sense of boundedness, this letter not only omits mention of telepathic understandings but also apologizes for the barrier that the letter itself is apt to present. "Forgive this heavy cobweb," he writes near the letter's close, "which I did not think of spinning, & which will put you too out of all patience with my prose" (LRWE 8:375). (This "heavy cobweb," aligning it with the heavy and loathsome "bounded world," indeed contrasts with the "web of transcendentalism a thousand times finer than spiderthread" that Emerson proposes, in the 1841 letter to William, to spin in his public lectures.) Still, the letter may strike one as more genuinely personal than the large volume of correspondence that passed between Emerson and Sturgis in the late 1830s and early 1840s. In not alluding to a transcendent interpersonal presence, Emerson invokes the mutual understanding of a specific friendship that has developed in historical time: "when we do not speak or write," he affirms, "it is out of a confidence that we know our party, & are known for our own quality, once for all."

Emerson's procrastination and silence as a letter writer become major themes in his later letters. Although he continued to maintain a prolific correspondence, comparatively few letters after 1850 possess the reflective capacity of those sent to his brothers, Aunt Mary, Sturgis, Carlyle, and others to whom he extended an epistolary friendship, and as a consequence few letters meditate upon the potentialities of the genre. His practice was given to business correspondence, occasional notes to devoted readers of his work, letters home to Lidian and his children from places as far removed as Paris, San Francisco, and Dixon, Illinois, and the oldest continuous exchange of all, that maintained with his brother William, which had long since ceased its discussion of philosophy to concentrate on family investments, the care of their mentally retarded brother Bulkeley, and the brothers' parallel course as patresfamilias. Despite this ongoing voluminous production, Emerson himself recognized that his work as a letter writer had fallen off in intensity and that even where a continuous contact was kept up there existed a silence within him that remained unbroken. He stood self-convicted of inadequacy to the supreme epistolary and, by extension, authorial tasks. Writing to Lidian from London in March 1848, in response to a request in a letter that does not survive, Emerson concedes and willingly generalizes his failings, his chronic inability to fulfill his own and other people's expectations of his performance:

> Ah you still ask me for that unwritten letter always due, it seems, always unwritten, from year to year, by me to you, dear Lidian,—I fear too more widely true than you mean,—always due & unwritten by me to every sister & brother of the human race. I have only to say that I also bemoan myself daily for the same cause—that I cannot write this letter, that I have not stamina & constitution enough to mind the two functions of seraph & cherub, oh no, let me not use such great words,—rather say that a photometer cannot be a stove. (LRWE 4:33)

No one familiar with the generous character of Emerson's letters would accuse them of relaying more light than heat, as his concluding line seems to suggest. Yet Lidian's letter, written in the course of a difficult and protracted absence, clearly has charged him with failure to provide, or must appear to Emerson to have done so. In any event, after protesting his capacity for domestic affection, he reverts to his oldest line of self-defense and explanation: "I foresee plainly that the trick of solitariness never never can leave me."

The solitariness that compelled the younger Emerson's prolific and experimental letter writing ultimately erodes his motive to correspond. Apologies for late replies become customary. To Alexander Ireland, May 12, 1850: "Forgive me that I never write. My eyes are not good, & I write no letter that is not imperative" (LRWE 8:253). To Charles King Newcomb, May 31, 1853: "I am always late, and now late even in excusing my lateness" (LRWE 4:361). To George Partridge Bradford, April 16, 1855: "I find it so hard to write letters, that nothing but errands of necessity can break through the spell" (LRWE 4:501). To Arthur Hugh Clough, May 5, 1856: "I have dreams lately that I have found or am finding my pen for writing letters, which has been long lost" (LRWE 8:485). The oldest correspondences were not excepted. To William Emerson, January 5, 1849: "I am so largely in arrears, in all my correspondence that I never write you in these months unless when an errand is to be done" (LRWE 4:127). To Thomas Carlyle, August 10, 1853: "My slowness to write is a distemper that reaches all my correspondence, & not that with you only, though the circumstance is not worth stating, because if I ceased to write to all the rest, there would yet be good reason for writing to you" (CEC 491). To the eighty-three-year-old Mary Moody Emerson he writes wistfully in a letter of December 10, 1857: "I am always meaning to take up that dropt thread of old correspondence, but the oppressive miscellany of my *business-letters* . . . has long ago destroyed almost all inclination to write. Carlyle, Helps, Caroline Tappan, and all the rest of my correspondents I have allowed to go. Yet I wish to be written to by you, & I prize every syllable of your records" (LRWE 5:91). The "wish to be written to" was insufficient to motivate in Emerson a recovery of the inclination to write substantial letters to those with whom he had once sustained intellectually demanding exchanges. Although he would remain a prolific writer of "business-letters," the litany of apologies goes on. To Paulina Nash Tucker, October 7, 1864: "I rarely write a note, or, if I must write, postpone it to the last" (LRWE 5:384). To William Hathaway Forbes, February 19, 1873: "I ought to have long since acknowledged your letters one & two so kindly ventured to an old scribe who, for the first time in his life recoils from all writing" (LRWE 6:235). The delayed reply and unbreakable silence that procrastination fosters measured the time that got away from him, and he occasionally records a shiver at his loss of contact as well as at his submission to what he regards as a deathward trend. To his brother William he opens as follows in a letter of December 30, 1857: "Tis dangerous to think of what spaces of time are coming to separate our letters in a correspondence that was once tolerably active" (LRWE 5:92). Yet in spite of his recognition of that danger the spaces continue to expand.

His diminished activity as a letter writer is paralleled by his increasing neglect of his journals; the abandonment of work in both genres signals the deterioration of his powers of concentration and memory, more and more apparent in the decade following the Civil War.[30] Emerson's decline as a correspondent emerges in his letters as the measure and metaphor of his decline as an author and as the index of his spiritual isolation, an isolation that his earlier letters deny on a metaphysical plane. It was not that Emerson became a hermit; in later life he became a conspicuous participant in activities involving his aging Harvard class, manifesting a sociability unimaginable in the Emerson of the 1830s and 1840s. Such social capacity perhaps became possible because the "colloquy sublime" was no longer something that he needed to seek. In practice, the spiritual conversation that Emerson sought to achieve in certain correspondences could never be satisfactorily sustained. Yet the most remarkable passages, those in which he thinks with the form as well as in the format of the letter, are those in which he meditates on his "proper life as Waldo Emerson" (LRWE 7:470), aspiring to fuller relations with his interlocutor, his society, and realities immanent and transcendent, than he knows he is ever likely to achieve. In such letters, Emerson acknowledges the tragic dimensions of life in their greater and lesser intensities, engaging a genre that assumes isolation and acknowledges limits and that alternately gives rise to visions, on the one hand, of community and boundlessness and, on the other, boundedness and death. The irony of such contemplations makes for writings in which Emerson adapts a vision of full presence to the ongoing conditions of incremental mortal time.

4

A Letter Always Seemed to Me Like Immortality
Emily Dickinson

• •

Emily Dickinson's early correspondence is similar to Emerson's in that she participates—however ironically and inventively—in what for children of literate households was an obligatory genre. Her teenage missives resemble those of other nineteenth-century youth; although originality in her handling of language is evident in the writings of her young womanhood, her distinction in the field of adolescent lucubration might easily be overlooked. Her adult correspondence demonstrates that she took part in conventional exchanges of letters as well as the conventional dispatch of home-prepared gifts (flowers and foods) accompanied by short notes. Dickinson's mature practice reflects the customs of the day with respect to middle-class women's epistolary relations and the metonymies of female community that such relations constitute.[1] Her letter writing no more evolves in reference to a British literary epistolary tradition than does Emerson's.[2] Like Emerson she was influenced by the works of Bettina von Arnim; at base her theory and practice of letter writing derive like his from the oppositions of body to spirit articulated by Saint Paul. Conventional as Dickinson in many ways is, in others she is the least conventional correspondent that one could imagine, meriting full consideration as the boldest, most inventive, most critically astute nineteenth-century letter writer in English. Although she could never have entertained such a notion about herself, she is arguably the greatest theoretician of letter writing to be met with in American letters and literature.

No one's letters have been read more searchingly than have Emily Dickinson's, and for good reason: in the paucity of other documents that may be summoned to provide an account of her life, her epistolarium constitutes that life's primary biographical trace.[3] Although her 1,775 poems and their variants seem to abound in autobiographical reference, it is in her letters that Dickinson created anything like a sequential record of her days.[4] That record, as we have it, is a fragment, much of it deriving from incomplete transcriptions of autographs now destroyed, while her lost whole letters would almost certainly fill volumes—how many is anyone's guess.[5] Few of the letters that she received survive, and those that do only begin to suggest how her correspondents met the peculiar demands of her conversation by letter sheet. Nothing remains of several extensive correspondences she is known to have carried on; probably there are others lost beyond anyone's power to recognize their absence. Moreover, the sequence of 1,049 documents that make up *The Letters of Emily Dickinson* depends almost wholly on editorial intervention inasmuch as, after 1858, the poet customarily did not date her letters.[6]

In publication Dickinson's letters have inevitably been subjected to interpretive contextualization, much of which is now regarded as controversial.[7] Yet even where Johnson and Ward persuasively document the circumstances behind a particular holograph, the stories told by the letters remain ambiguous for purposes of biography. Readers still endeavor to identify the "narrative of Sue" contained in the sheets dispatched to Susan Gilbert Dickinson and to decipher the love story suggested by the three draft letters addressed to "Master."[8] Twice as many letters, all precisely dated, might, however, do little to reduce the biographical obscurities. As she demonstrates early in the correspondence that she initiated with Thomas Wentworth Higginson, evading his requests for a portrait and life story, Dickinson's autobiographical representations emphasize theme and pattern over biographical detail. "When a little Girl," she writes in an account of her education, "I had a friend, who taught me Immortality—but venturing too near, himself— he never returned—Soon after, my Tutor, died—and for several years, my Lexicon—was my only companion—Then I found one more—but he was not contented I be his scholar—so he left the Land" (LED

2:404). A theme (bereavement, abandonment) is herein developed through three variations; in this passage as in countless others, her letters exhibit a writer who understands the performative character of discourse that says "I." "When I state myself, as the Representative of the Verse," she later writes to Higginson, "it does not mean—me—but a supposed person" (LED 2:412). Wishing to discourage autobiographical readings of her poems, Dickinson may somewhat overstate the case. Yet she clearly intuits the split between what Barthes has called "the one *who speaks* (in the narrative)" and "the one *who is.*" Undoubtedly she recognized that the "supposed person" spoke in the letters as much as in the verse.[9]

For his part Higginson may well have regarded Dickinson's talk of a "supposed person" as so much personal evasion. From one of his three extant letters to her we know that he was nonplussed if not put off by the "fiery mist" in which she seemed to "enshroud" herself in what she sent him; to her seeming diffidence he would confess feeling "timid lest what I *write* should be badly aimed & miss that fine edge of thought which you bear" (LED 2:461). Yet however elliptical her letter's utterance and however often her epistolary prose might break into verse, Higginson would have assumed the "I" of the letter (if not the poem) to refer to the actual person with whom he maintained a palpable correspondence, and he would have distinguished between letters and poems on what seemed to him self-evident formal grounds. For latter-day readers an increasingly tentative boundary divides the letters from the poems. Even if Dickinson had not embedded poems in letters or regarded the poems as her "letter to the World," we would be prepared to recognize the poetic structure of her letters, to perceive in them such nonmimetic constructive textuality as also figures in the letters of her literarily less astute contemporaries, Sarah Hodgdon, Mary Trussell, and Virginia Reed. But as Dickinson scholarship has more and more focused on the historical contingency of her poems' production, her correspondence has attracted attention as the intersubjective narrative frame in which her poems were composed, circulated, and revised, and thus as a discourse that fostered her poetic achievement.[10]

While affirming the poetic textuality of Dickinson's letters and acknowledging the aesthetic and thematic continuities that subsist between the letters and the poems, I shall nevertheless examine her letters as letters: inscribed artifacts (to recall our working definition) that at some point in their history are meant to pass in accordance with some postal arrangement from "I" to "you," and that inscribe the process by which the "I" personally addresses a specific readership. Precisely in Dickinson's intently self-conscious inscription of that process lies the core narrative of her letters: a narrative that identifies separation, the condition in which letters are written, as the fundamental sorrow of human life and that forecasts reunion, in this life or another, as the ultimate redemption. In all but its strictly biographical aspects the narrative of her letters is well-defined. Ever reflective of the letter-writing process, this basic plot underlies the narratives of Sue and "Master," as well as those of Austin, Abiah Root, T. W. Higginson, Judge Lord, the Bowles, the Hollands, and the Cousins Norcross. Important differences of course characterize these correspondences and the relationships that they constitute. Still, her letter exchanges exhibit remarkably consistent tendencies. As her reclusive habits suggest, her epistolary narrative increasingly resisted the apparent resolution offered by literal reunions. A principle of deferral drives her epistolary discourse: reunion, presence, closure become objects of perpetual postponement. Early and late Dickinson projects "immortality" as this narrative's one redeeming prospect.

Because I am interested in examining the themes and variations of what I have designated as her letters' core narrative in a representative selection of her correspondence, and because I believe there is little to be gained from fixating upon enigmatic examples, my analysis avoids those quicksands of Dickinson criticism and biography known as the "Master" letters. These three documents, which Johnson and Ward date "about 1858," "about 1861," and "early 1862?" appear to be drafts of letters to a lover with whom relations have become strained in the extreme, but there is no evidence that they duplicate letters that were ever actually sent, and even assuming that they do represent moments in an exchange, there has never been any agreement as to the probable identity of the addressee. Inasmuch as these letters have been treated exhaustively (even obsessively) by other commentators, my discussion will make no more than passing reference to them, although what I have to say about Dickinson's epistolary practice certainly applies to these texts.[11]

My discussion of her practice begins and ends with the perception that Dickinson's letter writing is at once singular and exemplary, brilliantly and performatively self-reflexive even as it remains fundamentally congruent with her era's conventions. With an intensity that has few rivals, Dickinson illuminates the fundamental condition of the familiar letter: the mutual absence of correspondents, the presumption of loss on which epistolary rhetoric commonly constructs its compensations. To be sure, Dickinson is capable of a wide range of expression in her letters, and although we shall examine many statements and figures of grief, we may also see abundant examples of joy taken in her writing's unhampered invention, in its satire of personalities and social forms, and in its construction of friendship in absence. Yet condolence recurs as a dominant motif of her letters, and whereas death remains the supreme occasion for condolence, for Dickinson even the friend's brief absence compels a recognition of mortal bounds. In Dickinson, physical separation from another could induce sorrow on the order of a state of mourning; the most cheerfully written, most gratefully received letter irrepressibly serves as a memento mori. An arresting writer of condolences per se, Dickinson brings to all of her letters a sense that language arises in bereavement. Her conviction that words mitigate that condition is ever affirmed and yet never without strain. Repeatedly she seeks compensation in the capacity of language to formulate bereavement and invoke the full if ever doubtful presence that is immortality. Succeed though she may in condoling, her way is generally to widen the void and intensify the grief more conventional letter writing seeks to occlude.

The mournful cast and readiness to condole are anything but unique to Dickinson: along with those whose letters are literarily self-conscious, we have seen immigrants, pioneers, indentured and enslaved persons, mill workers, and soldiers decry the rigid contours of time and space and conflate earthly separation with death. Nor do the irreverence, moodiness, and playfulness of Dickinson's letters set hers apart from those of her contemporaries. However struck one may be by the performative phrase or psychological peculiarity of Dickinson's early letters to her brother and girlhood friends, their outpouring of local news and personal longing bears a generic resemblance to loquacities inscribed in countless other letters of the era. Singular in motive and eccentric in form as Dickinson's epistolary practice might appear, her surviving output well represents the varieties of her period's prolific letter production: family letters, letters of adolescent and adult friendship, love letters, letters of thanks and condolence; notes exchanged within the bounds of a neighborhood to accompany gifts and recipes, to provide an afterthought to a conversation, or to attempt to reconcile a conflict; letters that traversed a continental or oceanic distance and that are written with a somber awareness of the space the message successfully must cross and the time such crossing must take. Like many letters of the period, hers are as likely to be conveyed by the hand of one whose errand lies in the direction of the addressee as by a government postal service.

As with the Emersons, the Adamses, the Fullers, the Clemenses, and other actively literate families, epistles flowed copiously among Dickinson family members during absences from the household.[12] For the young Emily Dickinson as for the young of like households, correspondence with a sibling or parent provided initial opportunities for personal expressiveness and verbal experiment. In coining an image, in pursuing a metaphor, Dickinson was as uninhibited as we have seen the adolescent Emerson to have been. As with Emerson, who on occasion had to answer a brother's criticism of his epistolary excess, constraint for Dickinson pertained mostly to her reader's expectations—to her sense of how far she might violate such expectations and at what cost. In this she was exceptional neither as a nineteenth-century adolescent nor as a Victorian young woman. Although advice books of the period suggest that a rather stiff protocol governed the composition of personal letters of young women, Dickinson and other women of her class were by no means bound to prescribed forms. As Karen Lystra has shown, letter-writers and advice books were chiefly directed to persons who aspired to middle-class ideals.[13] A woman of secure upper-middle-class rank like Emily Dickinson would have possessed the social as well as literary confidence to hold herself aloof from their strictures. Letters, for Dickinson and her friends, were largely determined by the occasion for writing and the writer's relationship to the addressee. Depending on the exchange, formalities might be abridged, constraints suspended.

Although Dickinson's letters exhibit an unusual license and inventiveness, even her most striking performances are enabled by conventions that promoted a voluble improvisation among writers of varying social position and skill. In the absence of deferences required by the letter writers' relationship to one another, the flow of ink relaxed constraint. "As Father was going to Northampton and thought of coming over to see you I thought I would improve the opportunity and write you a few lines—." So begins her earliest surviving letter (to her brother Austin Dickinson, April 18, 1842), citing, in that most formulaic of epistolary openings, the "opportunity" of conveyance, and following with a recital of longing and news whose paratactic structure reflects a common tendency among familiar letter writers to favor statement over syntax: "We miss you very much indeed you cannot think how odd it seems without you there was always such a Hurrah wherever you was I miss My bedfellow very much for it is rare that I can get any now for Aunt Elisabeth is afraid to sleep alone and Vinnie has to sleep with her but I have the privilege of looking under the bed every night which I improve as you may suppose the Hens get along nicely the chickens grow very fast" (LED 1:3). Read in light of what future letters and poems would articulate as the horror of separation, the content of these lines bears the impress perhaps of what we might think of as Dickinson's singular personality, but, as has been shown, obsessive dwelling on separation is by no means peculiar to her epistolary writing. In a stack of letters written by other twelve-year-old girls of the era, this passage would not necessarily call attention to itself.

Although it exemplifies conventional practice, this letter to some extent does forecast Dickinson's subsequent course formally and thematically. Evincing the lack of compulsory structure found in familiar letters of any period, it suggests something of the flexible space letters would avail her expanding capacities for sustained coherence and ironic control. It illustrates what in her early practice was the priority of the singular utterance over the letter's overall unity, in contrast with her later preference for shorter, poemlike letters that combine seemingly paratactic utterances into a self-reflexive whole—a development in her writing that emerges as her need for control forbade the more sprawling compositions of her youth and young womanhood. Control would never mean genteel conformity, however; her aphoristic mature style affords measured if ever powerful means of speaking the mind freely. Her earlier letters more readily invest in the performance of the momentary statement, lavishly courting that statement's transgressive potential. As in Emerson's early epistolary practice, privilege in Dickinson's youthful letters is conferred on the author's expressive urgency: the irruption of thoughts beneath the quickly moving pen (or what is meant to pass as such) overrules syntax, whether of the sentence or of larger units of meaning. Such thoughts are allowed to generate their own brief syntax and provisional coherence. For the adolescent Dickinson as for the adolescent Emerson, the effect often is to subvert rational and moralistic expectations of discourse in territory claimed by the prerogatives of private first-person utterance.

A brilliant example of such claim staking occurs in a letter of January 29, 1850, to Abiah Root, an Amherst Academy classmate with whom Dickinson corresponded for ten years. Dickinson's possession of the epistolary occasion commences with the salutation and proceeds to a deliberate writing of the parameters of her text's intended confidentiality:

> Very dear Abiah.
> The folks have all gone away—they thought that they left me alone, and contrived things to amuse me should they stay long, and *I* be lonely. Lonely indeed—they did'nt, and they could'nt have seen if they had, who should bear me company. *Three* here instead of *one*— would'nt it scare them? A curious trio, part earthly and part spiritual two of us—the other all heaven, and no earth. *God* is sitting here, looking into my very soul to see if I think right tho'ts. Yet I am not afraid, for I try to be right and good, and he knows every one of my struggles. He looks very gloriously, and everything bright seems dull beside him, and I dont dare to look directly at him for fear I shall die. Then *you* are here —dressed in that quiet black gown and cap—that funny little cap I used to laugh at you about, and you dont appear to be thinking about anything in particular, not in one of your *breaking dish* moods I take it, you seem aware that I'm writing you, and are amused I should think at any such friendly manifestation when you are already present. *Success* however even in making a fool of one's-self is'nt to be despised, so I shall persist in writing, and you may in laughing at me, if you are fully aware of the value of time as regards your immortal spirit. I cant say that I advise you to laugh, but if you are punished, and I warned you, that can be no business of mine. So I fold up my arms, and leave you to fate—may it deal very kindly with you! The trinity winds up with me, as you may have surmised, and I certainly would'nt be at the fag end but for civility to you. This selfsacrificing spirit will be the ruin of me! (LED 1:86)

The passage is worth quoting at length for the complicated privacy that it establishes and the elaborate pact-making that it engages in. Following a salutation that would affirm, against the formulaic address, the "Very" dearness of Root, Dickinson invites her correspondent to share an intimacy whose special quality lies in the fact that it remains unsuspected by her parents, who cannot guess the society she has summoned. Having defined their intercourse against an image of parental censure, Dickinson invokes the presence of that ultimate and (in Connecticut Valley culture) fearsome authority: God, the Omniscient, reader of the inmost, wickedest thought. But she does so only to counter the genuine anguish such divinity inspired with the sarcastically aggressive authority she, as writer, asserts on the occasion of this letter's composition. Lacking the other half of this correspondence, we cannot judge Root's collusion in such impiety, although later letters suggest that she would grow thereafter conventionally "wiser" than Dickinson, "nipping in the bud fancies" that her correspondent "let blossom"—that she would prefer the safe shore while Dickinson increasingly loved "to buffet the sea" (LED 1:104). In this letter, however, the writer appeals to Root's sardonic solidarity, enlisting her dish-breaking capacity in serious iconoclasm, and although Dickinson acknowledges the possibility that Root will laugh at her conceits, she proceeds in the confidence that her letter will compel her correspondent's sympathies.

Without transition, Dickinson next asserts that "I am occupied principally with a cold just now, and the dear creature *will* have so much attention that my time slips away amazingly." With this line begins an extended personification of her cold as seducer: a traveler from the Alps who accosted her while on an evening walk and begged for hospitality. Referred to as "it," the traveler is nevertheless said to be unaccompanied by "husband" or "protector," making its gender ambiguous. Ignoring the traveler and returning home—so she reports her adventure to Root—no sooner did she throw off her bonnet and shawl than "out flew my tormentor, and putting both arms around my neck began to kiss me immoderately, and express so much love, it completely bewildered me" (LED 1:87). In sexualizing the physical invasiveness of her cold's sudden onset, Dickinson may be parodying the erotic confidentialities that pass between young women.[14] Yet she also affirms that confidentiality, thereby reinforcing the letter's underlying theme of unsuspected and outlaw subjectivity. As a performance, this letter asserts outlaw subjectivity as a principle of authorship, calling attention to her pen's power to create, divert, seduce, transgress. Having concluded her fantasy on a cold, she warns Root of the subversiveness of such writing in language that at once parodies the current sermonic mode and identifies what she considers a genuine danger: "Now my dear friend, let me tell you that these last thoughts are fictions—vain imaginations to lead astray foolish young women. They are flowers of speech, they both *make*, and *tell* deliberate falsehoods, avoid them as the snake" (LED 1:88). Following a meditation on separation and death, she signs herself "Your very sincere, and *wicked* friend" (LED 1:89).

The letter epitomizes her epistolary performances of this period. In early letters Dickinson resorts to satire in general and sacrilege in particular in an effort to assert her own subjective space, to formulate her emphatic, even her eternal, difference from others, and to propose to her correspondents the terms of such intense, dangerous, and exclusive bonds as she then sought. At times the tone seems merely flippant: "'Yet a little while I am with you,'" she opens a letter of 1851 to Abiah Root, "'and again a little while and I am *not* with you' because you go to your mother!" (LED 1:129). Elsewhere her phrasing is not so much sacrilegious as brazenly heretical, which is to say profoundly if oppositionally religious, and many passages in letters to Susan Gilbert vibrate with an apocalyptic eroticism in which the absent Sue figures as the embodiment of heaven. In a letter of 1852 she reports that the thought of "Susie" preoccupied her during morning services: when the pastor "said 'Our Heavenly Father,' I said 'Oh Darling Sue'; when he read the 100th Psalm, I kept saying your precious letter all over to myself" (LED 1:201). In such passages Dickinson is less intent on attacking her culture's religious forms than inserting within them objects of worship that command her passionate assent, although the secrecy with which she performs her flagrantly unorthodox rites clearly contributes to their intensity.[15]

Heretical affirmation, trenchant satire of personalities and social forms, discourses that ridiculed and excluded others—such are only the more obvious manifestations of the power Dickinson exercised in taking up the epistolary pen. Yet simply to command the attention of her addressee was itself a power that she never overlooked or underestimated. "At my old stand again Dear Austin," she writes in a letter of 1851, "and happy as a queen to know that while I speak those whom I love are listening, and I am happier still if I shall make *them* happy" (LED 1:117). The tone is at once affectionate and imperiously acidic, for she replies herewith to a letter just received in which Austin has criticized her letters to him ("you say you dont comprehend me, you want a simpler style"), and the sentences that follow, which pointedly defy her correspondent's criticisms, simultaneously express the adoration and competition that constituted her relations with her brother. None of Austin's letters to her are known to survive, but it is clear that they offered an engageable texture, by turns wickedly amusing, collusively satiric, expostulating, solicitous. And certainly Austin was tolerant of, if not in fact entertained by, his sister's half-facetious bullyings: her barbed requests and critical observations, her blatant attempts to induce guilt. From a letter of 1853:

You did'nt come, and we were all disappointed, tho' none so much as father, for nobody but father really believed you would come, and yet folks are disappointed sometimes, when they dont expect anything. Mother got a great dinner yesterday, thinking in her kind heart that you would be so hungry after your *long ride*, and the table was set for you, and nobody moved your chair, but there it stood at the table, until dinner was all done, a melancholy emblem of the blasted hopes of the world. And we had new custard pie, too, which is a rarity in days when hens dont lay, but mother knew you loved it, and when noon really got here, and you really did not come, then a big piece was saved in case you should come at night. (LED 1:270)

As a literary performance, this passage presents a double cutting edge: one directed at the parents, who on the surface stoically forebear their son's callous neglect, all the while cultivating a hurt for which he will have to answer, and one directed at Austin, who, however excessive the parental disappointment, really should have come. The empty chair, the custard pie focus the disparity Dickinson perceives between the grief felt and the cause that gave it. She undoubtedly thought her maudlin assault on Austin funny, but she by no means absolves Austin of whatever guilt she succeeds in making him feel. Although she chiefly depicts the parents' disappointment, her sorrow in his failure to arrive is likely to have been—if anything—more grievous than theirs.

Much as she might laugh at the notion, she was not immune to reading the empty chair or the slice of custard pie as "a melancholy emblem of the blasted hopes of the world." Beneath the sensation of power to be attained in such emotionally manipulative rhetoric, her letters, particularly those to Austin and to Sue, mourn the writer's incapacity to seize the beloved object. Dwelling on the figure of the absent addressee, even her most vigorous and self-assured efforts to invoke and shape her correspondent's presence are touched by a certain desperation. Aggressive as her letters can be, they betray the suspicion that words and letter sheet are ultimately impotent in view of the vast separations that open up between people. "It did us a world of good—" she writes Austin in 1851, referring to his letter just received, "how little the scribe thinks of the value of his line—how many eager eyes will search it's every meaning—how much swifter the strokes of 'the little mystic clock, no human eye hath seen, which ticketh on and ticketh on, from morning until e'en.' If it were not that I could write you—you could not go away, *therefore*—pen and ink are very excellent things!" (LED 1:153). As though her quotation from the anonymous poem "The Life Clock" did not sufficiently merge the grief occasioned by her brother's absence with her anguished contemplation of the passage of time, Dickinson concludes this letter with news of the deaths of two young Amherst women: "It *cannot* be—yet it is so— Jennie Grout was buried yesterday—Martha Kingman died at four o,clock this morning—one and another, and another—how we pass away!" The truth, as she knows very well, is that Austin can "go away" (or "pass away") regardless of her ability to write to him, and that the mitigation of absence sought in the exchange of letters is provisional at best.

The power of letters was for Dickinson ever qualified. To the extent that a letter asserts a secret subjectivity or expresses blocked desire and longing for the absent, the writer confesses herself an object of forces beyond her control. We may see, as Dickinson herself did, how such object status reflected her place (privileged and eccentric as that place was) in the structure of an upper-middle-class Connecticut Valley Victorian household in which space and time were distinctly gendered and to be female was normally to be confined to a domestic realm. Dickinson herself represents her own object status as arising from a mortal condition over which an emphatically male God presided; what blocked desire was a power structure that manifested itself in her physical confinement to time and space, an isolation that required the material mediations of letter sheet and human language. As much a token of that isolation as an expression of the urge to break free of it, a letter was constitutionally inadequate to the ultimately metaphysical tasks imposed upon paper and ink. Early and late, the letter exchange existed for Dickinson as the intimation of a discourse fuller than was ever to be realized by material correspondence. She imagines, as we have seen, a telepathic communion that left no trace; she aspires to a seamless intersubjectivity which her confinement to space and time prevents her from verifying. "I have written you a great many letters since you left me—" she writes Jane Humphrey in 1850,

> not the kind of letters that go in post-offices—and ride in mail-bags—but queer—little silent ones—very full of affection—and full of confidence—but wanting in proof to you—therefore not valid— somehow you will not answer them—and you *would* paper, and ink letters—I will try one of those—tho' not half so precious as the other kind. I have written *those* at night—when the rest of the world were at sleep—when only God came between us—and no one else might hear. . . . Sometimes I did'nt know but you were awake—and I

hoped you wrote with that spirit pen—and on sheets from out the sky. *Did* you ever—and were we together in any of those nights? (LED 1:81–82)

For Dickinson, as for Emerson, friendship is never without a dimension of prophecy and the correspondence to which friendship gives rise exists as a prelude to a conditionless immortal communion. Yet Dickinson's burning question concerns whether the prophecy already has been realized: Did you receive my letters, and were we together in the night? Is there this fuller existence that embraces us now, of which desire (not doctrine) permits intuition? Are friendship and communication in fact possible on any other terms? As Dickinson's plaintive "*Did* you ever" suggests, there are few figures more desolate for her than that of the message (material or immaterial) that does not get through. In the abortive missive is so much lost being, so much death. Much of Dickinson's writing proceeds in the conviction that letters, poems, prayers, and the words of which they are made do not arrive at their intended destinations—not, at least, until long after their dispatch and then probably not intact. To write a letter was to reopen the question of what could and could not be done with words, what could and could not be done to appease desire and suspend an existential loneliness. For Dickinson, epistolary relations recurrently tested language and the social and metaphysical dogmas that language manages and mediates. All her life the letter genre engaged her in perpetuating an inconclusive inquiry.

PERUSE HOW INFINITE I AM

Dickinson would write twelve poems in which the writing or receiving of letters serves as a trope for the condition of language and the problem, more particularly, of establishing oneself in relation to the persons and powers that define one, such powers as for her seemed characteristically absent or inaccessible to direct interrogation.[16] Two poems especially articulate the attitudes that inform her letter writing and that give the motive to condole prominence in her epistolary rhetoric. Since its initial publication in 1890, poem 441 has been read as an apologia pro vita sua:

This is my letter to the World
That never wrote to Me—
The simple News that Nature told—
With tender Majesty

Her Message is committed
To Hands I cannot see—
For love of Her—Sweet—countrymen—
Judge tenderly—of Me (J 441)

Whether or not the poem ought to be read as a summary statement
of the Dickinson oeuvre, it does succeed in making two remarkably
sweeping propositions. First, that "This" (this poem, letter, or some
fuller body of writing that these lines represent) is "my letter to the
World," but that its "Message" originates not with "me" but with
"Nature," a female, oracular source of "News" subject to male neglect.[17] The poem's speaker is somewhat akin to the "Daisy" persona
of the "Master" letters, who addresses the Godlike "Master" from an
earthly realm at once opulent and desolate, but the poem voices a self-
deprecation to be found in other letters as well that she wrote to men.
In the speaker's alternating assertion and self-erasure, the poem dramatizes a paradox that inheres in all language but that is particularly
enacted in the epistolary exchange: that the messages of which one
would compose "my letter" are always to some extent already anticipated in the protocols one draws upon. Those protocols include the
letter genre itself with its peculiar form and phrasings, but also (as in
this poem) metaphors that identify Nature as a distinctly female realm,
or the scriptural tradition that Dickinson, like so many of her contemporaries, reinscribes with varying measures of irony and endorsement.
"My letter," no matter how much it becomes mine, derives from
sources outside of me and ends by residing with readers who at once
lay claim to my letter and judge the "me" whom their claiming voids.

Before one can pass beyond the opening clause of the first proposition, however, the second appears, with pointed concision, in the rela-
tive clause of line 2: the World "never wrote to Me." The writer seems
much less oppressed by the sense that she is preempted by the discourse of (her) "Nature" than by despair of adequate answer. Such an
answer would address her specifically, and would transform her reader
from a (male) predator of the object "me" into a writerly partner in an
intersubjective text, confirming her place with that of her reader in the
epistolarity that indemnifies individual isolation and mutual absence.
For her "letter to the World," the poet inscribes two readerships: one
figured, in what for the writer is the past tense, as absolutely unre-
ciprocating ("That never wrote to Me") and the other, in the present
tense that always attaches to the act of reading, as sternly adjudicating
("Judge tenderly—of Me"). Although she addresses this ever-present

readership, her claim never to have had a reply places her, as writer, in something of a posthumous relation to any actual reader of this poem. She is a letter writer who purportedly never was and now never can be a letter receiver. Hers is the despair of one cut off from a live exchange; hence her closing line's plea.

"This is my letter to the World" is not a letter, yet it reflects attitudes that operate throughout Dickinson's epistolary practice. For Dickinson the letter is a text of compelling (often sexual) urgency, written not so much to convey truth as to maintain and assess relation. Letters, inasmuch as they must pass through time and across space, confirm even as they mitigate separation, and there is ever the risk of misunderstanding: tonalities misheard, meaning misjudged, intimacy rejected. There is always the risk of epistolary silence: the letter, or its reply, has been lost in the mail, or one's partner has grown hostile or indifferent. There is the silence of the response that does not reciprocate one's own urgency. And there is the suspicion that letters must ever arrive as posthumous texts, inscriptions of always bygone moments and intensities. All such anxieties coalesce in the hyperbolic assertion that the world "never wrote to Me."

For Dickinson, the occasions of exception to the "never wrote" were ecstatic, however often she was in actuality the recipient of eagerly awaited and deeply satisfying mail. Sociable though such moments were, they required intense privacy:

The Way I read a Letter's—this—
'Tis first—I lock the Door—
And push it with my fingers—next—
For transport it be sure—

And then I go the furthest off
To counteract a knock—
Then draw my little Letter forth
And slowly pick the lock—

Then—glancing narrow, at the Wall—
And narrow at the floor
For firm Conviction of a Mouse
Not exorcised before—

Peruse how infinite I am
To no one that You—know—
And sigh for lack of Heaven—but not
The Heaven God bestow— (J 636)

Portraying letter receiving as an instance of the soul's shutting the door on all but her most select society, this poem belies the extent to which many of the letters Dickinson received were shared among family members or between friends.[18] Yet it is undoubtedly true to the manner in which some—among them many of the most gratifying—letters were received. The "Way" of reading letters is not simply the manner in which they are read, but the route one traverses by way of preparing oneself for the larger transport that the letter per se affords.[19] The way proceeds through a series of withdrawals, a seeking of progressively securer enclosures. Satisfactorily closeted, the recipient is free not only to draw her "little Letter forth" and "pick the lock" of its implied door (for, as communication sealed up in language, a letter necessarily offers resistance) but to enter and occupy a space of contrasting expanse: one that, in the poem's climaxing line, permits her to "Peruse how infinite I am."

This proposition, to students of Dickinson's letters and of correspondence generally, is incandescent: to read a letter is to peruse the infinitude of the reading "I," to perceive oneself imaged in the unfolding dimensions of an intersubjective epistolary space, contact with which reacquaints the self with a sense of unbounded circumference. The line that follows, "To no one that You—know—," qualifies the proposition intriguingly. One is infinite to someone, infinite by virtue of relatedness to another. Yet, to the poem's reader, or the reader inscribed as the second person in line 14, this other is explicitly identified as "no one that You—know—." Rhetorically, this statement, excluding the poem's reader from the core of relations at play in the epistolary exchange, reinforces the speaker's demonstration that the way to read letters consists of locking doors against all who should obtrude upon the self's chosen company. But by withdrawing all possible answer to the question "To whom?" she effectively encourages us to consider the identity of this "no one" whom we (cannot) know. Readily we may identify this "one" as the speaker's correspondent, in whose text the speaker may contemplate her infinitude, a correspondent who, even if name were known, would remain unknowable to us as a correspondent. We may, however, as well identify the "one" as the speaker herself—one whose identity, enmeshed in an epistolary partnership, is bound up in the text of the corresponding other. The whole force of the poem's rhetoric impresses upon us that neither the letter, its writer, nor its reader are to be known by the "You" of the poem.

What does such secrecy serve? The answer befits the paradoxical nature of epistolary compensations. Such secrecy serves "Heaven"—not the heaven to which God promotes the worthy, but the heaven of an intensely (perhaps impossibly) reciprocating human relationship.[20] But then the speaker sighs "for lack of" such "Heaven" because, however satisfying, a letter comes always as confirmation of the partner's absence. The infinitude of the speaker's self-perusal is thus qualified, in the final lines, by the emphatic reminder of what she lacks, and however defiant the clause of the last line, "Heaven" in this poem exists indeed as the desired transcendence of human limitations. However ecstatically a letter is received, its foretaste of heavenly reconciliations, or of lasting sublimations of earthly erotic impulse, at best makes one sigh for lack of Heaven in hand. Invariably for Dickinson, letter writing and letter receiving excite to the point of physical sensation the consciousness of her mortal bounds: her confinement to time and space, relieved by a language that can richly suggest yet never confirm a transcendent existence.

Dickinson's association of letters with life everlasting was perennial. "A Letter always feels to me like immortality because it is the mind alone without corporeal friend" (LED 2:460). So she opens to Thomas Wentworth Higginson in June 1869, replying to the letter of his quoted from earlier in which Higginson, along with confiding his uncertainty as to how to respond to her, apologized for his most recent lapse in the correspondence that had spanned seven years—a correspondence that Dickinson, in this same letter, claims to have "saved my Life." At this time Higginson was still a year away from materializing in the Dickinson parlor, and their friendship had been entirely epistolary, dependent on what she would proceed to define as that "spectral power in thought that walks alone" across the pages of letters. Writing thirteen years later to James D. Clark, Dickinson reiterates the proposition with only slight variation: "A Letter always seemed to me like Immortality, for is it not the Mind alone, without corporeal friend?" (LED 3:752). The context here is quite different: the correspondence with Clark had arisen out of what for both was the bereavement occasioned by the death in 1882 of Charles Wadsworth, their mutual friend, and the letter in which the phrase recurs specifically responds to what must have been Clark's letter to Dickinson soon after her mother's death—a condolence that appears to have been accompanied by something Wadsworth had written, making him a particularly immortal party to Clark's letter.[21] She repeats herself, then, at a time when her thought, even for her, intensely focused on mortality. "Her dying feels to me like

Emily Dickinson to Thomas Wentworth Higginson, June 1869.
Courtesy of the Trustees of the Boston Public Library.

A.M.

Amherst

Dear friend

A Letter
always feels to me
like immortality
because it is the
mind alone without
corporeal friend.
Indebted in our
talk to Attitude
and Accent -
there seems a
spectral power in
thought that
walks alone -

many kinds of Cold," she writes Clark, "—at times electric, at times benumbing—then a trackless waste, Love has never trod." The immediacy of death tested belief; understandably she covets every evidence of the "spectral power in thought that walks alone."

For Dickinson, a letter "always feels to me like immortality" because her correspondent's absence prefigured death. Or to put it less abstractly, more in line with the sensuous emphasis of the poet's own phrasing, such absence *felt* like death: that person's death to her, her death to that person, the death ultimately of everyone to one another. Absence as death is the fundamental trope of her epistolary writing. Separation anxiety constitutes a central topic of Dickinson biography and criticism, and that anxiety comes across in the letters as an obsessive and at times frantic state of being.[22] Yet concern with separation is, as we have seen, endemic to letters, and absence of a specific addressee is the condition from which letters are written. Whether or not the letter writer laments that absence, or prefers it to the addressee's presence, or, as is not uncommon, regrets yet desires estrangement, the condition of separation is intrinsic to epistolary writing. It need not be addressed explicitly. The fact of a letter itself acknowledges the mutual absence of correspondents and their intention to keep (in the common but significantly corporeal metaphor) "in touch." Although separation may go outwardly unacknowledged, it may obsess one or both correspondents; some of the most profound meditations to be met with in the familiar letter predictably concern that state: the isolation, the sense of mortality, that the effort to write a letter may seek to overcome. Such moments, infrequent and epiphanic with many writers, are almost the norm in Dickinson's letters, in which the genre of the familiar letter seems constantly intent on declaring and testing its basic discursive condition.

To write across such space and through such time as came between people prior to the age of telecommunications vividly enforced the sensation of physical separation, even as it induced writers to perfect epistolary simulacra of contact. Beginning one of the weekly letters that she sent to her brother when he was in Boston teaching school and studying law from 1851 to 1854, Dickinson explicitly registers the ambition of her writing vis-à-vis the constraints (here manifested by sister Lavinia's impatience) under which she writes:

> I cant write but a word, dear Austin, because it is already noon and Vinnie is waiting to go to the office for me, and yet a *single word* may be of comfort to you as you go travelling on. It should be a word big

and warm and full of sweet affection if I could make it so—Oh it should fill that room, that small and lonely chamber with a thousand kindly things and precious ministrations—I wonder if it *will*, for know that if it *does* not, it is bad and disobedient and a most unworthy type of its affectionate mistress! (LED 1:155)

The constraints on the writer inform the writing's ambition: she composes in view of Vinnie's imminent departure to the post office, which must not be delayed if the outgoing mail is to be timely in its several errands. Under those circumstances, Dickinson remarks that she "cant write but a word"; but from such rhetorical penury she rapidly conjures all that a single word may be, the plenitude that it may bestow should it prove the worthy type of its mistress. The aspirations Dickinson here places on the single word are striking given her later effort to economize in the interest of bringing out the opulence of her chosen words' effects. But in this comparatively prolix letter, language exists as the ultimate constraint, beyond the tyrannies of space and time that the epistolary word can transcend. As Dickinson suggests, that theoretical word, invoked by *shoulds*, is too apt to exhibit a volition of its own by which the mistress's will must miscarry.

Should the word fulfill its charge—what then? An utterance "big and warm and full of sweet affection" that could endow Austin's bachelor room "with a thousand kindly things and precious ministrations" is the word become flesh, the corporeal extension of the writer (as self-idealizing sister) across space and through time, a physical approximation of addresser and addressee that must obviate recourse to letter writing. As we have seen, the conceit that in composing and posting a letter one pays a visit, or that in receiving a letter one entertains a visitor, appears frequently in sustained correspondences and may be attributed in part to the metonymic turn by which the material letter offers itself as type or relic of its writer. Few correspondents, however, approach Dickinson in her fascination with that conceit, her insistence that her epistolary word embody herself at a distance through language that would simulate speech or through the gifts of flowers and bread that might accompany her word—or, conversely, that the letters she receives represent the best her correspondents can do distantly to embody themselves. As well, few writers exhibit her feel for the "spectral power" at play in the epistolary exchange, her sense that letters ever exist as tokens of the denial of the correspondent's bodily presence. Again, the immortality that a letter "feels like" derives from the "death" that this denial prefigures for Dickinson. But as she settled into the reclusive patterns of her maturity, such immortality—the metonymic presence of the correspondent in the letter that required the absence of the corporeal friend—provided distinct advantages over the panto-mimes of social contact in which the corporeal friend commonly ab-sented herself or himself from Dickinson's exorbitant expectations.

In the letters written to Austin Dickinson and Susan Gilbert before their marriage, Emily Dickinson frequently characterizes the epistolary relation as the necessary but always unsatisfactory surrogate for the seeming immediacies of voice, eye contact, touch. "You sat just here last Sunday," she writes Austin, sedulously observing his absence from the present week's sabbath routine, "where I am sitting now and our voices were nimbler than our pens can be, if they try never so hardly" (LED 1:156). "How vain it seems to *write*," she remarks to Susan Gilbert, "when one knows how to feel—how much more near and dear to sit beside you, talk with you, hear the tones of your voice" (LED 1:176). The theme recurs late in life, long after Dickinson had stopped seeing all but a few people and had made the letter the exclusive medium of many friendships. "Had it come all the way in your little hand," she writes Elizabeth Holland in 1881, confirming the arrival of a Christmas greet-ing, "it could not have reached us perfecter, though had it, we should have clutched the hand and forget the rest" (LED 3:721).

Yet it is not the friend's unconstructed presence (if such could exist) for which Dickinson truly longs. Her wistful scenes of immediate contact are remarkable in that, beyond the imagination of friends re-united, they commonly depict a perfection of relations wholly depen-dent on her inscribing pen. Recalling Austin's presence in the house the week before, Dickinson idealizes the routine of the home from which no member is absent. In imagining her reunion with Susan Gilbert, Dickinson strategically represents their relation as inhering in a contact that erases what she knows to be the normal boundaries language maintains between individuals who live as even the most intimate neighbors. "Susie, forgive me Darling, for every word I say—my heart is full of you . . . yet when I seek to say to you something not for the world, words fail me. If you were here—and Oh that you were, my Susie, we need not talk at all, our eyes would whisper for us, and your hand fast in mine, we would not ask for language" (LED 1:211–12). In this passage, Dickinson collapses the distinctions between written and spoken words; both are inadequate to a communication "not for the world." We may well believe that she thereby represses the articulation of a homoerotic passion whose undisguised statement (if such were possible) neither she nor Gilbert, as individuals deeply inscribed by the world, could hear. In any case, the act of communicating with Gilbert is envisioned as a utopian scene in which conversation figures as a perfect understanding established by such physical contact as may never in this life take place.[23]

Words for Dickinson ultimately fail of their charge to become flesh, and the exchange of language serves to confirm as much as to allay the mutual absence of friends. The passionate accord and wordless eroticism that characterize what Dickinson figures as her essential bond of friendship with Susan Gilbert measure the exorbitance of her requirement and indicate the extremes to which she registered the absence of the loved one. Her letters to Gilbert compulsively acknowledge the possibility that they may not again meet in this life. Safer, her phrasings often suggest, to consider sudden death probable, and their current absence to one another as a permanent earthly condition. Better to look forward conditionally: "and when you come *if we all live till then*" (LED 1:203; italics added).[24] Against such meditation—encouraged by the celerity with which Dickinson's contemporaries succumbed to pneumonia, influenza, and tuberculosis—her youthful epistolary voice rings with the pain of premonitory bereavement. A delayed reply was the occasion for panic as well as for wit: "I watch your letters Susie, to see if they grow saintlier, and more like Susie *Spirit*, than my dear earthly child. Forgive me a smile, Susie, on a subject near my heart, but for the last few weeks and days—they *are* so evanescent that I cant see them *at all*; dear Susie, *please* be corporal, it would so comfort me!" (LED 1:169). Please be corporal: write me to confirm your continued earthly existence; the letter, after all, possesses materiality and exists as personal metonym. But beyond the longed-for epistolary embodiment of what for now must remain an incorporeal friendship, be my corporeal friend.

The immortality with which letter writing and receiving became so profoundly associated in Dickinson's mind compensated not only for the death that separations prefigured but for what Dickinson came early to recognize as the impossibility of such wordlessly corporeal reunions as the letter writer fondly projected. If the word failed to become as flesh, flesh failed too as a medium of full presence. That being the case, the near approach effected by words afforded satisfactions surer and more controllable than those to be found in the occasions of contiguous personhood. Dickinson was acutely aware of the cost of such a recognition; in later life, she openly (if indirectly) confesses the anguish of her self-sequestering custom. "Dont you know you are happiest while I withhold and not confer," she writes to Otis Phillips Lord in 1878, "—dont you know that 'No' is the wildest word we consign to Language?" (LED 2:617). Her friendship with Lord, known only by some fifteen draft fragments left from what clearly had been a prolific correspondence, suggests that in the realm of potentially erotic relationships (a realm that she seems never to have irrevocably vacated) Dickinson was prepared by longstanding practice to content herself with the beloved's inscribed language. Blocked by the wild summary "No," desire nevertheless continued to flourish in its reliably prolific verbal form. Anticipating her weekly letter from Lord, she invokes a highly sexual trope in characterizing her life as so much "Fever with nearness to your blissful words" (LED 2:618). Having barred the possibility of corporeal intimacy, she finds a measure of delight in contemplating the conjugal existence that Lord evidently proposed and that she herself may have seriously entertained.[25]

The strangely flirtatious abnegation that characterizes her relations with Lord reflects an inveterate seeking of epistolary satisfactions as well as a long habituation to the notion of her friend's ultimate absence, whoever that friend might be. Her elaborate and artful efforts to articulate and thereby deny the absence and mortality of her intimates acquire a certain discipline in the years following Susan Gilbert's marriage to Austin. An accomplished and notably dispassionate rendering of the perfect reunion occurs in a letter that the poet wrote when she was twenty-five to Elizabeth Holland, a longtime friend and regular correspondent whom Dickinson saw eagerly if infrequently. In letters to Holland, whose physical presence was not an object of fixation for Dickinson, the association of her addressee's absence with death never becomes frantic, and the writer confides her compensatory image with a self-awareness and detachment that may well derive from the pleasure taken in the artistry of the picture. "Don't tell, dear Mrs. Holland," she begins playfully,

> but wicked as I am, I read my Bible sometimes, and in it as I read today, I found a verse like this, where friends should "go no more out"; and there were "no tears," and I wished as I sat down to-night that we were *there*—not *here*—and that wonderful world had commenced, which makes such promises, and rather than to write you, I were by your side, and the "hundred and forty and four thousand" were chatting pleasantly, yet not disturbing us. And I'm half tempted to take my seat in that Paradise of which the good man writes, and

begin forever and ever *now*, so wondrous does it seem. My only sketch, profile, of Heaven is a large, blue sky, bluer and larger than the *biggest* I have seen in June, and in it are my friends—all of them—every one of them—those who are with me now, and those who were "parted" as we walked, and "snatched up to Heaven." (LED 2:329)

This letter is important to an understanding of Dickinson's vigorously self-reflexive imagination of "Heaven," particularly of the defiance with which she embodied heaven in the perfected forms of such beloved earthly objects as bloomed and faded all about her under the rule of mutability.[26] But to the reader of her letters, it also represents Dickinson's growing power to create an epistolary compensation for the friend's absence, a compensation in which the ideality of a relationship need not be put to the rigorous tests of frequent social contact.

Dickinson proceeds to foreground the motive of this letter, which serenely contemplates the particular absence of her addressee amid a world governed by the laws of change and loss, and all against the enchanting (if for her ever suspect) promises of life everlasting. "Dear Mrs. Holland," she writes, renewing her salutation at the close of the second paragraph, "I love, to-night—love you and Dr. Holland, and 'time and sense'—and fading things, and things that do *not* fade." To love intransitively, in the abstract, as Dickinson here first professes to do, is to love in the absence of beloved objects, the lonely situation of the letter writer, a circumstance in which the human estate, as Dickinson often reminds us, is experienced in all of its mortality. But Dickinson's profession, which becomes transitive, first taking "Dear Mrs. Holland" and then her husband and then all things mortal and immortal, as direct objects, moves quickly to assert the act of loving as a godlike act—as the ultimate substantiation of the object loved which, left to itself, will positively fade. As she had written to Sue in a letter of 1852, "we shall not be separated, neither death, nor the grave can part us, so that we only *love!*" (LED 1:210–11).[27] Dickinson's epistolary purpose, as she matures as a letter writer, is boldly exhibited in the letter of August 1856 to Elizabeth Holland: to affirm love and to offer condolence for the death that our earthly absences from one another anticipate, earthly absences that no mere bodily contiguity can quite overcome. Supercilious and resentful as her letters sometimes are, they consistently strive to achieve a measure of transcendence over the emotional complications that characterize her mortal dealings with epistolary partners.

Condolence, from first to last, is the most consistent single purpose of Dickinson the letter writer. To condole, etymologically, is to grieve with another; to grieve with another is to console that person, reminding the bereaved of the communities that exist beyond the breach opened by loss: for Dickinson, the immediately mortal, ultimately immortal company that one keeps. She or he who would condole must be an initiate: "For the comprehension of Suffering," Dickinson writes to a neighbor, thanking her for her note following the death of her father, "One must ones Self have Suffered" (LED 2:527). So routinely do her letters treat the mutual absence of correspondents as premonitory of death and immortal life that her condolences proper seem only a slightly more specialized form of epistolary expression. Love that must affirm itself against a now probable, a now factual death, words that would reconcile sorrow with desire or seek to assuage those states of isolation beyond reach of language, are Dickinson's preeminent epistolary themes.

Her first surviving condolence exhibits her early recognition of the limitations of the epistolary medium, anticipating the grieving love letters she would later write to Sue: "*Can* I console so far off," she writes in April 1850 to Jane Humphrey on hearing that her friend's father was not expected to live, "wont the comfort waste in conveying, and be *not*, when my letter gets there?" (LED 1:94). Nothing, Dickinson here suggests, short of the corporeal friend can comfort the bereaved, but in later letters that incorporate her own accumulated sense of bereavement she reveals her understanding of the unapproachability of the grieved heart. As death separates one from the departed, so too it distances the bereaved from his or her companions in life. "One who only said 'I am sorry' helped me the most when father ceased," she writes to Elizabeth Holland in 1881, "—it was too soon for language" (LED 3:713). "When I am most grieved," she begins a condolence to her Aunt Katie Sweetser on the occasion of her cousin Henry's death in 1870, "I had rather no one would speak to me, so I stayed from you, but I thought by today, perhaps you would like to see me, if I came quite soft and brought no noisy words." And, according to the common refrain of such messages, there is virtually nothing to say: "when I am most sorry, I can say nothing so I will only kiss you and go far away" (LED 2:469). She represents her letter thus as performing a wordless physical gesture that imposes minimally on the space of grief.

Having represented it so, she nevertheless goes on to offer explicit comfort. ("Who could ache for you like your little Niece—," she asks, supporting her claim to presume, "who knows how deep the Heart is and how much it holds?") As though to mute the potential noisiness of her words, Dickinson condoles in short entries whose compression images the voice at once as speaking and refraining from speech. The rest of the letter is as follows:

> I know we shall certainly see what we loved the most. It is sweet to think they are safe by Death and that that is all we have to pass to obtain their face.
> There are no Dead, dear Katie, the Grave is but our moan for them.
> Were it to be the last
> How infinite would be
> What we did not suspect was marked
> Our final interview.
> Henry had been a prisoner. How he had coveted Liberty probably his Redeemer knew—and as we keep surprise for those most precious to us, brought him his Ransom in his sleep.
> Emily. (LED 2:469)

Dickinson's condolence draws upon two commonplaces of such messages: that we are sure to see the deceased in an afterlife, and that death, in this instance, has come as a release from suffering.[28] Any familiarity with Dickinson's uneasy faith in such afterlife as could truly appease the human desire for immortal existence makes obvious that she writes, here, in support of her addressee's need to believe. At the same time, her phrasing makes plain that she seeks also to confirm what she herself is willing if never simply able to accept. "I know we shall certainly see what we *loved* the most": her assent grounds itself in that verb which, when paired with a human subject (as we observed in the letter to Elizabeth Holland), affords that subject nearest access to godlike power and conditionless life. Letter writing upholds love, and love, Dickinson affirms, upholds the existence of the deceased as one who retains a visualizable (perhaps even a literally visible) identity—as one whose face may be obtained beyond the blind passage that is death per se. Poem J 1164, which this letter embeds, develops the theme further in its use of the word "interview": eye-to-eye contact, an exchange of views grounded in an exchange of language. The conversation that we could not at the time have suspected to be our final interview with the deceased may now, by virtue of being the last in a mortal series, be retrospectively regarded as the first in an immortal sequence, hence "infinite," our relations to be picked up from that point in a perfected eternal existence. It is thus that we move beyond the wordless moan of the gravesite; it is thus that Dickinson, in this extraordinarily artful letter, restores language and community to the occasion of death, doing so without recourse to "noisy words," content to achieve a companionable silence in the presence of grief.

That the newly bereaved were subject to an impenetrable solitude and silence appears to have been a prevalent Anglo-American assumption. "In the newness of bereavement we are deaf to consolation" (LRWE 7:269), writes Ralph Waldo Emerson in October 1836, writing at a time when the deaths of his first wife and brothers Edward and Charles constituted an active memory. Shortly thereafter, in a belated condolence to an old friend, he speaks of the comforter's corresponding aphasia: "I have not attempted to write to you since I heard of the death of Anne Jean, for death makes us all dumb" (LRWE 7:273). "What can we say in these cases?" asks Thomas Carlyle in a condolence written to Emerson on the occasion of his son Waldo's death. "There is nothing to be said,—nothing but what the wild son of Ishmael, and every thinking heart, from of old have learned to say: God is great!" (CEC 318). "I had not the heart to telegraph," writes Henry Adams to Clara Stone Hay shortly after John Hay's long-expected death. "I can say nothing. You will understand it" (LHA 5:685). Such was the refrain of Adams's many condolences which, after December 6, 1885, the day Marian Adams committed suicide, made more or less tacit reference to his own induction into the "vast fraternity" of "Hearts that Ache" (LHA 4:5).

To condole, there must be a grief in the bereaved party that one may confidently address, a grief receptive to another's loving attention. In a letter to her cousin, the Reverend Perez Cowan, on the occasion of his sister's death, Dickinson writes as a fellow sufferer and would-be comforter frustrated by the bereaved party's refusal to voice his pain, which she cannot think honestly admitted inasmuch as her cousin does not present the aspect of someone beyond comforting. "You might not need assistance?" she queries challengingly. Not to need assistance, for Dickinson, is to deny the human bond, and her figure for this denial is the refusal to talk one's native tongue. "You speak with so much trust of that which only trust can prove, it makes me feel away, as if my English mates spoke sudden in Italian." Four months later she would write the letter to Katie Sweetser just discussed, speaking, to what she imagined as her aunt's desolation, precisely of "that which only trust can prove." Here, however, she writes as though Cousin Cowan's trust has left her alone to bear the occasion's proper sorrow, and that it is she who therefore requires his condolence. "It grieves me that you speak of Death with so much expectation," she exclaims. "I know there is no pang like that for those we love, nor any leisure like the one they leave so closed behind them, but Dying is a wild Night and a new Road" (LED 2:463). Although offering "assistance," this letter would dismiss the facile comfort, insisting that sorrow be experienced (first) as an uncompensatable state and allowed to exact its due. "I like a look of Agony," she had written some eight years earlier, "Because I know it's true" (J 241).

It is not without compunction that she impeaches the candor of her cousin's bereavement. "The subject," she confesses after treating it in several of the concise paragraphs typical of her mature epistolary style, "hurts me so that I will put it down, because it hurts you." Yet her purpose has been to speak in behalf of the grief that indicts trust, that causes her (at least) to distrust Jesus when he speaks of his Father.[29] Toward the letter's end, she adverts to the notion that the epistolary word makes a poor substitute for the presence of the conversing voice. "We bruise each other less in talking than in writing," she reflects, "for then a quiet accent helps words themselves too hard." That she may establish the commonality that permits comfort, Dickinson is prepared to bruise her bereaved addressee. Yet much of the grief expressed in this letter is peculiarly that of the letter writer, for whom the sensation of immortality proceeds from a consensus that she cannot achieve with her cousin. Doubtful that she and her correspondent can reach an accord, Dickinson writes as one who bears an unrequited grief in the midst of a bereavement greater than any specific loss, and that exists for her in her loneliness as the ontology to which all deaths and all absences make ultimate reference.

HOW SIMPLY AT THE LAST THE FATHOM COMES

I have been arguing that Dickinson's epistolarium derives from a state of bereavement that is reconfirmed in the act of writing to those whose bodily presence is, for whatever reason, withheld, and that love and immortality exist for her as realities to be invoked, with varying measures of confidence and anguish, in compensation for this bereavement. To this state one can of course assign no single biographical cause. In youth Dickinson experienced separations as intensely grievous events; bereavement as a condition of life seems especially to have been decided by the loss of a partly real, partly imaginary male lover.[30] In letters to Austin she reports the deaths of contemporaries but is unable to discuss her sorrow. The demise of her "tutor" Benjamin Franklin Newton is registered in a postscript; we can only uncertainly conjecture all that she leaves unsaid: "Oh Austin, Newton is dead. The first of my own friends. Pace" (LED 1:236). Letters in which she explores bereavement in the light of deaths that touch her directly date only from her early forties, when family members and close friends begin to die. In these letters, the central emotional reflex that was her capacity to grieve, and by which she reads the bereavement of others, achieves a complex articulation in which her position as letter writer and letter receiver remains tropologically suggestive.

In these letters, Dickinson represents her own dolor as a state in which she inconsolably confronts the disembodiment of the departed soul—a turn of events made horrific by the fact that she is dispossessed of the material means to communicate. "I dream about father every night," she writes her cousins Louise and Frances Norcross two years after Edward Dickinson's death, "always a different dream, and forget what I am doing daytimes, wondering where he is. Without any body, I keep thinking. What kind can that be?" (LED 2:559). Her concern with "where" Edward Dickinson is has less to do with whether or not there is an afterlife in which he continues to exist than with the inconceivability for her of a bodiless, locationless existence.[31] We may surmise that to anyone who had sustained as many friendships through the mails as Dickinson had by this point in her life, and who was therefore used to the absence of the corporeal friend mitigated by the friend's metonymic presence in the material letter, the idea that a loved one abides (if at all) in a space impervious to the epistolary exchange must have been bereaving in an absolute sense. A recurrent motif of her correspondence is the restoration of absent friends, not only the person with whom she is corresponding but third parties who are likewise absent. Writing in the immediacy of bereavement, Dickinson typically figures the deceased as a traveler with whom communication and reunion have been thwarted. "We don't know where she is," Dickinson writes of her recently deceased mother, evincing again her abhorrence at imagining the dead as beyond location, "though so many tell us" (LED 3:750). Ultimately, the bereaved must discard their mortal sense of time, space, and embodiment. "Mother has now been gone five Weeks," she later writes. "We should have thought it a long Visit, were she coming back—Now the 'Forever' thought almost shortens it, as we are nearer rejoining her than her own return" (LED 3:754). Amid such paradox, the writer projects her own decease as a journey from which she too will not return.

In Dickinson's last years events increasingly forced the " 'Forever' thought" upon her. Envisioning her own decease as a journey undertaken beyond mortal bounds that would culminate in the restoration of those loved and lost provided a certain speculative consolation; inasmuch as she retained a capacity to love readily and intensively, there were compensatory constructions to be put on "forever" as long as a loved one's death did not appear absolutely imminent. Writing to a tired and unwell Otis Lord a month after the death of Charles Wadsworth, she laments the fact that she and Lord had not found one another sooner but then proceeds to celebrate their late intimacy as a prophecy of "forever": "The time before it was—was naught, so why establish it? And all the time to come it is, which abrogates the time" (LED 3:728). Nevertheless, in what is probably her next letter to him, written after hearing first that Lord was near death and later that he had rallied, she speaks of her "rapture" upon learning of his "return, and of the loved steps, retraced almost from the 'Undiscovered Country' " (LED 3:730). The "forever" of an immortality that redresses separations incurred in mortal time figured less compellingly than the sensation of relief produced by the news that her friend for the present had been spared time's inevitable abrogation.

Lord's death in 1884 deeply grieved Dickinson but came as no surprise. Perhaps nothing could have shocked her after the loss to typhoid fever of her eight-year-old nephew Gilbert in October 1883, no event again force the " 'Forever' thought" with such withering trauma. This death plunged Dickinson into a grief for which she was so unprepared that it called forth her most rhetorically strained efforts to affirm immortality. The condolence that she writes on this occasion to Susan (Gilbert's mother) passes between two who share the inconsolable immediacy of bereavement. Endeavoring to write beyond sorrow, to console by means of a sequence of prophetic utterances that seek in Gilbert's death final proof of an unconditional existence, she closes as she can the breach between desire and confirmation. The letter in full:

Dear Sue—
The Vision of Immortal Life has been fulfilled—
How simply at the last the Fathom comes! The Passenger and not the Sea, we find surprises us—

Gilbert rejoiced in Secrets—

His Life was panting with them—With what menace of Light he cried "Dont tell, Aunt Emily"! Now my ascended Playmate must instruct *me*. Show us, prattling Preceptor, but the way to thee!

He knew no niggard moment—His Life was full of Boon—The Playthings of the Dervish were not so wild as his—

No crescent was this Creature—He traveled from the Full—

Such soar, but never set—

I see him in the Star, and meet his sweet velocity in everything that flies—His Life was like the Bugle, which winds itself away, his Elegy an echo—his Requiem ecstasy—

Dawn and Meridian in one.

Wherefore would he wait, wronged only of Night, which he left for us—

Without a speculation, our little Ajax spans the whole—

Pass to thy Rendezvous of Light,

Pangless except for us—

Who slowly ford the Mystery

Which thou hast leaped across!

Emily. (LED 3:799)

To proclaim the death of a child as the vision of immortal life fulfilled is extreme, but if we ask on what grounds she makes this statement—which absolutely denies the reality of death—the answer is that she cannot admit, either to the child's mother or to herself, the possibility that the child has died. In sustaining this proclamation, which would erase the distinction between mortal and immortal life, Dickinson characterizes Gilbert retrospectively as one whose immortality could not be contained by mortal bounds. In so doing she articulates the Romantic commonplace that children partake of immortal mysteries and do so without the "speculation" that characterizes the adult mind.[32] Adult that she feels herself to be, Dickinson in this letter identifies with the deceased; to her life's end she preserved the child persona in herself, and her own life abounded in the untold secret of her poems and epistolary contacts. Yet the breach nevertheless reappears: if there is no substantial distinction between mortal and immortal life, differences still obtain between the child who may spontaneously pass to his "Rendezvous of Light" and the adult who, however sympathetic with the child-mind, must "slowly ford the Mystery"—a delayed gratification of the hunger for truth that has its analogue in the always delayed condition of epistolary disclosure. Although the letter argues that the difference is temporary and hence insubstantial, the grief in this letter is the more terrible for her effort to repress it, and it remains moreover the old grief of loss complicated by the persistent doubt that the vision of immortal life finally will be fulfilled.

To the end of her life Dickinson periodically entertained the sensation that her vision of immortal life had been or would shortly be fulfilled, and epistolary contact was commonly the medium of such sensation. "A Letter is a joy of Earth—," she writes about 1885, "It is denied the Gods—" (J 1639); but so miraculous to her were the communications that traversed the forbidding distances between individuals that she represents the epistolary act as always potentially a species of divine visitation. This was particularly so when a letter confirmed love or concerned in some way a deceased beloved person with whom she could almost believe herself in contact. Her correspondence with Charles Wadsworth's friend James D. Clark focuses ever on the deceased Wadsworth and reads as a kind of epistolary séance; when Clark dies, Dickinson's correspondence with his brother Charles memorializes James Clark and Wadsworth both. When James Clark writes enclosing something of Wadsworth's authorship, she refers to the enclosure as a "Letter from the skies" and speaks of her inveterate association of letters with immortality. Later, when Clark sends her what may well have been Wadsworth's last volume of sermons, Dickinson writes: "To thank you is impossible, because your Gifts are from the Sky, more precious than the Birds, because more disembodied" (LED 3:761). Here, disembodiment is favorably associated with the life that persists beyond the body's dissolution, and she proceeds to represent Wadsworth's text as confirmation that mail, by whatever indirection, arrives from the immortal realm. "The Page to which I opened," she writes Clark, "showed me first these Words. 'I have had a Letter from another World'" (LED 3:762).[33] Bereavement established one in proximity to that world. Increasingly for Dickinson, letters serve as the link between bereaved persons living in isolation, completing their lives' slow ford of the mystery—a crossing that might at any moment venture within hearing of a summons.

Dickinson's last letter, probably written a few days before her death and received after she had entered a coma, enacts this process so memorably that it counts as one of the most interesting epistolary moments on record. The recipients were her cousins Louise and Frances Norcross. In full:

Little Cousins,
     Called back.
          Emily. (LED 3:906)

She here alludes to Hugh Conway's popular *Called Back*, a mystery
novel in which human love, partaking of the divine, triumphs over
crime, blindness, forgetfulness, loss, and death—the moral of the story
being that love recalls us to our proper immortal relation with one another.[34] The letter presents an intriguing parallel to her self-depiction
in "This is my letter to the World" as one who would write as part of a
larger system of exchange. Addressing her cousins as the orphaned
children they were when she first took an interest in their welfare, she
directs to them a condolence on the occasion of her own death.

There is nothing especially dolorous here: to die, in her figuration, is
to be "Called," as though across space and through time, "back" to the
full, disclosed presence of our common immortality, alienation from
which had ever been the occasion for her letters to the world. The
voice says only so much as to state and explain what upon the letter's
receipt would be its own absence, to record a final disembodiment of
the speaker and her voice. The voice thereby places itself beyond the
language it no longer needs as a compensation for the fading and
absenting of beloved objects. Few messages could ever be so affir-
matively posthumous, so rhetorically in command of their occasion.
Even the nonepistolary reader perusing the letter at more than a century's distance must be struck by the wit exhibited in extremity, as well
as by the recognition that she to whom the world supposedly never
wrote should represent herself finally as the assenting object of an
otherworldly call. How consistent with Dickinson's lifelong practice
that she should seize a last opportunity to pen an utterance that might
feel like immortality to her recipients—that might uphold the "mind
alone" to those who should mark the departure of her elusive corporeal friendship.

Such communication is truly exceptional and must reinforce the
impression that Dickinson's practice as a letter writer is a highly individual one. Yet its distinction lies in her articulation of the spaces that
divide all correspondents from one another and the process by which
letter writers shape and negotiate such space. Dickinson's letters are
singularly lacking in the discussion of ideas and trade only lightly in the
gossip that constitutes the stock of many correspondents. Rather than
ideas or gossip, her letters specialize in themes, themes that are profoundly self-reflexive and that compel Dickinson to probe the very

project of human language in the dramatic interaction that is the epistolary exchange. Aware as she is of the absence that letter writing creates in spite of its intention to extend presence, her practice persists, and thereby affirms the compensatory value of language as well as, more specifically, the motive generosity of epistolary discourse, which she identifies as love and regards as the agent of immortal life. Still very much the practice of a mid-nineteenth-century New England woman for all of its inimitable brilliance, Dickinson's letter writing has the wonderful merit of taking none of its procedures for granted. Our examinations of other letter writing are illuminated by the themes that such skepticism voices and exemplifies.

5

I Write Now d'Outre Tombe
Henry Adams

. . . .

Henry Adams's letter writing presents a study in contrast to Emily Dickinson's spare and resonant epistolary prose. Whereas Dickinson proceeds by compressed phrase and vivid trope, Adams favors an expansive monologic utterance. Dickinson constructs a voice of pregnant reticence, refraining as she can from "noisy words"; Adams, preferring other forms of subtlety and suggestion, commonly abounds in exclamations and aims at producing a dense flow of inspired and improvisational talk. Dickinson's letters avoid discussion of ideas and trade lightly if at all in gossip; Adams's letters traffic heavily in both. The contrasts between the two not only reflect a difference in gender but also the fact that each manifests an intensified version of their period's gendered behaviors. Dickinson exaggerates the upper-middle-class woman's confinement to the home, whereas Adams exemplifies the privileged male's geographic mobility and habit of treating the world as subject to material and intellectual appropriation. For Dickinson, the space that she and her writings occupy is private if not unsociable; recurrently she must appeal to men for information concerning the worlds beyond her home bounds. For Adams, the personal and literary occupation of public space is taken for granted, and it is with a set of prerogatives very different from Dickinson's that he cultivates the privacies that he does.

Such contrasts stem from the feature that most obviously distinguishes Adams's correspondence from Dickinson's: his view of the probable public destiny of his letters. The scion of a family nationally prominent for four generations, he wrote with the sense that his writings were always potentially in the public domain. His family's sense of itself was intensely bound up in its papers; not only did it maintain an archive but publication of its familiar correspondence commenced as early as 1840, when Henry's father, Charles Francis Adams, compiled an edition of his grandmother Abigail Adams's letters.[1] As he came of age the young Henry Adams had ample opportunity to participate in exchanges that contributed to public policy, and early letters record his presumption that his correspondence will one day claim a broad readership. Whereas Dickinson's practice chiefly arises from models common to middle-class women of her time, Adams writes with an emulative eye to private correspondences published on account of their literary merit. Never doubting that the content of his letters would assure their enduring interest, he was the more determined that his art as a letter writer should distinguish his epistolary production. Hence his great model is neither Abigail nor John Adams but Horace Walpole, who groomed his letters for eventual publication and whose social and political observations ever implicitly remind the reader that they are the constructions of a literary stylist superior to his objects of scrutiny.[2]

No other American has so aspired to produce a correspondence to rival the scale and artistry of the great eighteenth-century British letter writers, and Adams's success in this venture has been widely acknowledged.[3] But although the sense of public destiny that Adams brought to his correspondence encouraged a voluminous and literary epistolary production, it also provided for that production's greatest irony: the suspicion, increasingly articulated by his letters, that the world is devoid of a meaningful public realm, and that literary expression is probably meaningless except when generated for a known, private, like-minded readership. Inasmuch as the claiming of confidential, intimate, utopian space figures among the letter's genre-specific themes, there is nothing anomalous in Adams's privatization of literary discourse. Nor is privatization characteristic of his later practice alone: narrowly confidential as his correspondence becomes, Adams's insistence upon the superiority and self-sufficiency of the private utterance exists in latent form among his earliest surviving letters. What distinguishes Adams is that his authorship begins with the inverse assumption: that letter writing is a valuable activity inasmuch as it allows one to explore social concerns and equip oneself to act on the public behalf, and that a letter acquires more than private value to the degree that it incorporates polemics, analysis, and narrative. No writer of Adams's generation was more prepared to put literary language at the service of public life, and the familiar letter was the genre of initial trial in his framing of such language.[4]

At the very beginning and very end of his career, Adams authored minor works that visibly emerge from his epistolary practice; in the dissimilarities between them may be seen much of that career's peculiar development. The first is a series of travel letters from Austria and Italy addressed to his brother Charles Francis Adams Jr., with the understanding that Charles, exercising editorial discretion, would arrange for their publication in the Boston press. Dispatched from Vienna, Naples, Rome, and Palermo over a two-month period in 1860, Adams writes as an observer of manners, personalities, and political conditions, secure in his moral superiority as an American as he marks the progress of republican insurgency among the Italian states. As novice author, Adams assumes the existence of a readership whose views may be edified by what he has to say. Although the letters hardly unite around a consciously determined thesis, they reflect the conviction that private discourse is readily and valuably publicized and that an observant American's experience of Europe certainly pertains to a common national identity. Fifty years later he would again engage a rhetoric of epistolary familiarity in a text intended for a nonfamiliar if not entirely public readership. *A Letter to American Teachers of History*, a pamphlet that Adams sent to historians and university administrators, translates the second law of thermodynamics into a prophecy of society's decline and death. Forthright in acknowledging that the thesis may interest few besides Adams, the *Letter* implicitly tests the hypothesis that discourse itself is an entropic system in which epistolary delivery alone preserves an intellectual urgency that can foster debate. Openly discouraging its recipients to reply, however, Adams is ambivalent to dialogue, and the experiment represents a rejection of all writing that is not private and emotive.[5]

In the fifty years that separate the *Courier* letters from *A Letter to American Teachers of History*, much occurred that serves to explain

Adams's abandonment of public discourse. As members of the third generation descending from John and Abigail Adams, Henry and his brothers found themselves unable to fulfill hereditary expectations that one or more of them should hold high public office; as young men they watched their family's prominence diminish as each presidential quadrennium brought their father no closer to succeeding his father, John Quincy Adams, in the White House. Before Henry Adams was thirty, he had disavowed political ambitions per se. By the time he was forty, he had led a brief career as a political journalist and spent seven years at Harvard teaching medieval history and editing the *North American Review*. In 1878, he established for himself a new career as biographer, historian, and occasional novelist committed to ascertaining the nation's future in view of its ideological idealism, corruptible institutions, and rapid development of wealth and mechanical power. Adams's withdrawal from his family's wonted political activities by no means entailed an abandonment of public concerns. His magnum opus, *The History of the United States during the Administrations of Jefferson and Madison* (1890), accounts for the formation and assesses the prospects of an American national character, and Adams began this work thinking it would be his supreme contribution to what he was willing to imagine as a renascent postwar United States.

The abandonment of public discourse is partly explained by Adams's inability to sustain his vision of an America emerging from the turpitude of the Grant era to figure in the world as a new order of human civilization as well as an international political power. Even before his wife's death in 1885, he had become increasingly convinced that American culture was impervious to the influence of such intellectual and artistic ideals as he could articulate. Avowedly democratic as those ideals may have been, they were founded in the notion of an egalitarian society that exists to support a hierarchy of merit; in the decades after the Civil War, Adams was equally unprepared for the rise of a corporate oligarchy and the emergence of a mass society in which non-Anglo-Saxons increasingly figured. As Joanne Jacobson has shown, letter writing for Adams is an ongoing exercise in the recontainment of class identity and hereditary privilege.[6] Such recontainment involved a steady withdrawal from the visibility and responsibility of a public authorship, a rejection of the possibility of an intelligent readership that is forecast in the image of the mechanistic passivity of the American mind with which the *History*—his last work to see conventional publication in his lifetime—concludes. If Adams had begun his nine-volume magnum opus with the idea of writing for "a continent of a hundred million people fifty years hence" (LHA 2:535) who could respond thoughtfully to his critical but nevertheless affirmative representation of the Jeffersonian era, by the time he completed it he was certain that it should find only a small, obscure, specialized audience.

Adams was midway through the writing of the *History* when Marian (Clover) Hooper Adams committed suicide. Her death so profoundly imbues his vocational crisis that in explaining the course of his subsequent career one cannot separate his grief as a husband from his disappointment as an author. This personal catastrophe existed for him as the adumbration of what was wrong not only with America but with Western industrial culture generally. Although Adams avoids mention of his wife in the letters of his widowerhood, bereavement is the overwhelmingly dominant theme, alternately associated with the loss of opportunities to refashion a national culture and the unavailability of specific addressees for intellectual, spiritual, and erotic companionship. Clover Adams—an embodiment of promises and deprivations, ideals and flaws—exists as an implicit signified of these more nameable absences. A prominent feature of Adams's later letters is his willingness to establish Clover as the more or less explicit signified of the life carried on so long in her absence, a life that itself has been a living death inasmuch as he claims to have died with her. Insofar as the paradox of "absent presence" is intrinsic to the letter's discursive condition, Adams's epistolary practice provides endless opportunities to perfect his conceit of a posthumous life. Life and death, presence and absence, become interchangeable terms for one who supposedly writes "d'outre tombe." In the final phase of his career as a letter writer, Adams constructs a private utopia of grief in which all of his lost companions reunite.

The bereavement that Adams's letters espouse as their great and consuming motif places his correspondence on thematic ground common to Dickinson and Emerson as well as to legions of anonymous writers whose letters represent a varied inscription of mortal occasion. For Adams, who had begun by assuming that his private correspondence should ultimately emerge as public text, but who ended by "publishing" his nonepistolary works (*Mont Saint Michel and Chartres*, *The Education of Henry Adams*, *A Letter to American Teachers of History*) through guarded circulation within his networks of private correspondence, bereavement entails a lost public estate that it does not involve for the other writers considered in this book. Still, loss of friends and

loved ones to distance, time, and death is thematized in Adams's correspondence in ways that conform to genre patterns even as his practice
enlarges our sense of the ways in which the letter inscribes such experience. Reluctant to embrace metaphysically compensatory terms—be
they Emerson's "eternal mind," Dickinson's "immortality," or the various invocations of an afterlife commonly found in popular letter writing—Adams nevertheless develops the idea of a community of sufferers, a secret society of "Hearts that Ache" that unites humanity
across the social and political barriers of a nearly unsalvageable public
life. Steeped as this notion obviously is in material privilege, it does not
preclude Adams's recognition of the suffering endured by people not
of his class and race. In what for Adams is the universal commonality
of private suffering—the unity in life that he discovers and theorizes
primarily through the medium of the condolence letter—animosities
dissolve and exclusivities momentarily recede.

Yet it would be wrong to presume that Clover's death instantly
transformed Adams's epistolary practice and the course of his authorship generally: made it inward where it had been extrovert, despairing
where it had been hopeful. Public mindedness survives residually to
the end of Adams's life; an inward-tending despond is present in his
earliest extant epistolary expression. As with Emerson and Dickinson,
our task in reading Adams's letters is to discern the ways in which the
letter exchange determined his understanding of what it meant to be
present and absent to others, and how that understanding shaped his
production as a letter writer while it conditioned the thematic possibilities of his authorship in other genres. In Adams's correspondence, not
only are presence and absence to others more intensely politicized
than in the correspondences of Emerson and Dickinson, but the distinction between the terms acquires new degrees of complication. Like
Emerson and Dickinson, Adams defies the notion that his being is
subject to spatiotemporal confinement and regards the letter as his
medium of extended presence, but he is much less prone to invoking a
Pauline presence-in-the-spirit transcendent of time and space. His defiance rather is shaped on the one hand by his mobility as an inveterate
traveler and, on the other, largely in consequence of his not being fixed
to a particular locality, by his cultivated autonomy as a letter writer: the
ritual subordination of space, time, and the presence of others to the
epistolary affirmation of his literary self-presence. Adams is the most
modern and prophetic letter writer of the three. In what he represents
as the ease with which he moves from place to place and in the absence

generally of reflections on the barriers that time and space present, we see the emergence of a culture that is more mobile, less confined, less certain of differences between here and there, presence and absence. Assertive self-presence and geographic mobility are features that he shares with writers of such different class and regional origins as Jack London and Ernest Hemingway.[7] Finding himself regularly in the position of having to correspond over long distances, Adams's engagement of the epistolary genre encouraged him to develop an identity that defined itself in relation to its absence from specific places, persons, occasions, and opportunities. Present to himself in absence to particular people and circumstances, he acquired in young manhood a sense of doubleness that his subsequent experience confirmed, and expressions commonly associated with his widowerhood surface in his youthful letters with peculiar clairvoyance. Adams's letters provide all along a structure in which bereavement may flourish; his earliest dispatches appear at times intent on constructing a prophecy of disappointment. First and last, disappointment and bereavement serve nonetheless as the conditions of an ongoing epistolary self-invention.

AS IF I WERE COUNTED OUT OF SOCIETY

Adams's earliest surviving letters date from his twenty-first year. Growing up in a large, epistolarily active family he no doubt engaged in all manner of letter writing from early childhood through late adolescence. But where the chance preservation of documents allows us to see Emerson and Dickinson take up the pen as children under their parents' roofs, by the time Adams first comes to view as a correspondent he has left home and put an ocean between himself and his geographic origins. Following his graduation from Harvard in 1858, Adams went to Germany to study Roman law at the University of Berlin, a plan thwarted from the start by his nonmastery of German. In the series of dispatches to his brother Charles Francis Adams Jr., there exist spirited accounts of misadventures as well as experimentations in admissible utterance comparable with what we see in the letters Emerson and Dickinson wrote in youth. "What one writes is considerably influenced by the accidental state of his mind at the instant of writing," Adams theorizes to his brother Charles, "and it is not strange if, among so many letters, when I am hurrying to put down the first thing that comes into my head . . . I say many silly things" (LHA 1:18). Like the young Emerson and the young Dickinson, Adams exploits the genre's liberatingly paratactic structure, although in his case the early performances are those of a man out of his teens who has already acquired considerable command of the epistolary occasion. The letters from Berlin and Dresden represent him meeting occasions as challenging as any he would have met with formerly. In our first view of Adams as a correspondent, moreover, we see him registering a situation he would inscribe recurrently ever after: identifying himself as one who is absent—from home, family, friends, the structure of a presumed normality.

As a young man dispatching letters from a strange European city, Adams constructs a life for himself among distressingly alien conditions: a language that he does not easily learn, a people whom he finds uncongenial. Exhibiting an observant eye and an aptitude for narration as well as an ability to revise plans, his letters demonstrate confidence in their protagonist-author's capacity to order an unfolding experience, a confidence reinforced by the weekly ritual of synopsis in which, writing at length to family members, he produces chapters in continuing narratives that structure events both expected and unforeseen. What anchors those narratives is the residence of family in America with whom he, as fellow Adams, can identify and imaginatively join in the reading of his European missives. But such anchorage requires a regular exchange, and in his earliest surviving letter, written from Berlin in November 1858, we see that a lapse has rendered him susceptible to the distant traveler's common fear that his or her existence abroad is not supported by acts of remembrance at home: "I humbly apologize to you for the remarks in my last letter," he writes to Charles, "which were written under the supposition that you had forgotten me. Your letter was satisfaction itself" (LHA 1:2). Whatever the incoming mail has to say, a basic satisfaction lies in its confirmation that his own letters represent him afar with a sufficiency that compels a response.

In his first letters from Berlin, as he responds to Charles's news of courtships and engagements among their Boston acquaintance, Adams exhibits a detached absorption in the little world of rumored pairings from which he has absented himself in undertaking his two-year sojourn. Ever in the process of adjusting to life in Berlin, he writes as one between worlds. Yet despite his obvious interest in home events and anxiety over the uncertain prospects he faces in Berlin as a non-speaker of German, he expresses a contentment in being abroad that is only enhanced by what he hears from home: "though I have been having a delightful time here and have enjoyed life to the hubs, still I have never felt quite so glad at being out of Boston as I felt after reading that epistle" (LHA 1:6). So he proclaims at the beginning of a letter to Charles, with implied reference to his own unhappiness in the now vacated field of courtship. As Charles's epistle brings Boston to him, it upholds a contact that affords Henry the pleasure of representing Berlin, constructing his delight in novel scenes in self-assured and self-congratulatory letters home, certainly a chief source of his purported enjoyments. Toward the end of the letter he reverts to the matter of news from Boston. Admitting that "it is rather amusing to hear what is going on" with respect to his contemporaries' alliances, "still," he observes, "I can't say that I should care much if I didn't hear a word except from the family, while I am away. I am however always very glad to hear from home" (LHA 1:9). He is happy to have Boston at a distance as long as such detailed intelligence as he receives from Charles continues.

Writing from Germany in these earliest of his surviving letters, Adams assumes what is to become a lifelong task: maintaining an identity apart from its accustomed frame of reference while opening that identity to growth and change in view of new experience. If the fresh scenes of overseas travel unfailingly captivate his attention, geographic separation from home associations does little to diminish the urgency of what he has left behind. His accommodation of the resulting divided consciousness gives rise to a sensation of multiple placement: being in more than one place at one time, vividly absent in one setting while spectrally present in another. Adams's sense of multiple, dispersed, and more or less real being is in large part the consequence of travel and varied residence, but it is always the peculiar construction of the epistolary genre to which Adams the traveler makes constant resort, and it persists in varying circumstances throughout his life. Even letters written from a fixed residence will convey something of the traveler's headlong momentum; when "at home," the mature Adams typically describes himself as between travels or longing for travel, conscious in any case of the sensation of moving in time.

Adams's sense of being in more than one place at one time is complicated by the persistent fear of having missed the opportunity of being wholly in one place at the right time. For this reason, early and late, his letters constitute a registry of disaffection. As pleased as he initially represents himself to be with his Berlin excursion, absence from those scenes in which his Boston contemporaries are passing through the stages of prenuptial crisis generates a rhetorical position in his letters that anticipates disaffections to come: estrangement from his male contemporaries who fought in the Civil War while he served in London as his father's private secretary; alienation from friends and acquaintances after Clover's death; even the sense, first voiced in middle age, that the work of his generation was completed and the field now belonged to a younger and more vigorous crowd. From Dresden in April 1859 he writes to Charles: "I'm getting to distrust myself about young women, from my six months want of practice, and to feel as if I were counted out of society and never should reappear in it. There's a younger set even than I, now coming on; great God where will you be if I'm antiquated two winters hence!" (LHA 1:35). In such a superficially facetious remark Adams reveals a capacity to imagine himself as a detached observer of a life in which he may have preferred to have taken a more active part. A pose of exile and superannuation already begins to assume characteristic profile.

In this same letter that registers distress over being counted absent among the trivial if engrossing realities of Boston, Adams creates the image of a full, alternative life elsewhere; if he is absent in Boston he is nonetheless on occasion richly present to himself in Germany. The construction of alternative experiences that offer intense if short-lived satisfaction as well as the sense of other identities emerges as a pattern in Adams's later travel letters. Having come to an end of a winter in Berlin that had not gone according to plan (rather than attend lectures in German on Roman law at the University of Berlin, he has had to enroll himself in a Berlin secondary academy to acquire the language), Adams has indulged in a hike through the Thuringian Forest with two other Boston friends. The weather was snowy and the young men resorted frequently to wine, beer, and cigars to keep up their stamina. "You may think this wasn't much fun," Adams writes, "and indeed I believe I was the only one who really enjoyed it, but the glow, the feeling of adventure and the novelty; above all, the freedom and semi-wildness after six months in Berlin, made it really delightful to me. I haven't felt so well and fresh for ever-so-long" (LHA 1:37). Much of the pleasure derived from the fact that the journey "had been made wholly without plan. None of us knew six hours ahead what we were going to do," and the company "were all pleasant and indifferent to everything except what was pleasant" (LHA 1:38). The adventure needed no justification as a contribution to a larger, more meaningful narrative.

Yet when the vacation is over, Adams and his friends are content that it should end, as all have studies to resume and none "cared to lose more time" (LHA 1:38). Adams's youthful preparations for a yet-to-be-defined role in American public life are too compelling at this point to admit any but momentary detour. Longer, more complicated digressions might, however, be undertaken under cover of a pragmatic purpose, as is the case with Adams's Italian journey of spring 1860, an episode of first importance in his development as an author, traveler, and Adams *fils* who would make a name for himself at a distinct distance from the rest of his clan. Following the example of his brother Charles, who had been serving as Washington correspondent of the *Boston Advertiser*, Henry undertook the experiment of writing a series of letters for publication in the Boston press as he traveled from Vienna to Rome across regions contested by Austria, Piedmont, Naples, and the Vatican. The sojourn to exotic and politically volatile realms would at the same time be a first trial of his ambition to appear in public as an author. The step between private and public correspondent was one before which Henry hesitated, preferring to take it in the dark; observing to Charles that "this trip may perhaps furnish material for a pleasant series of letters" (LHA 1:106), and designating his brother as their principal addressee, he charged Charles with the tasks of editorship, censorship, and publication. Annoyed to discover that the first installments had been printed above his initials, he would remind Charles in a note accompanying the fifth dispatch that "the letters are private letters which might be published, but anonymously" (LHA 1:148).

At the beginning of the series, which commences with the rail journey from Dresden to Vienna, Adams takes the tone of the seasoned traveler inured to a sojourner's fortune. He provides a condescending portrait of the Austrian lieutenant with whom he shares a compartment and a sampling of the national types found along the valley of the Danube. His brief stay in Vienna is highlighted by the chance sighting of the Austrian emperor and empress, before whom he characterizes himself as awestruck, although his prose readily classes the moment among the ephemera of travel impressions. Venice itself exists in his letters as a spectacle of architectural and atmospheric effects conforming to tourbook expectations. Padua, Ferrara, Bologna, and Florence flash by in detailed, reductive commentary. Only with his arrival in Rome does Adams come to a place that breaks his commentary's momentum. "From ruins, from palaces, from history and art," he writes after a three-and-a-half-week break, "I am just waking up again to the course of life. In the Belvedere, or among the fragments of the Forum, one forgets who he is and what he is living for" (LHA 1:144).

Although the capacity of Rome to enchant Boston youth was well-known, the suggestion that it harbors the power to obliterate the self and its voluble ironic verbal resource is significant, even as the author, in making that suggestion, reasserts the egocentricity of the traveler's discourse. Phrases flow and the surface of experience continues to offer itself as a page easily read, but Adams has intimated that the objects of study offer resistance.

Rome, at once the seat of an ancient civilization and site of a contemporary political unrest, receives from Adams only a slightly more reflective consideration than that found in the accounts of the earlier and briefer stays on his itinerary. The mysteries of the city, which he conjures in set fashion by wandering among the ruins of the Forum, visiting the Colosseum at night, and touring the Campagna on horseback, speak deeply to Adams because he is at the time immersed in reading Gibbon's *Autobiography*. It is noteworthy that, in the course of this epistolarily active journey in which letter writing serves the purpose of feeling out possible careers as an author, Adams first articulates for himself a literary vocation that would fix his attention on such ultimate realities as Rome suggests while disengaging him from the family preoccupation with politics. In a letter not meant for publication, he reports to Charles that he has been reading Gibbon: "Do you know, after long argument and reflexion I feel much as if perhaps some day I too might come to anchor like that. Our house needs a historian in this generation and I feel strongly tempted by the quiet and sunny prospect, while my ambition for political life dwindles as I get older" (LHA 1:149). Although it would be a long time before he could come into that "quiet and sunny prospect," he has already gravitated toward interests more compelling than those his family and region have to offer. Unready to distance himself from the prejudices of the *Courier* readership, Adams as letter writer has begun to cultivate estrangement from conventional values and expectations.

If his evolution as an author is to be charted by the orders of distance that he establishes between himself and his regional and class origins, the most significant event recorded in these letters is his journey to Palermo in the immediate aftermath of Garibaldi's successful siege. "I would see a great drama in the world's history; I would take at last a part in the excitement of the day" (LHA 1:161): with such aspirations he concludes a letter posted from Naples as he embarks for the Sicilian capital, as though his placid life among the Boston bourgeoisie and his steps in their well-worn European paths had insulated him from such great dramas as he had read by the light of Gibbon's page in the monuments to a vanished civilization in Rome. Five days later, in a letter datelined Palermo, he confesses that he had left Naples "in a state of grand excitement, feeling a good deal as if I were going to an unknown world and might never come back" (LHA 1:162). The motif of crossing from a known to an unknown world and paying for such passage with one's life is a recurrent theme of his epistolary practice, one that articulates a desire for experience that affords escape from deadeningly predictable careers. In arriving at a city that bore fresh signs of convulsive change, in being taken to converse with Garibaldi, he represents himself as achieving a success well off the path and purchased at considerable personal risk, a success that his previous letters in this sequence, with their descriptive passages and brief anecdotes, had never anticipated as a probable climax.

"Here I was at last, then," Adams writes of his dinner meeting with Garibaldi, "at the height of my ambition as a traveller, face to face with one of the great events of our day. It was all perfect." In defining what made for this moment's perfection Adams enumerates its scenic attributes as though the ambition of the traveler is to write history:

> There was Palermo, the insurgent Sicilian city, with it's barricades and its ruined streets with all the marks of war. There was that armed and howling mob in the square below, and the music of the national hymn, and the five revolutionary cannon. There were the guerilla captains who had risked their lives and fortunes for something that the worst envy could not call selfish. And there was the Great Dictator, who, when your and my little hopes and ambitions shall have lain in our graves a few centuries with us, will still be honored as a hero, and perhaps half worshipped, who knows! for a God. (LHA 1:168)

As a paragraph arising in an epistolary text, this passage is interesting for several reasons. In journeying to Sicily Adams represents himself as attaining his closest proximity to "great events" at the same time that he achieves the furthest distance from what he regards as the experience of his Boston readership. Yet, having achieved such nearness to a real action and such absence from the world of his audience, Adams proceeds to create a position abstracted from the Sicilian scene, a position in which he and his readership may jointly engage in the contemplation of this drama as a moment of historical record. In doing so Adams writes with the recognition that epistolary texts submit themselves to delayed reading and that by the time his account can reach his readership the day's event is past. Adams, however, historicizes further. Convinced of the significance of what he has witnessed in far-off Sicily, he is moved to reflect upon the probable absence of himself and his kind from the historical record that will celebrate Garibaldi; geographically distant from his audience, he imagines himself at one with it as an eminently forgettable historical entity. Whatever its merit, Adams suggests, only the gaudily spectacular moment is likely to withstand the oblivion that "a few centuries" will bring. Despite his recognition of Garibaldi's personal dignity and obvious gifts of command, Adams appeals to his readership's provincial perception of European revolutionary leaders, a perception compounded of fascination, class fear, condescension, envy.

The distance he contrives when "face to face with one of the great events of our day" is preserved to the end of the series. "It is something to have seen the raw elements at work, though one is no element oneself," Adams avers in the final letter written a week later in Sorrento (LHA 1:176), and for the moment he is content to refrain from attempts to define that "something" further. In concluding the Italian letters he reinforces a spectatorial position exempt from the immediacies of revolutionary Italy; he takes refuge in a consciousness that, in the presence of much that would estrange him from what he knows and make him feel the force of epistolary distance, reduces the exotica of the foreign setting to a commonplace frame of reference. In his final paragraph he abandons interpretive commentary for factitious sentiment: "If you ever come here and smoke your last cigar and watch your last sunset with the waves of the bay breaking under your window, and take your final leave of a book of life that has been all rose-color, you will probably feel as solemn as I do, and will finish with Italy by reflecting that our good God is really good, but that we have ourselves something good and immortal in us, which Italy calls out and strengthens" (LHA 1:177–78). This is a peculiar moral to derive from the social observation, political analysis, and historical musing of the series. Yet the sense of closure with which Adams writes is emphatic, as though he wishes that the lesson were encyclopedic and emblematic of what one carries off from a full and completed life.

The letters from Italy are important inasmuch as they exhibit in Adams a distinct tendency to understand the world historically; in Rome, Adams articulates not only his calling as a historian but an ambition to rival the narrative accomplishments of Gibbon. At the moment that Adams envisions this development in what he already looks upon as his literary rather than political vocation, he has begun to adopt a position as a writer that is characteristically detached and epistolary, that perceives the authorial act as the creation of a record that will be read at distances of space and time from the place and moment of inscription. The presence of life in the moment of the epistolary act leads inevitably to a sense of that moment's passing and the author's absence not only from contemporary and future readers of the text but from the moment of inscription that will have passed by the time the text is read. If as a tourist in a country in which historical transition is visible Adams becomes receptive to the spectacle of history, as a letter writer he becomes aware of the historical process by which language substitutes memory of the present for the present itself in view of an absence that comprehends both writer and reader. He already intuits that discourse generates historical and biographical process.

The historical mindedness that emerges in Adams's letters from Europe and the conscious epistolarity of his historical testimony become salient in letters he would write over the course of the next five years as he found himself living in varying proximity to "the great events" of secession and Civil War. Not long after his departure from Sorrento, Adams was back in the United States and situated, as the secretary of his father the congressman, to witness the course of what promised to be the country's dissolution along sectional lines. In December 1860, he wrote to Charles a letter in which he formulates an ambition that would inform his prolific correspondence with his brother for years to come:

> I propose to write you this winter a series of private letters to show how things look. I fairly confess that I want to have a record of this winter on file, and though I have no ambition nor hope to become a Horace Walpole, I still would like to think that a century or two hence when everything else about us is forgotten, my letters might still be read and quoted as a memorial of manners and habits at the time of the great secession of 1860. At the same time you will be glad to hear all the gossip and to me it will supply the place of a Journal. (LHA 1:204)

As in the scene that Adams offers as the climax of his adventures in Sicily, he simultaneously identifies himself as an observer in close proximity to a momentous historical transition and as the deceased chronicler of a record bequeathed to distant posterity. What for his contemporary addressee is meant as a series of private letters containing the latest news and gossip is projected as a future public text by which he may achieve a degree of literary immortality. Whereas he knows he can make his letters interesting to his living correspondent, he can only strive to create a memorial that will be consulted by future readers, hence his disavowal of ambitions that are indeed formed in view of the enduring value of Walpole's epistles.[8] As with the letters from Italy, Adams designates Charles as the addressee of documents that he ultimately intends for a large public audience, although in this case the readership is "a century or two" in the future. As for the contemporary public, Adams is reaching the Boston and New York readership of the day by means of political correspondence published anonymously in the *Boston Advertiser* and reprinted in the *New York Times*; unlike the letters from Italy and from Washington ostensibly addressed to Charles, the political correspondence does not arise out of what is supposed to be a private exchange.

The letters that Henry Adams writes to Charles between December 1860 and May 1861 chronicle the activities of moderate Republicans aimed at preserving the federal union against the pressures of Northern abolitionists and Southern secessionists to force an open and almost certainly military confrontation. Considerations of long historical perspective are less prominent now than the partisan journalist's running account of unfolding events. "I feel in a continual intoxication in this life," Adams confesses to Charles in January 1861 amid discussions of a possible face-off in Charleston Harbor. "It is magnificent to feel strong and quiet in all this row, and see one's own path clear through all the chaos" (LHA 1:221). As one whose political correspondence sought to shore up support for his father's position, Adams had cause to consider himself a participant in as well as an observer of events. But the sensations of living in immediacy to a great historical event and of taking part in the fray were to be short lived. In May 1861, Charles Francis Adams left Washington to assume his commission as Lincoln's minister to England, and Henry, in the capacity of his father's private secretary, began a seven-year residence in England that would give fresh incentive for maintaining a prolific correspondence.[9] His letter writing of the London years would confirm his commitment to epistolary rituals by which he revised his identity and reestablished his bearings in a world of increasing geopolitical complication—a world of competing national hegemonies with which he would ever afterward maintain the semblance of a personal relationship.

In the first years of the London mission, the diplomacy of Charles Francis Adams was principally directed at preventing Great Britain, which had proclaimed its neutrality in the conflict prior to the new minister's arrival, from taking the further step of recognizing the Confederate States of America. Although outwardly occupying the unofficial and juvenilizing position of his father's private secretary, Henry Adams was able to preserve some sense of taking part in events by serving as a special unsigned correspondent for the *New York Times*, an activity that he necessarily concealed from his father. As he sought through such writing to foster public confidence in Lincoln's foreign policies, he was also drawn to publish, again under the cloak of anonymity, impressionistic accounts of English life. When the Boston *Courier* inadvertently identified him as the author of "A Visit to Manchester: Extracts from a Private Diary"—a piece in which he had complained of the graceless economy of the London social reception—he found himself the subject of burlesque in the London *Times*. Exposed as the author of the *Courier* article, Adams could not risk the much more damaging exposure as the special *New York Times* correspondent and so terminated activities as a secret propagandist. Reduced to the roles of amanuensis and factotum, he found himself isolated from the political drama that was being settled on the American battlefield as well as from the amusements that British society had to offer, and his letter writing facilitated the recurrent meditation of chronic disconnection.

His isolation was by turns relieved and intensified by the connections he preserved through a heavy volume of correspondence. During the war Adams made efforts to maintain ties with his male contemporaries in military service: Harvard classmates such as Benjamin Crowninshield, Nicholas Anderson, and Henry Higginson as well as his brother Charles, who accepted a commission as a cavalry officer in December 1861. Through this correspondence Adams strove to represent himself among the members of his generation as they set themselves to a great public task, yet such contact tended more to enforce his sense of absence from his country's historical decisions in the making, particularly after the London *Times*'s embarrassment of him forced his withdrawal as a political correspondent. "My pen is given up," Adams writes dolefully to Charles in March 1862. "Here I am, more dry-nurse than ever, dabbling a little, a very little in society; reading a little; copying a great deal; writing nothing, and not advancing an inch. I envy you who at least have an enemy before you. My enemy is only myself" (LHA 1:285). From his loathing of the Henry Adams whose public mortification required his retreat to what he considered an emasculatingly domestic sphere, he finds little relief in helping his father with the challenges of their diplomatic task. The life of military action seems much more attractive: "Hard as your life is and threatens to become," he writes Charles in July 1862, "I would like well to share it with you in order to escape in the consciousness of action a little of the struggle against fancied evils that we feel here" (LHA 1:305).

Although Adams contemplated returning to the United States and obtaining a commission, he weathered his season of inanition as family attaché and became reconciled to a long-term English residence. His letters balance sensations of estrangement from the scenes of military conflict with his conviction that, at whatever distance, he shares in the common fate of his nation and generation: that "the country has been so turned upside down now, that all the world will be as little able to go back into a path as I am" (LHA 1:304). "The future is a blank to me as I suppose it is also to you," he writes to Charles in November 1862; and after reporting that he observes in himself an eroding faith in his sense of personal purpose, he goes on to propose the terms of a collective purpose that may serve to rescue all whose paths have been confused by the war. Writing with reference to a postwar America, Adams calls for "a national set of young men like ourselves or better, to start new influences not only in politics, but in literature, in law, in society, and throughout the whole social organism of the country" (LHA 1:315). Such in fact Adams would set about trying to create as a reformer, journalist, and editor in postwar America. In the meantime, the diplomatic mission would recover its self-confidence, and Adams, concluding that his hand was "not made for a sabre," felt utilized in his duties as personal secretary. "My place is where I am," he affirms in May 1863, "and I never was so necessary to it as now. All thoughts of escape even for a day, have vanished" (LHA 1:348).

Increasingly assured of the success of the diplomatic mission and the Unionist effort generally, Adams set about preparing himself for the labors of postwar America, which for him lay in the clarification of the possibilities of democratic polity. With the idea of contributing to "a national school" of his own generation (LHA 1:315), he read widely in European social philosophy and considered the course his family's postwar career should take. At the same time that he was plotting his assumption of a publicly engaged career, however, he was naturalizing himself to the position of spectator, outsider, and distant traveler that his voluminously sustained epistolary practice allowed him to cultivate even as it served to maintain American connections. Adams's development as an author during the London years had always to contend with his debilitating conviction that he is absent from his country's great unfolding drama, that the circumstances in which he finds himself as private secretary to his father in London are juvenilizing and emasculating, and that the world of British intellectual society, the one field of independent existence open to him, must be navigated with cautious attention to the codes that regulate social behavior and that put even the most prepossessing American at disadvantage. The conditions of his life in London elicit from him recurrent expressions of despair, but his long-term literary response to these circumstances is a resistance that asserts an independent, self-sufficient being, a personality that is not so much exiled as voluntarily present somewhere else.

The letter, a genre of detached, distanced utterance that affirms the writer's absence in one place while asserting his presence in another, is instrumental to Adams's literary development throughout this period. The genre allows him to mark out for himself a place apart in which geographic separation confirms intellectual aloofness. Inasmuch as Adams locates others in relation to positions he is increasingly adept at constructing for himself in the moment of inscription, he develops a consciousness of the discursive nature of geographic location and an awareness of the letter writer's power to map the world with himself at its center. The writer that Adams is becoming affects indifference to the claims of geography; such is consistent with his affected indifference to the claims of history that we see in his dispatches from Palermo and that anticipates the position of scientific historian that he would attempt to define over the next fifty years. Where he is in space and time remains secondary to whatever primary locus he establishes as epistolary observer.

As epistolarian, Adams becomes adept and indeed imperious in constructing a self-presence capable of answering the implicit argument that he can only maintain a phantasmal existence apart from Boston, or Washington, or the battlefield, or from his family's ambitions. Such self-presence is consciously affirmed in what for Adams is a cultivated literary artistry, one that may be seen in the long narratives that he embeds in letters to his brother Charles as well as in deliberate refinements of style. In a passage from a long account of his vacation in the Hebrides in 1863 he inscribes a self-justifiable, independent existence in language that aims at Wordsworthian poetic effects: "I enjoyed immensely this evening sail on the Hebridean seas. Civil wars, disgust and egoism, social fuss and worry, responsibility and anxiety, were as far at last as the moon. They left me free on the Sound of Sleat. I felt as peaceful and as quiet as a giant, and saw the evening shades darken into night, and phosphoric waves of light swell in the air and under the boat, with a joyful sense of caring not a ha'penny when I had my breakfast" (LHA 1:381). Much of the force of this passage derives from the fact that he is representing this existence to his brother the cavalry officer, for whom he describes such privileged moments without apology.

Adams's image of Charles, a man of action, reading his letters in camp is instrumental to his assertion of a full alternative life elsewhere, and on no occasion was this assertion more vigorous than when he writes to his brother in the aftermath of Lincoln's death. Receiving word of the assassination in Rome, where Adams was accompanying his mother and siblings on a two-month Italian tour, his first response is one of shock, and a brief letter written to his father in London brings back the old feelings of uselessness and displacement: "I have never felt so much as to-day how out-of-place I am, and how little I have to do here. Roman history, even, doesn't console me" (LHA 1:494). Two weeks later, however, he writes to his brother from a secure frame of self-presence, and although he is struck by the incongruity of the correspondents' respective experience, he claims, by virtue of his sojourn in Rome, a privileged perspective from which to view the recent American catastrophe:

> I can't help a feeling of amusement at looking back on my letters and thinking how curiously inapt they have been to the state of things about you. Victories and assassinations, joys, triumphs, sorrows and gloom; all at fever point, with you; while I prate about art and draw out letters from the sunniest and most placid of subjects. I have already buried Mr. Lincoln under the ruins of the Capitol, along with Caesar, and this I don't mean merely as a phrase. We must have our wars, it appears, and our crimes, as well as other countries. . . . History repeats itself, and if we are to imitate the atrocities of Rome, I find a certain amusement in conducting my private funeral service over the victims, on the ground that is most suitable for such associations, of any in the world. (LHA 1:494)

Such utterances as insist on his entitlement to be amused prepare for the manifestoes of independence from family that Adams would write in letters to Charles just after the war. Although the pressure to conform to family expectations was too strong for Henry to resist—he and Charles would form a partnership as reformers, and at his family's insistence Henry would accept a position teaching history at Harvard in 1872—the self that Adams constructs in his letters claims absolute prerogative not only over the course his career will take but how that career in all its vacillations is to be interpreted. Responding to his brother's charges that he has lost his bearings, Adams adopts a defiant tone: "I have never varied my course at all. From my birth to this moment it has been straight as an arrow. Such as I am, I am complete. . . . I shall get along; and if I am in the end what you in your sublimity call a failure, I shall still have enjoyed what I, in a spirit of more philosophical and milder tendency, consider a rounded and completed existence" (LHA 1:515). So he wrote from London in December 1866. In November 1867 he states more explicitly his intended departure from the paths chosen by his brothers Charles and John: "I claim my right to part company with you both. I never will make a speech, never run for an office, never belong to a party. I am going to plunge under the stream. For years you will hear nothing of any publication of mine—perhaps never, who knows. I do not mean to tie myself to anything, but I do mean to make it impossible for myself to follow the family go-cart" (LHA 1:557).

The task of defining a life apart from his family would take years to accomplish, and there would never be a time when Adams would not have to explain his departure from hereditary expectations. In his first years back in the United States after the war, however, he would not follow through on the wholesale divergence that he had announced in his letters to Charles. Soon after returning to Quincy in September 1868, he established himself at some distance from his family by moving to Washington; there, in an atmosphere peopled by the memory of his ancestors, Adams took his stand on the rock of traditional family doctrine: strict constructionist constitutionalism, hard-money fiscal policy, and ideals of public service that transcended party and regional politics. Relaxing his philosophical detachment, Adams pursued notoriety as a journalist in the cause of civil service reform. Motivated by a desire to rid government of a corruption that threatened the viability of democratic polity, and harnessed by the notion that such work might prepare the way for his family's return to the presidency, Adams was the more intensely engaged in his tasks by virtue of the combative excitement of the moment. Soon after publishing his first "Session," a harshly satiric review of the 1868–69 legislative proceedings, in the *North American Review*, he crows of his success to his British friend Charles Milnes Gaskell: "For once I have smashed things generally and really exercised a distinct influence on public opinion by acting on the limited number of cultivated minds" (LHA 2:31–32). As much as by long-term ambitions for himself or his family, he appears to be held in his tasks by the momentary pleasure of living and working independently in Washington.

NOTHING CAN SURPASS THE QUIET
DISAPPEARANCE OF OUR LIVES

In the continuing correspondence with Charles Francis Adams Jr., Henry Adams addresses prospects of reform as each wrote exposés of the graft that swiftly metastasized throughout the body politic from the first days of the Grant administration. Although prepared to converse with his brother on matters concerning joint ventures of a political or financial nature, he closed off discussion relating to how he should conduct a career and zealously asserted his temperamental aloofness: "You work for power. I work for my own satisfaction. You like roughness and strength; I like taste and dexterity. For God's sake let us go our own ways and not try to be like each other" (LHA 2:33). The satisfactions of taste and dexterity, the gamelike amusements of political journalism in which scores were tallied with cynical relish and an affected indifference to the long-term course of events, were pleasures that he could not share with his brother but could develop at length in letters to his British friend Charles Milnes Gaskell. Relations with Gaskell, an aristocrat four years his junior, were formed during the latter part of the London residence. Over the course of the next twenty-five years Gaskell became Adams's most regular transatlantic correspondent, replacing Charles as his distant confidant.

Although Gaskell would serve briefly as a conservative member of Parliament from his native Yorkshire, this friendship had little basis in political conversation. Rather, it arose out of Adams's need during the London years of extrafamilial and cosmopolitan connections—the disposition to stake out alternative existences. From its beginning the association with Gaskell fostered the arrogance Adams assumed more and more in exchanges with his brother Charles during the later phase of his London residence. In letters to Gaskell mandarin posture constitutes fellowship as Adams seeks to emulate the mannered aloofness of Gaskell's class. It would have been impossible for Adams to write to

Charles as he wrote to Gaskell: "My poor boy, this world is a disappointment altogether. Let us quit it punctually next Sunday" (LHA 1:563). His discourse with Gaskell would quickly shed such obvious (and Walpolian) mannerism, although the remark presages what he would represent in this correspondence for many years to come as the ennui of his life and occupations.[10] The bored and uneventful existence that he claims to lead is considerably belied by the reformist agenda, scholarly projects, and literary aspirations to which he would consistently give himself from 1868 to 1885. By professing boredom with a life of highly ambitious undertakings, Adams manifestly sought relief from its unrelenting routines and disciplines, and found a temporary escape from the severe focus of his intellectual energies.

A letter of January 1870, written during Adams's residence in Washington as a freelance political commentator, exhibits his construction of an alternative existence enabled by the letter genre and suggests his capacity to invent selves dispersed over a geography configured by epistolary relationships. With Gaskell as audience, Adams could write freely, and seemed intent on penning passages that would have been absolutely inconsistent with the personality that he inscribes in family correspondence and that are indeed out of character with the repertoire of selves that appear in the bulk of his sixty-year epistolarium. "You would have been amused to see me the other day acting as groomsman at a great wedding here," Adams writes, invoking Gaskell as observer and sharer of a scene of macabre and decadent satisfactions. At the wedding Adams has been paired with a bridesmaid

> just on the thresh-hold of twenty, and in fact not without fine eyes and no figure. Perhaps in your vulgar mercenary eyes her chief attraction would be £200,000. In mine her only attraction is that I can flirt with the poor girl in safety as I firmly believe that she is in a deep consumption and will die of it. I like peculiar amusements of all sorts, and there is certainly a delicious thrill of horror, much in the manner of Alfred de Musset, in thus pushing one's amusements into the future world. Shudder! oh, my friend, why not! You may disbelieve it if you like, but I assure you it is true that every sentimental speech or touching quotation I make to her, derives its amusement from the belief that her eyes and ears will soon be inappreciative. Is not this delightfully morbid? I have marked it for a point in my novel, which is to appear in 1880. Meanwhile my attentions are not limited to this, or any other, individual. I sometimes wonder how I ever cared for anyone. My heart is now as immove-

able as a stone, and I sometimes doubt whether marriage is possible except as a matter of convenience. (LHA 2:60)

Among the nearly five thousand surviving letters of Adams's authorship, these sentences are unique for the cultivated perversity of the amusement derived from what passes as a conventional flirtation. Yet the passage restates themes that have become well-established in Adams's letters and that receive development over the long term. In writing to Gaskell, who has nothing invested in ideal notions of the Adams family or American destiny, Adams creates a personality wholly abstracted from the manifold commitments to which he holds himself even as a young man supposedly on his own in Washington. In characterizing his political activities he emphasizes the pleasures of destroying adversaries rather than the ultimate goal of recalling a corrupt nation to its idealistic possibilities, and in portraying his circulation as an eligible bachelor (for an Adams son, a necessary stage in fulfilling the expectation of establishing a family) he depicts himself as organically unfit for making alliances. As he represents it to Gaskell, his relation to the life that he leads in Washington is supremely ironic: he is absent from a sincere participation in its forms, and is present only in such cynical amusements as he can confide to Gaskell—such pleasure as he and Gaskell share as observers of his phantom life. In the consumptive girl we may recognize Adams's recurrent imaging of borders between one existence and another, a theme discursively imaged in the epistolary exchange that he maintains with Gaskell as one who occupies a wholly other world.

The letter of January 13, 1870, makes for distressing reading inasmuch as it is impossible to see Adams gleefully speak of "pushing one's amusements into the future world" by virtue of the doomed bridesmaid without thinking of the doomed Marian Hooper Adams— at this point little more than an acquaintance—whom Adams would marry in two and a half years. Before Clover committed suicide in 1885, Adams would engage in a sober exploration of future worlds in the light of the doomed if not quite suicidal heroine of his second novel, *Esther*. One is struck by this letter's anticipation of the novel writing that lies ahead for Adams, a literary activity that departs from the program of professional authorship that he had set for himself in the year he returned from London and that he would pursue under elaborate concealments. The erotic fascination with the death of women (à la Musset or Poe) would not, however, recur in future correspondence; in July 1870, Adams watched his sister Louisa die of lock-jaw, and the shock no doubt purged all possibility of light conversation on the subject. Although he might write Gaskell in the course of his vigil at his sister's oddly festive deathbed in Italy and declare that the ordeal had "its amusing side" (LHA 2:74), when his sister failed to recover, a badly shaken Adams gave an account of her last days and then, judging by his surviving correspondence, had nothing more to say of the experience until he wrote *The Education of Henry Adams* thirty-five years later. By that time his grief over Louisa's death had become assimilated to his anguish over Clover's.[11]

On returning to the United States after a lengthy stay at Wenlock Abbey, Gaskell's home and Adams's resort in the weeks following Louisa's death, he accepted Charles Eliot's offer to appoint him assistant professor of history at Harvard and editor of the *North American Review*. Over the next seven years Adams would marry and travel extensively—as far west as Utah, as far east as Egypt; he would become absorbed in routine duties as teacher and editor and guide the *North American Review* toward a vigorous engagement of contemporary issues.[12] While Adams continued his involvement with the reform movement, he made himself an authority on Anglo-Saxon legal institutions and then turned his attention to the Jeffersonian era of American history; at the same time, he was singlehandedly establishing Harvard's doctoral program in history. Adams's energies in this period were thus largely given to academic activities. On the whole, he found the decade following the Civil War at once stimulating and anticlimactic: although the magnitude and diversity of political corruption centered in Washington disgusted him and impelled him to join with others in the civil service reform movement, such causes could hardly approach the adventure and grandeur of the Civil War years, which acquired during the Grant era the aura of a heroic age in which the diplomatic battles fought in London were almost as glorious as the military engagements on home ground. For Adams the sense of anticlimax was further compounded by the fading probability that his father would make a run at the presidency.

During this period of heavy academic and editorial activity Adams attempted to exert the kinds of intellectual leadership that he had envisioned in London; through his efforts as editor of the *North American Review* he published rising (if generally conservative) intellectuals of his own generation in the interest of starting new influences. At the same time he quietly prepared for the sustained labor that would necessitate his resignation from Harvard and the *North American Review* and that would culminate in the nine-volume *History of the United States during the Administrations of Jefferson and Madison*, a work that in its conception reflected a capacity to entertain visionary notions of an American futurity. Yet throughout his seven years at Harvard, Adams lived what he insisted on representing to his British friends as an uneventful and unfulfilling existence. "Life has become gray, monotoned, calm as a monk of Wenlock," he writes Sir Robert Cunliffe in his first year as a professor at Harvard. "Nothing can surpass the quiet disappearance of our lives. I lose all patience when I think how little we do that is worth remembering" (LHA 2:101, 102). The complaint takes various forms, but perhaps the most recurrent phrase in his letters to Gaskell and Cunliffe is that he has nothing to say: "I have absolutely nothing to write about" (LHA 2:238); "Life here offers astonishingly little to write about" (LHA 2:234); "I have literally nothing to write that can possibly be of more than a very vague interest to you" (LHA 2:274–75).

Adams left Harvard and the *North American Review* at the end of the spring 1877 term, and moving to Washington began a period of prolific and experimental authorship during which he produced two biographies, *The Life of Albert Gallatin* and *The Life of John Randolph*, two novels, *Democracy* and *Esther*, as well as the nine-volume *History of the United States*. In setting up a household aloof from the vicissitudes that rendered most of capital society anxious, the politically and financially independent Adamses aspired to contribute to the intellectual and social life of a nation that appeared at last to be emerging from the scandal of the Grant administration. "As for me and my wife," Adams wrote Gaskell in November 1877, "we have made a great leap in the world" in moving to Washington, having "caught new ties and occupations here. The fact is, I gravitate to a capital by a primary law of nature." And in his sanguine view his nation was destined in coming years to figure internationally as a cynosure of human advancement. "As I belong to the class of people who have great faith in this country and who believe that in another century it will be saying in its turn the last word of civilisation, I enjoy the expectation of the coming day, and try to imagine that I am myself, with my fellow *gelehrte* here, the first faint rays of that great light which is to dazzle and set the world on fire hereafter" (LHA 2:326). In such language Adams registers an engaged presence that seldom appears in letters to Gaskell written during his earlier Washington residence and that contrasts with the note of chronic disaffection that dominates future correspondence.

The Washington residency led to the coalescence of the circle of friends known as the five of hearts: Henry and Marian Adams, John and Clara Hay, and Clarence King. The Adamses' and the Hays' periodic absence from Washington and King's increasingly rare presence made this group an epistolarily active one; their use of a custom-designed five-of-hearts stationery for brief in-town exchanges as well as for long-distance correspondence indicates the degree to which the letter served as the metonym of group identity.[13] This intensely private and indeed secretive circle is important to Adams's development both as a letter writer and as a public author. In his correspondence with King and John Hay, Adams was able to write with a license that he had exercised heretofore only in his correspondence with Gaskell and to cultivate a detachment from the Washington scene that kept the spectacle of capital life at a decided distance. Exclusivity not only encouraged the caustic commentary of in-group conversation but the anonymously published satiric novels *Democracy* (Adams) and *The Bread-Winners* (Hay). The valuing of private association over the occasions of public life comes out in sentences like the following: "The universe hitherto has existed in order to produce a dozen people to amuse the five of hearts. Among us, we know all mankind. We or our friends have canvassed creation, and there are but a dozen or two companions in it;—men and women, I mean, whom you like to have about you, and whose society is an active pleasure" (LHA 2:473–74). Such remarks would seem implicitly to repudiate ideals of a progressive democratic commonality.

Free as Adams was to realize what he had once referred to as "the quiet and sunny prospect" of the full-time historian and buoyed as he was in his ambitions by what he continued to perceive as his nation's potential, the restlessness that he reported in his letters of the Harvard years resurfaces in the correspondence of his new phase. Writing to Gaskell in anticipation of a trip to Europe for the purpose of conducting research among European diplomatic archives, he characterizes himself as ambivalent to fixed location. "I am now forty and the grave is yawning for me," Adams remarks in August 1878, secluded with Clover in their Beverly Farms summer home,

> but I would do my best to smile as I sat on its edge, and to talk as though I were still as young as when you and I first met. Every now and then in my bourgeois ease and uniformity, my soul rebels against it all, and I want to be on my wanderings again, in the Rocky Mountains, on the Nile, the Lord knows where. But I humbly confess that it is vanity and foolishness. I really prefer comfort and

repose. I should not now be meditating the passage of that miserable ocean, if it were not for my literary necessities. I am ashamed to seem restless. It is ludicrous to play Ulysses. There is not in this wide continent of respectable mediocrity a greasier citizen, or one more contented in his oily ooze, than myself. (LHA 2:344)

His 1879 visit to England was remarkable for the intensity with which he recognized the passage of time, an intensity exhibited by the emergence of a metaphor that is to become dominant in subsequent letters as well as in *Mont Saint Michel and Chartres* and *The Education of Henry Adams*: at a reception hosted by Lord Carnarvon he writes of having "sat in a corner and realised the feelings of ghosts, for no one remembered me and I enjoyed my invisibility too much to recall my memory. To be dead and gone, I now know, is not a painful sensation" (LHA 2:361). To be thus "dead" is to exercise what for Adams is the epistolary liberty of designating oneself as one chooses, more or less abstracted from a particular time and place; it is to be free to find life where one wishes and to assume recreational identities. In a letter written to Gaskell from Spain five months later, the ghost gives way to a self renewed by the exhilarations of travel: "whether my name is now Abd-el-adem, or Ben-shadams," he speculates, "or Don Enrique Adamo, I couldn't take oath, for I have been utterly bewildered to know what has become of my identity, and the Spaniards have been so kind to us that I feel as though I owed them a name" (LHA 2:382).

The sense of precipitate passage—through time, through space, through experience that is tremendously satisfying if ever vaguely disappointing and shadowed in the best moments by intimations of mortality—figures insistently in the letters of this period. Such preoccupations are generated by the prolific epistolary record by which Adams maintained relations with his several sets of British and American friends. The multiple selves—dead, alive, transcending space and time—that Adams fashions against the apprehension of a proximate death are the specific constructions of a continuous engagement of the letter genre. The portrait of a life-in-progress in the following paragraph arises out of the satisfactory experience of friendship, travel, and ambitious literary projects, as well as the fear that life is passing too quickly. But it arises fundamentally from a consciousness produced by the life's continuous epistolary textualization:

It is not only the fugaces annos, but the fugaces continentes, that bewilder me with the sense of leading several lives. Just at present, however, life seems as real and enjoyable as ever. Indeed, if I felt a perfect confidence that my history would be what I would like to make it, this part of life—from forty to fifty—would be all I want. There is a summer-like repose about it; a self-contained, irresponsible, devil-may-care indifference to the future as it looks to younger eyes; a feeling that one's bed is made, and one can rest on it till it becomes necessary to go to bed for ever. (LHA 2:448)

As reported to his friends, the fullness of life is real, but there is ever the awareness of its ghostly ephemerality.

Adams's most interesting development as a letter writer in the half decade before Marian Adams's death lies in his exploration of the boundaries between life and death, for him an increasingly vanishing boundary. "Your letter announcing Frank Doyle's death grieved me sadly," he writes to Gaskell in January 1883. "Death gets to be such a daily matter as one advances in the world that now I hardly know who of my friends are dead and who are living. They are all equally alive to me at this distance, for I remember everything as it was, and a few changes in such a trifle as life make no impression on the mind" (LHA 2:489). "Your letters are a necrology," he writes to Gaskell in June 1883, responding to his British friend's most recent news of the deaths of people he had known in London twenty years earlier—a period that in retrospect exists for Adams as an era abundant in youthful contacts. His spatial separation from Gaskell and Cunliffe has increasingly merged with the separation in time between the present and the past in which his friendships with them were formed. By now it is commonplace for Adams to identify with what is past and deceased: "I feel as though I had also passed over to the next world, and you were notifying me of the latest departures" (LHA 2:504). "History grinds itself out like saw-dust," he reports to his friend Sir John Clark in December 1884. "Nothing could be pleasanter or less heroic than our lives in this small capital," he affirms of an existence that has become reduced to hard, ongoing literary labor and concern over Clover's mood. "My wife is worse than I am. Nothing will induce her to contemplate any change except final cremation, which has a certain interest of new experience" (LHA 2:560).

One week short of one year later, Clover would embark upon the final change and in so doing sharply define the border between life and death that Adams's epistolary conceit had blurred. Clover's death was preceded by her father Dr. Robert Hooper's death in April 1885, and throughout the summer and fall of 1885 Adams witnessed the deterioration of Clover's condition that culminated in her December suicide. The letters Adams wrote to his wife as she attended her father belie an anxiety half-suppressed by a running account of daily life in Washington—weather conditions, social contacts, progress of the house they had commissioned H. H. Richardson to build for them on Lafayette Square—as though the letter's purpose were to recall her from her deathbed vigil to the quotidian minutiae of their life in Washington. That life is desolate in her absence: "certainly this solitary struggle with platitudinous atoms, called men and women by courtesy, leads me to wish for my wife again. How did I ever hit on the only woman in the world who fits my cravings and never sounds hollow anywhere? Social chemistry—the mutual attraction of equivalent human molecules—is a science yet to be created, for the fact is my daily study and only satisfaction in life" (LHA 2:608). So Adams writes in a paragraph that comes as close as any to professing his love for her.

After Clover's suicide, the conceit that he had died with her would become a permanent feature of his letters, although the passage that he was actually to embark on was into the world of the bereaved. In the immediate aftermath of her death Adams's epistolary language is of course incommensurate with the experience; it does, however, assert his need to shield himself from the force of death to unmake his yet-living identity: "Wait till I have recovered my mind," he warns Rebecca Gilman Dodge, a would-be comforter in the first hours of bereavement. "Tomorrow I *must* be myself; and I can't think yet" (LHA 2:640). The solitude that he elects in this moment is to be permanent, although relieved by an apocalyptic sense of commonality and community served by the experience of death and the epistolary contacts that address it. Death and the condolence letters that follow induct Adams into a new, yet perennial society. "The great calamities of life leave one speechless," he writes in response to Anna Barker Ward.

I have not a word to say. During the last two weeks I have learned something more about life than I knew before, but the saddest discovery of all was that I did not stand alone in my extremity of suffering. The whole of society seemed to groan with the same anguish. My table was instantly covered with messages from men and women whose own hearts were still aching with the same wounds, and who received me, with a new burst of their own sorrows, into their sad fraternity. My pain seemed lost in the immensity of human distress; and all these people were still carrying on their daily lives, as I must do. (LHA 2:644)

Although Adams's habitual social exclusivity would persist, one sees in such a passage a vision of human commonality, a "vast fraternity" of "Hearts that Ache" that contrasts with the gleeful contraction of the world to the amusement of the five of hearts: "For the last three months it has seemed to me as though all society were coming to me, to drop its mask for a moment and initiate me into the mystery," he writes to Henry Holt in March 1886 (LHA 3:5). In the life that would follow, the spectacle of human distress would recurrently prompt a sense of common suffering that would serve to overrule snobbish predilections.

AS A GHOST I AM RATHER A SUCCESS

The suicide of Marian Hooper Adams on December 6, 1885, marks the great divide in Adams's life. Letters written in the hours, days, weeks, months, and years following her death cast Adams in the role of bereaved husband whose every communication makes tacit reference to an experience he cannot bear to articulate. In their rare mention of Clover and his married state, their constant implicit invocation of his loss, and their generalized characterization of the absence that defines his life, the letters anticipate the *Education*'s refusal to cite this experience directly. As we have seen, attitudes expressive of bereavement are part of Adams's epistolary repertoire from the beginning: absence from occasions or persons that afford life and meaning, estrangement from opportunities that offer intense definition, even the sense of living a posthumous life—such themes are on their way to becoming constant refrains of Adams's correspondence in the letters he wrote from Germany and Italy prior to the secession winter. His longstanding concern with presence and absence, separations in space that increasingly become separations in time, and the uncertain borders between life and death, make for a continuity between letters written before and after Clover's death. Yet despite his propensity to generalize the themes of loss, absence, and the steady approach of death, there is no mistaking the extent to which the letters written after December 1885 reflect a specific loss and the catastrophic transformation of an epistolary identity.

Exhibiting a more extreme detachment, a more expansive self-invention, greater verbal license, and a surer if at times more hazardous approach to intimacy, the post-1885 letters are qualitatively different from those written before. They proceed from a subjectivity radically differentiated by grief: over and over Adams will claim that he is dead to the world even as he reserves the ghost's option of returning to a semblance of life. As the sorrow that Adams's letters represent isolates him from his companions, it affords him the freedom to speak intimately to them, and never more intimately than when friends and acquaintances are bereaved in their turn. Arising from what his letters identify as extremities of solitude, his correspondence is at liberty to construct more elaborate orders of intersubjectivity than it could have attempted prior to Clover's death. Already a prolific correspondent, Adams's production of letters increases after 1885 as they become his principal means of relieving loneliness; that production increases again after 1890 when, the *History* completed, letter writing is the medium by which he narrates a life of ambitious travel, variable residence, and restless intellectual inquiry. In the thirty-three years that remain to him, Adams sustains his most important friendships through letters written with weekly and at times daily regularity and that display a diarist's compulsion to represent the texture of day-to-day life. As life for Adams largely becomes a matter of epistolary relation, he does much to define and realize the potential of the letter genre.

Only a lengthy catalogue can account for the variety of expression found in the correspondence written between 1886 and 1918. Best known are the voluminous travel letters that Adams wrote from Japan, the South Seas, the Caribbean, the Middle East, the Balkans, Russia, Norway, France—letters that combine anecdote with anthropological observation, ongoing meditation on the course of Western history with reflections concerning the specific friendships that his correspondence inscribes and sustains. Almost as well known are the letters of satiric observation of the political and social life of Washington and—given the notoriety of their anti-Semitic remarks—those obsessed with the social dissolution and escalating militarism of France, Great Britain, and Germany, the conspiratorial activity of international bankers on the one hand and Socialists on the other.[14] In addition to travel narrative and social commentary, Adams's epistolarium comprehends economic treatise and geopolitical analysis, social diary and personal advice, as well as historiographical speculations directed to colleagues in history.[15] As his correspondence extends more and more to children and young adults, he writes letters of avuncular affection and playfulness. And as each year death figures more prominently among his circle of acquaintance, he produces an increasing volume of condolences.

The variety of expression reflects the diversity of his epistolary relationships as well as the range of interest and sensibility found among his correspondents. Anyone who could so busily and multi-fariously engage his contemporaries obviously succeeded in emerging from the extremity of grief; for Adams, grief was above all measured by the degree to which the sufferer became encased in a silence that language was powerless to break. By no means reclusive, Adams represented himself as facing the world chiefly through his correspondence, and letter writing, a sociable activity that always reaffirmed the solitude of epistolary inscription, allowed him to perpetuate and elaborate his conceit of having already died. His notion of living a posthumous existence was particularly aimed at absenting him from a public life that had been the hereditary realm of his family, a realm that in his view had inadequately acknowledged his own singular merits but that had claimed, through the agency of gossip columnists, his private tragedy as public spectacle.[16] Unwilling to withdraw from the social, political, and intellectual currents of his day, Adams led the semblance of a public life by means of an extensive discursive network fashioned of epistolary thread, a network that simultaneously asserted his foregone absence and continued presence. After the publication of the *History*, the rest of his literary work would emerge from his study through the restricted circulation of private epistolary channels. Literary expression for Adams had become systematically privatized, an extension of the familiar letter.

Although Adams maintains abundant connections, it is to a comparatively small number of correspondents that he directs the bulk of his letters, and those with whom he is in continuous contact revolve among interlocking circles of acquaintance. In the years following Clover's death, John Hay and Elizabeth Cameron emerge as the correspondents to whom Adams directed his most urgent and voluminous communications. Clarence King—with Hay and Hay's wife, Clara, one of the old five of hearts set—was perhaps the recipient of letters as urgent but only remnants of that correspondence survive. Anna Cabot Mills Lodge, the wife of Senator Henry Cabot Lodge, Adams's former graduate student and *North American Review* coeditor, is an important if less frequent correspondent.[17] The daughters of his brother-in-law Edward Hooper and the children of friends (Martha Cameron, George "Bay" Lodge) emerge as correspondents for whom Adams would construct the figure of Uncle Henry. His younger brother Brooks emerges in the 1890s as a fellow speculator on the decline of Western civilization. With Robert Cunliffe and Charles Milnes Gaskell he would continue to exchange letters until Cunliffe's death in 1905 and his own death in 1918. Just beyond the epistolary relations within these inner circles there are other notable correspondences: those with Henry James and Edith Wharton (although little survives of the former and evidently nothing of the latter), those with Bernard Berenson and Theodore Roosevelt, as well as those with numerous wealthy society women who prized his ironic conversation and accessible sympathy. Such correspondences reflect the writing in other, more continuous exchanges.

In the first five years of his widowerhood, Adams's friendship with Elizabeth Cameron, the beautiful and increasingly estranged wife of Senator J. Donald Cameron of Pennsylvania, became the focus of affections that caused him to doubt the proposition that he could sustain a life of spectral substance and forsworn pleasures. The idea of Elizabeth Cameron tempted Adams as nothing else to abandon the cultivated presence-in-absence for which the epistolary text served as model. Because their relationship tested the premise that Adams had died to the world, the thematic, formal, and theoretical interest of Adams's letter writing is most clearly to be seen in this correspondence.

Elizabeth Sherman Cameron became a friend of the Adamses in 1881, soon after she had arrived in Washington with her husband, a member of a Pennsylvania political dynasty who succeeded his father in the U.S. Senate. She was herself the daughter of a politically powerful Ohio family (General William T. Sherman was one uncle, John Sherman, a U.S. senator, another, while her father, Charles Sherman, was a Cleveland judge), and her marriage with Donald Cameron, a widower twenty-four years older than Elizabeth with six grown children, was an alliance wholly of political convenience.[18] Henry and Clover Adams admitted her instantly to their circle, and Adams and Hay made her the subject of facetiously courtly attentions. Catherine Brooke, the beautiful and naïve young Westerner of *Esther*, is thought to have been modeled on Elizabeth Cameron.[19] After Clover's death, Cameron's solicitudes as neighbor and friend constituted Adams's chief source of comfort. The nineteen-year age difference between them invested their attachment with ambiguities that would take years to clarify.

Apart from the letters that he wrote to his wife during her two-month absence in Boston in the spring of 1885, Adams had never in his previous correspondence really developed the theme of personal longing for another. In letters to Gaskell and Cunliffe written from Boston, Adams expresses longing for the company of his British friends, but the object of desire has more to do with escape from present burdens or with recapturing moments of youth that stood outside the current of family and professional responsibilities than with an erotic interest in the addressee. Even the letters written to Clover express desire for her presence reticently, and only after an extensive catalogue of daily events, as though the epistolary medium were an awkward measure for a couple accustomed to the unwritten language of constant companionship. By contrast, the relationship with Cameron was always to some extent epistolary: even when both are at home in Washington, brief notes pass between their houses conveying such information as succeeding generations would exchange by telephone. Although this relationship would be one sustained by texts passed over thousand-mile separations, the habit of writing extends to such routine communications as the invitation to tea, and that habit sustains a friendship in which the two are more consistently present to one another through the medium of writing than through the physical and conversational proximities of in-person companionship.[20]

In the letters Adams wrote to Cameron in the first two years of his widowerhood one observes him shed what in previous letters had been the formal if affectionate tones of a mock-chivalric attention and adopt a familiarity and confidentiality that confess a growing emotional dependence that he will eventually proclaim explicitly. His attachment to Elizabeth extended also to her daughter Martha, born in 1886, whom Elizabeth had intended originally to name Marian; Clover's recent death and Donald Cameron's virtual desertion of his second wife and infant daughter fostered the rapidly developing familial character of their friendship with Adams. The quasi-familial relation was reinforced by Adams's successful effort to settle Elizabeth and Martha, during the latter part of the summers of 1886 and 1887, in the Beverly Farms house that he and Clover had built to serve as a summer home while he was at Harvard and that he could not now bring himself to enter. In 1887, while he attended his declining mother and toiled away on the final volumes of the *History* in Quincy, Elizabeth and Martha resided near enough to be under his care while remaining peculiarly off-limits. Elizabeth had begun to occupy a vacuum in Adams's life, although by means of a delicate reciprocity of movement she would persist in occupying it at a distance and never really offer to abrogate the absence that gave that vacuum enduring structure. Her persistently distant presence in his life, and his in hers, is the new theme in this period of his letters, and as a theme it foregrounds his own epistolary practice and articulates the discursive conditions of their exchange.

A letter Adams wrote from Quincy in September 1887 to Cameron in Beverly exhibits the emerging patterns of their correspondence and suggests the extent to which, as an epistolary construct, the friendships with Elizabeth and Martha will have abiding reference to his relationship with the absent Clover.

> I am homesick to see you, but unless you take matters into your own hands . . . I shall see nothing of anyone. . . . I am alone here, and my mother is not a good subject for masculine care. Also I am victim to a female called a caligraphess . . . meaning a type-writer; whom I am slowly killing with five hours a day of type-writing, in order to hurry my journey to the Celestial Empire. . . . If you could only come over for Sunday, you would make life another thing, and I would come to town Saturday afternoon to get you. But I know you are too much occupied. (LHA 3:76)

"I am homesick to see you," Adams begins significantly: whereas homesickness typically involves separation from loved ones, the word's primary definition denotes a longing for a place identified with those who are missed. Beneath Adams's homesickness for Elizabeth and Martha, with whom he constitutes "home" through occasional meetings in various places but not by virtue of a continual presence in a place consecrated to family life, is his homesickness for Beverly and his erstwhile life with Clover. As the letter continues, he speaks of his nearly solitary care of his ailing mother, his constant labor over the *History*, and the long, open-ended journey that looms beyond completion of the magnum opus—a journey that figures for Adams as an enduring separation from Cameron and his old life and that foreshadows his own death. Adams's "female called a caligraphess" contributes to the theme that he is paired with people and situated in circumstances that he does not want, and cannot have whom and what he desires (Clover, Elizabeth; a life free of bereavement and restlessness). Against such prospects as seem to forbid a convergence with Elizabeth and Martha, Adams tantalizes himself with what he represents as an impossible "if": "If you could only come over for Sunday, you would make life another thing. . . . But I know you are too much occupied."

This letter's lament is developed with expansive and artful freedom in epistles addressed to Martha Cameron; such letters, although meant to speak to a child and crafted for what Adams supposes to be a child's sensibility, are inevitably also addressed to the parent who must relay the message to the child too young to read for herself. "I love you very much, and think of you a great deal, and want you all the time," he writes to Martha in September 1888, proceeding to limn a fable of loss, grief, and decline: "I should have run away from here, and looked for you all over the world, long ago, only I've grown too stout for the beautiful clothes I used to wear when I was a young prince in the fairy-stories, and I've lost the feathers out of my hat, and the hat too, and I find that some naughty man has stolen my gold sword and silk-stockings and silver knee-buckles. So I can't come after you, and feel very sad about it" (LHA 3:137).[21] Such writing engages in a rhetoric of emotional appeal and elaborates an allegory of personal sorrow. The brief narrative registers a fallen estate, a loss of virility, an alienation from preferred heroic narratives (now "fairy-stories"), and the inaccessibility of the beloved object as a consequence of misfortune (*"So* I can't come after you, and feel very sad about it"). Such avowals of loneliness cannot help but invite the addressee to allay that loneliness and to affirm the restorability of friend to friend. Convinced as Adams may be that his essential solitude will persist, the letter exchange affords the possibility that his correspondent at least will dispute his conviction that those he loves are fated to diverge from his path. In writing to Martha, Adams can proceed as if the adult lament could be contradicted by the child in whom the capacity to perceive impossibilities is not yet developed. Letters to Elizabeth exhibit the consciousness that the language of nearest approach is apt to alienate the addressee, yet Adams finds ways to speak to Elizabeth as though the seeming transparency of the affectionate word addressed to the child might also serve (although he suspects it cannot) to convey a far more complicated emotion to the adult. "Give Martha my tenderest love. Propriety forbids me to send as much to her mamma, so I remain only conventionally hers" (LHA 3:142). In testing the borders of epistolary protocol, Adams as ever explores the possibility of Cameron's presence in his life; in exploring those possibilities, he probes what are for him the borders between life and death.

Cameron's words and actions in the years ahead would neither confirm nor refute his suspicion that their lives were destined not to converge. Yet for her and Martha alone was the fiction of a posthumous existence to be suspended: "The rule that nothing matters much, does not apply to you," Adams would write from Quincy in July 1888

(LHA 3:130). Through the epistolary medium that he would more characteristically use to assert his absence from the world, he inscribes the extendable presence of Elizabeth and Martha in his life and his in theirs. "You and Martha are my chief companions," he writes in June 1889, referring to a recent photograph of mother and daughter, "you in red Japanese silk, Martha in green—and you smile at me on my toilet table, to my great comfort and enjoyment" (LHA 3:184). Against the pervading absence of his solitary travels he is moved to write in affirmation of Cameron's presence-at-a-distance. From Ottawa, where Adams was conducting research in September 1889, he addresses Cameron in lines that demonstrate how instrumental the letter is to his efforts to preserve human contact: "My only excuse for writing is that I really must imagine you to be somewhere about. My only surviving notion of happiness is the sense that some one, to whom one is attached, is sitting in the next room. In the Russell House at Ottawa such a sensation is not within bounds of sanity; but a letter is a sort of substitute for it" (LHA 3:196). Noteworthy here is the concession that near attachment may bring him no closer to Cameron than a next room: solitude for the bereaved Adams is irreducible.

In embarking on the journey to the South Seas, Adams was to separate himself from Cameron by thousands of miles, yet continue to speak not only as though she were as near as the next room but as though nearer approach might be possible almost as a consequence of their separation. No voyage that Adams ever took was as complexly motivated as the one he ventured upon in the company of John La Farge in August 1890, and from which he would not return to his Washington residence until February 1892. As early as 1881, he had projected a flight to Polynesia as a kind of afterlife beyond his completion of the *History*. By 1890, Clover's death all the more impelled him to quit settings associated with her memory in search of the renewal that he was accustomed to finding in travel. The long diary letters that he sent to Elizabeth Cameron and John Hay provide abundant evidence of intellectual renewal as Adams copiously documents his sojourn in Hawaii, Samoa, Tahiti, and Fiji, describing landscapes and atmospheric effects, noting people and customs, constructing as he can their precolonial history, and narrating at length his many and varied adventures of island exploration. These letters, for all their limitations as ethnographic representation, figure among Adams's most accomplished literary achievements. The series of letters to Cameron, while telling the story of his absorption in Polynesia and the recovery of appetite, stamina, and intellectual tone, recurrently if ever reticently propose that the most compelling reason for his distant travel is the increasingly dangerous character of his relation with her. As these letters address an uncertain and emotionally adulterous relationship, they endeavor to emplot a future acceptable reunion.

Adams's departure for the South Seas was prolonged by the long rail journey to San Francisco and a wait of several days for the *Zealandia* to sail. As the moment of embarkation neared he experienced acute homesickness for Elizabeth, Martha, and the Beverly Farms home that he had not entered since Clover's death.[22] The break with the old life was not to be simple. Writing in June to Lucy Baxter, his mother's companion, Adams had spoken of the upcoming voyage as a form of death and himself as "a man about to commit suicide" (LHA 3:242); yet launched on the Pacific and engulfed by seasickness, his thoughts fixed on home, and he images Cameron's most recent letter, arriving in the last mail pouch and reaching him after the ship had left port, as an object to grasp in his misery: "All night I lay on my face in my clothes," he writes on August 26, "clasping your letter between my hands, and only after twentyfour hours did I indulge in the pleasure of opening it" (LHA 3:268). Here there is only recoil from the death the journey represents, and the letter in this instance (first as unopened fetish) secures a future beyond the bout of nausea that constitutes an initial increment of the voyage. A month later, writing from Honolulu, Adams would explicitly state his need for Cameron's epistolary attentions: "I must say—what you must understand without saying—that I am something more than dependent on your writing. Now that I am here I find what I expected to find when I came away—that you are my only strong tie to what I suppose I ought to call home. If you should go back on me, I should wholly disappear" (LHA 3:285).

Negotiating his geographical separation from Cameron involved reaffirming her distant presence through acts of attention that vividly imagine her life at Beverly or Washington, and that prompt her to reciprocal acts of attention that in turn affirm his distant presence to her. "Here we are then," he writes from Hawaii on September 2, "and you can imagine me, as though the verandah at Beverly looked over palms and tube-roses to the south seas, and I were seated on it, in a Japanese kimono, writing to you in the early morning, while La Farge still sleeps within." The oddness of the circumstance has less to do with their absence from one another than with the distance that enforces separation: "Everything seems natural and easy except that you and Martha should be five thousand miles away" (LHA 3:271). In November, images of Samoa and Washington combine as Adams meditates his absence from accustomed haunts: "I am depressed by the thought that this letter will find you in Washington," he writes from Samoa, "while I shall be still looking out on my village-green at Vaiale, and confusing my brain with a queer medley of pictures, among which your house will pirouette with Mata-afa's" (LHA 3:328). Although the compelling spectacle of the Pacific islands claims its share of his attention, the epistolary exchange with his American correspondents would stimulate his active visualization of the places from which he had absented himself. Given such epistolarily cultivated homesickness, the "suicide" that he had equated with his departure would remain reluctant and inconclusive.

Adams's homesickness was both relieved and reintensified by episodes of engagement in the phenomena of Samoa and Tahiti that alternated with periods of boredom and depression. One dimension of his interest in South Seas culture lay in the erotic spectacle of female undress and the Rousseauian utopia that it suggested; for years Clarence King had talked of the uninhibited Edenic sexuality of such supposedly archaic cultures as those of the Polynesian islands. Adams probably never wished for anything other than a voyeuristic relation to this feature of South Seas life, yet the native dances that the missionaries had not yet suppressed became for Adams a focus of a rejuvenated sensibility. On October 9 he writes as follows to Elizabeth Cameron of his attendance at a *siva*: "The mysterious depths of darkness behind . . . the sense of remoteness and of genuineness in the stage-management; the conviction that at last the kingdom of old-gold was ours, and that we were as good Polynesiacs as our neighbors,—the whole scene . . . gave so much freshness to our fancy that no future experience, short of being eaten, will ever make us feel so new again" (LHA 3:290–91). This passage recalls the account of his winter tramp through the Thuringian Forest some thirty years before that had restored a temper enervated by a winter spent in Berlin (the very rhythm of the sentences bear striking resemblances: "You may think this wasn't much fun, and indeed I believe I was the only one who really enjoyed it, but the glow, the feeling of adventure and the novelty; above all, the freedom and semi-wildness after six months in Berlin, made it really delightful to me. I haven't felt so well and fresh for ever-so-long" [LHA 1:37]).

In Samoa, Adams became naturalized sufficiently to sign himself

"Akamu" (after the Samoan pronunciation of his name) in some letters, and in Tahiti, the friendship he developed with the Tevas, the Tahitian ruling family, culminated in their adoption of him, ritualized in their bestowal of the name "Taura-atua." As traveler he had always been open to the development—ever an epistolary construction—of alter egos. But such engagements were always limited by the impression that the Polynesian experience was a succession of theatrical effects that served little purpose but to divert his mind from the reality Cameron represented. Even when he was most captivated by the Samoan or Tahitian scene, Adams made reference to its "stage-management." "As usual, the scene is preposterously like a stage-decoration," he writes of a set of waterfalls sighted during a tour of the Samoan island of Upolu, minutely described in his letter to Cameron (LHA 3:353). The reality of such scenes is qualified; there are limits to how fully he can be present in them, and without evidence that people at home are thinking of him he feels scarcely present to himself. In the following passage he represents "my existence" as self-aware and responsive to surroundings only in partnership to reciprocal attentions, a proleptic epistolary reflection:

> *You cannot fill up the background of my existence here without imagining me* every evening towards sunset, paddling my canoe far out on the reef, or floating on the long ocean-swell in the harbor, waiting for the sunset, and *thinking of you and Martha and all that may or may not be happening at Washington.* The contrast is almost laughable between this velvety, oily, half-dead or half-vegetable atmosphere, intellectual and physical, where even the ocean-water is warm to the touch, and even the stormiest sunsets are soft violet in tone, and the heaviest rainy horizons are strong purple over a purple ocean, and *your winter in La Fayette Square which comes before my mind as the more real of the two.* (LHA 3:388; italics added)

Throughout his South Sea travels he writes of experiencing a geographically dispersed existence. "As the winter approaches I seem to think more and more about you and Martha," Adams writes on October 23, "and long more to see you. The contrast between my actual life and my thoughts is fantastic. The double life is almost like one's idea of the next world." Much of Adams's thought in Polynesia is invested in identifying what that next world is to be and plotting a passage to it. Just as he had earlier regarded his departure as a sort of death and afterlife, so now he assessed the existence that would follow the South Seas excursion as a proposition in which the chance for life perilously involved the renewal of contact with Cameron. Further on in the letter of October 23 he writes: "I dare not think about next summer, if you go to Europe, for I cannot foresee whether it will be possible for me to get there, and, if I did get there, I cannot help foreseeing that I should have done better not to go. Please tell me what to think, for I am distracted in mind, and being naturally as near a fool as is manufactured, I feel too much or too little when I ought to see as a matter of course what is the correct and proper conventionality" (LHA 3:299). Here as elsewhere he puts Cameron in the position of having to coauthor the plot that would bring them together or confirm him in a life of solitary, deathward wandering.

Adams concluded an "extravagantly bulky" and generally buoyant diary letter written between November 9 and 25 with a six-stanza poem that continues the argument that the life left behind is more vivid to him than the one in which he now finds himself, but that in spite of his keen longings for what is temporally past or geographically distant "Death is not hard when once you feel its measure" (LHA 3:340).[23] Cameron's reply is consistent with her manner of responding to Adams's other letters from the South Seas. "Your dear letter made me happy for many days, and the verses I keep by me. They are dear, but too sad." Answering his recurrent claim that he has died to the world of Washington, she writes: "You are not dead, but very alive,—a living presence by my side in many long hours, and I think, I *have* to think, that you will come back, oh, how I wish that it might be soon!"[24]

For their part, Cameron's letters to Adams cast the latter in the role of boudoir confidant as she registers her comings and goings, changes of dress, evening entertainments, whom she has seen in society, and so on. Each produces an epistolary diary addressed to the other. Compared to Adams's letters—the productions of a resourceful writer in scenes that bring out his singular gifts for description, anecdote, and ironic commentary—Cameron's letters are banal, but for Adams their repetitive account of social occasions, personalities, and gossip sustains her presence in his life. Arrivals of her dispatches were for Adams intensely life-affirming occasions. To the letter from her quoted above Adams responds on March 4, 1891: "I know no new combination of love and angel to offer you, and am reduced to sheer bêtise, which, at a seven thousand mile dilution, is exasperatingly stupid; but you can at least to some degree imagine what sort of emotion I might be likely to feel at having you take me by the hand and carry me on with your daily life till I feel as though I had been with you all the month." The effect of such sustained epistolary companionship was to make reunion imaginable, although the ground of their reunion would remain for Adams distressingly undefined. "When you say that you wish I would come back," he writes in this same letter, "I want to break in with observations on that subject which would soon tire you out. . . . If you think I ought to come home,—I am willing to accept you as judge,—I will agree to come. Can I say more than that?" (LHA 3:423).

From March 1891 on, the issue of whether he and Cameron would reunite was settled. Although questions regarding the nature of their relations had not been answered, Adams was now directing his letters to an Elizabeth whom he was expecting to meet in Paris toward late summer or fall. He was acutely conscious that, to reach her, he had to endure thousands of miles of travel in vessels that induced the worst seasickness and that he had to pass the perils of shipwreck and disease. In the end, owing to the infrequency of traffic between Tahiti and Fiji, he spent £400 beyond customary fare to sail by charter.[25] Actually to arrive in Cameron's presence seemed to him increasingly hypothetical; when he thought of her as a point toward which he wished to gravitate he felt immobilized not only by the geographic distance between them but also by constraints that he rightly feared would always render her inaccessible; "like the unfortunate Robinson," he had characterized himself in January just after his arrival in Tahiti, "I cannot get back to land" (LHA 3:382). For Adams, getting back to land required Cameron's active encouragement and coauthorship. On May 13 he writes from Tahiti: "if we ever do reach Europe, where something like neighborhood exists, I shall want to know all about myself, now that myself and I are two different persons; one a mere shadowy possibility in Washington; the other an almost equally thin shadow in unknown or uncertain night. You are the only person who can tell me what I want to know" (LHA 3:472). What he wanted to know concerned their coordinate movements and convergence in space; it concerned what Cameron should will of their relationship, which alone could recall him from the deathly sensation of geographic dispersion.

Closing the distances that stretched between them involved questions of what each had become in their absence to one another and the extent to which their respective disappointments continued to shape occasions for friendship. The miscarriage of mail, the possible failure to coordinate plans, the uncertainty of Cameron's whereabouts in America and Europe, and the perils of the imminent voyage combine to make the prospects of convergence doubtful; much is asked of the letter exchange as a medium of friendship and self-identity. "Shall I really ever escape from here, and shall I see you again, and will you be the same, or am I the same, and is La Fayette Square really where I dreamed it?" Adams asks in the final Tahitian diary letter. "Only when the monthly packet arrives from San Francisco, I realise that my old life is still going on" (LHA 3:479). Toward the end of the letter Adams considers the odds: "I have not an idea where you are, or are to be, or where I should address to you . . . I mean to post this letter here, before sailing, so that, if we go to the bottom of the ocean, you may have the last news of me" (LHA 3:480). Fighting the conviction that his chances for life are dead, he closes the letter on this affirmation: "My only source of energy is that I am actually starting on a ten-thousand-mile journey to see—you!" (LHA 3:482).

The disappointment of their October meeting in Paris is a well-known matter of biography: Cameron was not to be approached for intimate conversation and generally imposed the constraint of a third person's company (usually that of Martha—epistolarily an enabler but in person an inhibitor of intimacy) on her meetings with Adams.[26] Following their reunion, Adams retreated to London, where later he would meet again with Cameron as she prepared to return to the United States. From Gaskell's estate, Wenlock Abbey, where Adams had retreated twenty years earlier after watching his sister die of lock-jaw, he renewed his correspondence with Cameron, and did so in view of an education in bereavement that now included what he had hoped against his better judgment to have been a love affair with her. This letter marks a new phase in Adams's relationship with her, a confirmation of Adams to a solitude defined not only by his widowerhood but by what he now recognizes as Cameron's inability to occupy the space of Clover's absence. On the phrase "apocalyptic *Never*" Adams builds a narrative of loss that begins implicitly with Clover's suicide and concludes with Cameron's recent refusals (signified by the Paris and London addresses that he mentions) to meet with him:

A long, lowering, melancholy November day, the clouds hanging low on Wenlock Edge, and stretching off to the westward where you are streaming along the Irish coast and out to sea. . . . You do not read Mrs Browning. No one does now. As a collegian I used to read Aurora Leigh . . . and two lines have stuck: "Know you what it is when Anguish, with apocalyptic *Never*, / To a Pythian height dilates you, and Despair sublimes to Power?" The verse is charmingly preposterous and feminine, for a woman never recognises an impossibility; but an elderly man, when hit over the head by an apocalyptic *Never*, does not sublime to Power, but curls up like Abner Dean of Angels, and for a time does not even squirm; then he tumbles about for a while, seeing the Apocalypse all round him; then he bolts and runs like a mad dog, anywhere,—to Samoa, to Tahiti, to Fiji; then he dashes straight round the world, hoping to get to Paris ahead of the Apocalypse; but hardly has he walked down the Rue Bassano when he sees the apocalyptic *Never* written up like a hotel sign on No. 12; and when he, at last leaves London, and his cab crosses the end of Cork St, his last glimpse of No. 5A shows the Apocalyptic *Never* over the front door. More than once today I have reflected seriously whether I ought not at once to turn round and go back to Ceylon.

The problem as Adams sees it is that he must either count himself as dead or own up to a desire not to be appeased by companionship merely, a desire that he has never really stated for all of their epistolary intimacies: "no matter how much I may efface myself or how little I may ask," he admits, "I must always make more demand on you than you can gratify, and you must always have the consciousness that, whatever I may profess, I want more than I can have. Sooner or later the end of such a situation is estrangement, with more or less disappointment and bitterness." Yet even at this turn Adams strives for a deeper consensual understanding, aware of the limits of intersubjective accord: "I would give you gladly as many opal and diamond necklaces as Mr Cameron would let you wear if I could only for once look clear down to the bottom of your mind and understand the whole of it. I lie for hours wondering whether you, out on the dark ocean, in surroundings which are certainly less cheerful than mine, sometimes think of me" (LHA 3:556–57). In wondering whether Elizabeth Cameron sometimes thinks of him, Adams reverts as he has throughout his long circumnavigation to the most fundamental of epistolary questions.

I AM LEFT BEHIND WITH EVERY BODY
I EVER CARED FOR

The massive epistolary diary keeping addressed to Elizabeth Cameron would continue for the rest of Adams's life; by that practice he would sustain their one occasion for intimacy. Adams's wanderings were by no means at an end when he returned to Washington in February 1892. Over the next ten years he would undertake journeys to Mexico and the Caribbean; to Egypt, Lebanon, Greece, and the Balkans; to eastern Europe, Russia, and Scandinavia; to the Rocky Mountains and western Canada. In these years he also established the pattern of spending winter and spring at his Washington residence and summer and autumn in Paris, from which he would stage cathedral-viewing motor tours of Normandy and the Île-de-France. A great portion of the letters written over this period are thus travel letters, yet so frequently does Adams pass from residence to residence that it is unusual for him not to reflect upon a transit just accomplished or impending. But whereas the letters written during the circumnavigation of 1890 to 1892 have Cameron as their constant reference—their point of departure and their point of hoped-for arrival—the letters written after this period tend to define more purely discursive destinations: as Adams alludes to his movements between Paris and Washington, he also writes as traveler to the past of the twelfth-century Virgin and as someone who, approaching life's end, awaits transport to the next world. Confirmed by the "Apocalyptic *Never*" of his experience to a solitary existence, Adams can arrive in no place, attain the company of no person, that will release him from that solitude, and there is never a break in the flow of letters that at once inscribe and mitigate that condition.

It is in the years immediately following his return from the South Seas that Adams, insisting that he no longer takes any part in the world's business and that nothing can matter to him because he is dead, writes with savage satire of American and international politics, searching for signs of "Jewish conspiracy" in the economic collapse of the early 1890s, and lamenting the degeneration of the Anglo-Saxon in his genteel English and American heirs. In addition to and in spite of his uncritical indulgence of anti-Semite paranoia and his sweeping dismissals of contemporary life in favor of an elegiacally privatized twelfth-century past, the twelve years following his return were a period of massive intellectual effort that culminated in the two late masterpieces, *Mont Saint Michel and Chartres* and *The Education of Henry Adams*. Both works emerged from an ongoing epistolary commentary on worlds medieval and modern; both were printed and circulated privately, although the posthumous acclaim these books have won attests to a public appeal that Adams's growing insularity could not suppress.[27] *A Letter to American Teachers of History*, his nihilistic projection of the entropic tendencies of human existence, closed his accounts with professional colleagues. Against what Adams might have hoped, the *Letter* proved only too unanswerable.

From the soberly reflective concluding chapters of the *History* to the somber assertions of *A Letter*, Adams increasingly called into question the possibility of a public life that could structure itself according to ideals expressible in such ostensibly consensual documents as the Declaration of Independence and the United States Constitution. Although he had devoted himself in the 1860s and 1870s to the emergence of an enlightened democratic society, he had always assumed that private ambition stood ready to compromise public good; by the time Clover committed suicide he had begun to suspect humanity of an organic predisposition to failure in every detail of its political, social, psychological, and physiological life. Although he would call himself a Conservative Christian Anarchist, Adams could never subscribe to anarchy: he would contemn the world of his time but enjoy too many material privileges to dispute the provisional necessity of a coercive public order. Yet politics for Adams was the organization and civic accommodation of hatreds more or less personal; although public order might guarantee a measure of peace, the bond of one human being to another was for him essentially apolitical. That bond rested on a transcendent sympathy for others, the ability to identify another's loss as one's own. Expecting in young manhood to establish a name as a social critic and historian, Adams came by his middle years to the conclusion that Dickinson and Emerson (all sufficiently privileged to ignore the political implications of an ample private life) had also reached: that social bonds were forged in realms apart from public or politicized space, and that the letter was preeminently the text of such social bonds as might exist.[28]

For Adams as for Dickinson and Emerson, death serves as the preeminent occasion for the epistolary affirmation of the human bond— an affirmation of one presence for another in spite of the temporary absences in this life that presage the permanent absence of death. From December 1885 on, Adams's letters recurrently project the vision of a secret society united in a mostly tacit understanding of the ways of grief, a community whose only outward manifestation is the condolence by which the sympathizer's words penetrate the otherwise unbreachable solitude of bereavement.[29] As Adams had written to Anna Barker Ward on December 22, 1885: "The whole of society seemed to groan with the same anguish. *My table was instantly covered with messages* from men and women whose own hearts were still aching with the same wounds, and who received me, with a new burst of their own sorrows, into their sad fraternity. My pain seemed lost in the immensity of human distress" (LHA 2:644; italics added). A month after seeing his own table covered with such messages Adams wrote to the newly bereaved Thomas F. Bayard: "in all the world I doubt whether another person exists, beyond your family, who sympathises with you more keenly than I do . . . within the last few weeks I have learned that, in the mass of human distress, trials like yours and mine can be endured, since so many men and women do endure them" (LHA 3:3).

Such trials could be endured, as Adams would live to demonstrate, but the pain of loss could not be assuaged and in the condolences that Adams was to write in the coming years the autobiographical reference to his own loss would become more and more pronounced. To Robert Cunliffe, who had lost his wife, Adams wrote on March 28, 1898: "the thought of you continually recurs to remind me how I have had to tread that path before you, and how infinitely useless all attempt at consolation was, and still is. Yet the one slight relief which I then felt, was in the expressions of sympathy which made me a little less terribly conscious of total solitude. It was something to know that others had suffered like me. It was almost a relief to think that others had got still to suffer" (LHA 4:555–56). To Lord Curzon, whose late wife, Mary, had once been a member of Adams's breakfast circle, Adams confesses that he writes as much in reference to his own revived pain as to his addressee's:

I had not the heart to write to you while the whole world was overwhelming you with condolence, and even now I write rather to quiet my own memories than with any idea of quieting your pain. Twenty years ago when I went through the same suffering, I found relief only in the sudden revelation that I was not alone; that others were nursing the same acute memory of intolerable loss, like a secret society that silently opened its arms to let me in. I have lived in it ever since, and in twenty years search have found no other life worth an effort; but this is my weakness, and I sincerely trust will not be yours. . . . I do not understand how we bear such suffering as we do when we lose them; but we have to be silent, for no expression approaches the pain. (July 30, 1906; LHA 6:23–24)

In all such expressions Adams affirms the silence and solitude that encompass the sufferer—the failure of language to address pain and the inaccessibility of the sufferer to comfort—as well as a sense of membership in the human family that only comes through intense but epistolarily expressible suffering. Adams wrote with special passion of

29 August, 1909

23 Avenue du Bois de Boulogne

My dear Sister
            I could not tele-
graph! No words would come.
I turned round at once and
came back here to see Sturgis and Mrs Roosevelt and
Mrs Wharton, and to ask
what had happened. I got
back here a few hours ago,
and have not been able to
see Sturgis, whose door was
barred, but have seen Mrs
Wharton and Mrs Roosevelt,
and am more in despair
than ever. As you know,

Henry Adams to Anna Cabot Mills Lodge, August 29, 1909.
Courtesy of the Massachusetts Historical Society, Boston.

this paradox when the poet George "Bay" Lodge died suddenly at thirty-six, leaving a wife and two children, his parents, Anna Cabot Mills Lodge and Henry Cabot Lodge, as well as Adams and other friends in mourning. "I could not telegraph!" he exclaims to Anna Lodge on August 29, 1909: "No words would come . . . the only relief I have ever found in it, is the sense that others are suffering too, and in this crushing calamity we are all one. . . . You are not alone! To me, the sense of solitude is the hardest to bear of all the inflictions of life" (LHA 6:266). To Elizabeth Davis "Bessie" Lodge, Bay's widow, Adams writes with an even more focused autobiographical reference: "What is worse, your miseries so acutely recall my own, of times that I shudder to remember, as to make me afraid to write at all . . . if you are like me, as I remember how my mind went to pieces under the shock, you will turn from one mood to another without rest, and will want affection at one moment as violently as you want solitude at the next" (LHA 6:267). Writing to Bessie again three weeks later, he invokes the image of the society of sufferers and the value, even the pleasure, of a suffering that preserves the memory of the one lost: "Even in the worst depths of solitude, I was surprised to find that almost everyone, beyond child-hood, was nursing some memory, or hiding some wound, that was never spoken of, but made the deepest feeling in life. . . . Nothing helps except to think of the happiness we have had, and even that is a kind of self-torture. I am old enough not to try to make the suffering less. The suffering is itself almost a pleasure that one does not want to forget" (LHA 6:279).

The suffering is a pleasure because, as it signifies the absence of the beloved, it affirms the beloved's lasting presence. "To me the dead are the only live companions," Adams wrote to Mary Cadwalader Jones on January 10, 1907. "I live with them almost wholly, and when two or three more have gone, I shall live with them entirely. . . . The world goes its way, and I am left behind with every body I ever cared for, as outside of life as they" (LHA 6:41).[30] The beloved person's absence—whether that person be Clover or the geographically distant but epis-tolarily present Elizabeth Cameron—blurs the line between the living and the dead, as epistolary discourse blurs the line between presence and absence. "I should only make it worse by talk," Adams writes to Henry Cabot Lodge in September 1915 after the death of Anna Lodge, yet he follows the remark with one that suggests that Clover has ex-isted for him all along as the perennial and ultimate addressee in his many correspondences: "I have gone on talking, all that time, but it has been to myself—and to her" (LHA 6:702). Discourse preserves memory of and relationship with the absent. "If it were not that I could write you—you could not go away," Dickinson wrote to her brother soon after he had entered what for her was the vast universe of death that lay beyond the confines of the Amherst home (LED 1:153). Adams's confession that he has "gone on talking" likewise argues that discourse substantiates the existence of an addressee whose more or less fatal departure is not subject to the writer's control.

In writing letters to his absent intimates Adams constructs a society of the bereaved whose collective mourning succeeds in preserving the vivid impress of the deceased—a private world that for Adams stood outside politics and history and that drew its being from the death that would eventually encompass all. Herein lay the true relevance of the second law of thermodynamics. In his last decade as a letter writer Adams compulsively notes the deaths of his contemporaries and juniors, constantly updating his own "necrology," and erasing as ever the line dividing the living from the dead. "Life gets to be charmingly gay and delirious towards eighty," he writes to William James in 1910. "I lose a friend every day, except when I lose two, and in the last month or so, I've lost so many that I have no longer a vehicle of communication with anything but the next world" (LHA 6:335). The "next world" that is death does not entirely eclipse the "next world" of twentieth-century life, for Adams an alternately entropic and explosive but ever alien prospect from which his death in any case will render him absent. For the most part, then, Adams's solipsistic assertiveness as a letter writer had subverted the public world to which a Walpolian correspondence must eventually be offered, yet three years before his death he envisioned an epistolarium to be published as a monument to the private society that he had turned to in abandoning more public ambitions. The suggestion occurs in a letter of November 10, 1915, to Elizabeth Cameron:

I write now *d'outre tombe* for another matter. You know that for ten years past I have tried to drape myself and my friends neatly for their final tableau before the audience that is to take stall-seats in the movie-show when we go. Slowly it is getting itself done. . . . As far as I know, you are the only letter-writer and letter-receiver living, and if you have kept your letters, you must have tons which you can select to print together with your own. I have all your letters for thirty years in a box. You can easily choose volumes of them to be copied, and unite them by a mere thread of editing. You need not publish or print, unless you like. Just lock them up, and name a literary executor.

I suggest this—supposing you to have preserved the letters,—as much because it would occupy and amuse you for years, as to immortalise you or us. I do want you and Nanny to stand by the side of John Hay and Clover and me forever—at Rock Creek, if you like,— but only to round out the picture.

Of course, if you can't, say no more. Sometimes I succeed, sometimes I fail, and my failures are far the most common. Only—I would like to feel you there, with Clover and me, and Nanny, and Hay, till the St Gaudens figure is forgotten or runs away. It is all that I have left. (LHA 6:703–4)

The letter, startling for its willingness to mention Clover by name, projects an intensely privatized heaven, yet suggests that the visionary tableau has some value as a public image. In the *Education*, he had demonstrated the desire, albeit ambivalent, of being remembered as an Adams scion and historian. Eight years later he seems genuinely interested in perpetuating his memory as a member of a social set that cohered through acts of mourning and letter writing, and one can only wonder what public impression Adams hoped to create by making their private papers available—assuming that such papers had been preserved. Clearly there would be a wealth of political commentary in those letters, much of it of the court gossip variety, and there would be relentless and generally unsparing criticism of the political culture of Washington: ongoing indictment of the ethics of government, running disparagement of Washington society's deportment and tastes.

Nevertheless, the cardinal lesson would undoubtedly concern lives that endured in progressive alienation from an emerging national culture, from a world transformed by the demographic and technological forces that Adams had sought to define in the *Education*. To the extent that such correspondence reflected the tendencies of Adams's own letters, loss of national opportunity and the mortality of friends and loved ones would coalesce in a poetics of private bereavement. In view of what for Adams was the growing incoherence of public life, the private life had to serve as an ultimate frame of reference.

More than at publication, perhaps, he aimed at bringing his friends together in a metonymy of gathered letter sheet that could serve as an approximate realization of the fancied reunion of his circle at the Rock

Creek tomb. Offhand as his proposal to Cameron may seem, it reflects a serious reconsideration of the terms of epistolary immortality, one that attenuates the Walpolian ambition but leaves it substantially intact. On such ground he addressed what he could still confidently look upon as the probable public destiny of his correspondence.

Conclusion
Letter Writing in the
Era of Telecommunications

· ·

Already, by cable, telegraph, and telephone, no two towns in
the civilized world are more than one hour apart. We have even
girdled the earth with a cablegram in twelve minutes. We have
made it possible for any man in New York City to enter into
conversation with any other New Yorker in twenty-one
seconds. We have not been satisfied with establishing such a
system of transportation that we can start any day for anywhere
from anywhere else; neither have we been satisfied with establishing such a system of communication that news and gossip
are the common property of all nations. We have gone farther.
We have established in every large region of population a
system of voice-nerves that puts every man at every other man's
ear, and which so magically eliminates the factor of distance
that the United States becomes three thousand miles of
neighbors, side by side.
—Herbert N. Casson, *The History of the Telephone*, 1910

Except where beginnings and endings are heralded by abrupt and
cataclysmic change, eras of human experience resist confinement to

neat chronological boundaries. Especially when we define a period by the prevalence of specific practices, the determination of the point at which one era ends and another begins is complicated by the fact that the continuation of old ways may long overlap with the inception and establishment of new. Even as Henry Adams lived, persisting in an epistolary practice that recalled distinctly eighteenth-century protocols of letter writing and letter exchanging, new technology-driven models of communication had sufficiently emerged that by 1910 the telephone already had a history and, in Herbert N. Casson, a prophetic historian. Given the lengthy coexistence of different orders of communications technology, the overlap of eras certainly characterizes the history and periodizing of letter writing.

When does the era of telecommunications begin? If we date it from the year that the first telegraphic cable was laid (1843), we find that Emerson and Dickinson lived at the beginning of this period and that Adams, in whose Washington residence a telephone was installed probably no later than 1908, lived at a time when the first true strands of what exists today as the global telecommunications network were being woven.[1] Although each exemplified the practice of earlier epistolary traditions, telecommunication was becoming a part of their worlds. "Yesterday the *time* all over the kingdom was reduced to Greenwich time," Emerson writes Thoreau in 1847, citing what would prove to be the first step toward the possibility of coordinated, reciprocal action taking place at far removes over a national, international, or intercontinental expanse.[2] "At Liverpool, where I was, the clocks were put forward 12 minutes. This had become quite necessary on account of the railroads which bind the whole country into swiftest connexion, and require so much accurate interlocking, intersection, & simultaneous arrival, that the difference of time produced confusion. . . . The proceeding effects of Electric telegraph will give a new importance to such arrangements" (LRWE 8:136). "However slow the steamer," Thoreau writes in response to this letter, skeptical, as we saw in chapter 1, of the very notion of a transatlantic communication, "no time intervenes between the writing and the reading of thoughts."[3] For Thoreau (as for a younger Emerson) the inherent necessity of a communication exempted it from such spatiotemporal considerations as slowness and celerity, and it is against such material innovations as steamship and telegraph that he affirms the fundamental ideality of thought.

For her part, Dickinson laments the slow and imperiled passage of letters in ways that recall similar lamentations in the letters of John

Winthrop, Abigail Adams, and other correspondents who wrote long before anyone had begun to dream of technology whereby people could communicate instantaneously over geographic space. Like Emerson and Thoreau, she imagines telepathic understandings that transcend time, space, and death. Nevertheless, she was able to characterize what in her day had already become an Information Age:

> Myself can read the Telegrams
> A Letter chief to me
> The Stock's advance and Retrograde
> And what the Markets say
>
> The Weather—how the Rains
> In Counties have begun.
> 'Tis News as null as nothing,
> But sweeter so—than none. (J 1089)

Read in conjunction with "The Way I read a Letter's—this—" (J 636), "Myself can read the Telegrams" argues that there is a qualitative difference between newer and older forms of communication and that the form affects the matter of communication. Ironic, equivocal, Dickinson suggests that ease, speed, and frequency of transmission render the content of messages proportionally less valuable, even if "News as null as nothing," given the human need to be informed by evidence of a world beyond the self's boundaries, be "sweeter so—than none."

Unlike Emily Dickinson, who is known to have communicated by telegraph only once and then only by proxy, Henry Adams made regular use of the telegraph, especially to announce his arrival in port or to confirm an intended rendezvous.[4] Death emerged as another and increasingly obligatory occasion for dispatching telegrams. "Bitterly sorry not to be with you," he cables John Hay from Paris on receiving word of the accidental death of Hay's son Adelbert in 1901, although the telegram did not substitute for the condolence that Adams duly wrote and sent the next day (LHA 5:258–59). Yet he could resort only to letter writing on learning by telegram of the death of George Cabot "Bay" Lodge in 1909, and his inability to make use of the swifter medium provides a measure of his isolation and grief. "I could not telegraph! No words would come" (LHA 6:266), he begins a letter to Lodge's mother, Anna Cabot Mills Lodge, explaining why he could not perform what by then had become a conventional response to such tidings. To Bay's widow, Elizabeth Davis Lodge, he takes the explanation further: "I have not telegraphed. Forgive me! I could not telegraph to *you* a miserable phrase without meaning, at a moment when I was helpless to say a word of encouragement even to myself" (LHA 6:267). Such apologies exhibit Adams's recognition that the speed of the telegraph might better have served his sense of urgency in getting a message conveyed even as they indicate a suspicion of the message—"a miserable phrase without meaning"—that the telegraph transmits and a preference for the longer and explicitly grieving condolence that arrives in the form of hand-inscribed letter sheet with what by new measures of expeditious transmission amounts to delay.

The clipped, compressed, paratactic nature of the telegraphic message was an object of passing fascination to Henry James, who in *Portrait of a Lady* portrays Ralph Touchett's initial awareness of Isabel Archer's existence as arising from cryptic references in the disjointed phrases of his mother's telegrams from America:

Tired America, hot weather awful, return England with niece, first steamer decent cabin.

Changed hotel, very bad, impudent clerk, address here. Taken sister's girl, died last year, go to Europe, two sisters, quite independent.

"They say women don't know how to write them," Ralph remarks to Lord Warburton, "but my mother has thoroughly mastered the art of condensation."[5] Ralph's quotation of what "they say" on the subject of women and telegrams suggests the degree to which this first medium of telecommunication was associated with male activities: commercial, political, journalistic, military—associations confirmed by Dickinson's "Myself can read the Telegrams." Yet Mrs. Touchett is at once congratulated and criticized for condensing syntax out of her utterance to the extent that her messages "admit of so many interpretations." (One phrase in particular—"quite independent"—is indeed to provide interpretive focus throughout *Portrait*.) In contrast not only to the language of telegrams but of much conventional correspondence as well, James's letters revel in the expansive and subordinated phrasing that characterizes his prose generally; like Adams's letters, James's typically unhurried missives define for themselves the time and space of writing. Even his telegrams resist the severities of condensation, as we see in his October 1912 dispatch to Logan Pearsall Smith: "Deeply regret have just been put to bed with bad attack of shingles where apparently I must remain for some days the doctor rigid and my sick condition fatal to any decent hospitality."[6] A half dozen modifiers might easily be trimmed from this message. Samuel Clemens, in responding to an 1866 invitation to lecture in Carson City, is far more succinct: "Been on sick list off now—I accept for Saturday with many thanks—will be there tomorrow."[7]

Perhaps it is ironic, then, that in 1892 Henry James should have been the means by which his sister Alice's last recorded utterance, which she whispered in his ear the day before she died, was telegraphed to William James in America: "Tenderest love to all farewell am going soon."[8] That her life's last message should be cabled rather than set down on letter sheet and sent by mail reflects a need to speed it on its way while it remains the living statement of the still undeceased speaker. Yet such a "need" is no doubt created as much as facilitated by a rapid transmission technology. Alice James's last words bear a resemblance to the telegraphlike message that Emily Dickinson sent from her deathbed to her Norcross cousins some ninety miles distant—but with this difference: Dickinson's farewell ("Called back") is in the simple past and represents a completed action, whereas the tense of Alice James's valediction—future with a modifier suggesting imminence ("am going soon")—implies that her death may not have occurred before the report of her condition has traversed the Atlantic, and that those to whom she sends love will be aware of her passing more or less as it transpires. The era of telecommunications has succeeded in making a sense of global simultaneity part of everyday awareness, and we can see that sense of simultaneity emerge in just such bulletins of family news as Henry James dispatched from England to his brother in America.

If the era of telecommunications begins long before the hand-inscribed exchange shows signs of receding, the perpetuation of older forms of correspondence extends well into the twentieth century and, despite the common perception that "nobody writes letters anymore," the older forms remain with us still. To be sure, the telephone long ago made obsolete the small change of correspondence—spontaneous invitations, lines sent to confirm or adjust a meeting time—and eliminated the multiple daily mails that kept up a rapid circulation of such messages within the late-nineteenth- and early-twentieth-century urban community. Although messages of this sort could always imply much more than they stated, the major function they performed has for over a century been served by technologies that expand the live conversation far beyond the small circumference in which a person may hear, speak, and be heard. Affordable long-distance telephone has undoubtedly reduced the volume of family letters and correspondence between friends committed to sustaining relationships over distances that prevent regular meeting. Moreover, the letter has become increasingly occasional and automated, as the genres of the greeting card and the Christmas family newsletter prove. Changing conditions in the experience of space and time have meanwhile lowered the intensity of the letter's older, genre-reflexive themes. Given the increasing ease with which distances are crossed and given the accessible alternative means of establishing and maintaining long-distance contact, twentieth-century letters less commonly lament the deathlike loss of a correspondent to the immensities of geographic space.

Problematic communications of a nonfamiliar or intimate character are still the province of a written exchange, as are many communications in which distance and formality need to be preserved. Some correspondents will surely continue to write letters in the interest of constructing and controlling certain forms of intimacy as well as creating the preservable record of a relationship. Perhaps the phobic relation that many individuals have been known to bear to the telephone—an aversion resulting in a preference for a slower, written communication—will be reconfirmed by voice mail and other deferrals that telephone users increasingly must negotiate; perhaps, too, such phobia will extend to the telephonelike dialogue of much e-mail. Whatever one's preferences, the concurrent existence of different orders of accessible epistolary media creates a situation in which practices overlap and interact and the choice of one medium over another is inherently meaningful. To write rather than call, to call rather than write, to write or not by e-mail are decisions made with respect to the time frame in which the message must be conveyed, the status of interpersonal relations, rhetorical advantages and disadvantages, and many other considerations more or less complicated.

Perhaps for many in the twentieth century, communication has proceeded by whatever means have happened to be available and the question of options has not always been very complicated. Options exist by improvisation: in the early 1960s, an Armenian immigrant who could not afford intercontinental telephone conversations and who in any case lived in fear of spies communicated by a code in which meaning was conveyed by the number and pattern of reciprocal telephone ringings.[9] Many others probably have made similar telegraphic use of the telephone, maintaining some form of contact with loved ones and associates in distant regions or countries. Considering what even at mid-century was the multitude of ways to maintain connections, it is surprising to learn of instances in which a life not deliberately reclusive has managed to become obscure. Withholdings of information, conspiracies of silence, are one thing, but instances in which an individual inadvertently disappears seem anomalous in a century that maximizes interpersonal access. Elie Wiesel relates an anecdote about letter writing, telephone calls, and lapsed contact that seems much more likely to have occurred in the late nineteenth than the middle of the twentieth century. "He died of cancer of the liver," he writes of his friend Itzu Junger. "But nobody told me. I thought he wasn't writing back to me because he was too busy, so I kept on writing for some time. Two or three years later I was in New York again and tried to get in touch, but his number had been disconnected. I called his sister in Brooklyn, and she burst into tears. I had been writing to a dead man."[10]

Given the increasingly compelling reality of electronic contiguity in everyday life, it is less likely now than ever before that one should lose track of someone with whom one is determined to remain in touch. Yet it is perilously easy for people who routinely speak telephonically or who regularly transmit and receive e-mail to assume that all other potential speakers and letter writers are likewise "wired"—that telephone and Internet totalize the world. For there remain, of course, large parts of the world unserved by the Internet, and even in affluent Western countries severely marginalized people (homeless persons, individuals confined in hospitals and prisons) generally lack access to electronic terminals and are thus excluded from the electronic community. Correspondence nevertheless exists for such people. For years, activist groups have encouraged individuals in the middle-class mainstream to correspond with prisoners. In *Dead Man Walking* (to cite what has become a well-known book), Sister Helen Prejean writes at length about her epistolary relations with death row inmates. A 1996 issue of *Friends Journal* carries an article that discusses protocol to observe in corresponding with prisoners and mental patients, and there exist Internet sites that solicit pen pals for inmates—an unusual instance of the electronic medium promoting an old-fashioned paper-and-ink epistolary exchange.[11] In the concerted efforts of people who regularly write to harshly isolated and deprivileged individuals, older forms of epistolary practice vigorously if marginally survive.

The endings and beginnings of eras are more matters of collective perception than verifiable realities. Until and unless postal systems and other opportunities to convey material correspondence disappear, it is unlikely that older forms of epistolary writing will absolutely cease. Yet it is undeniable that electronic correspondence has taken the place of much old-fashioned letter writing at the same time that it has innovated the conception and possibility of epistolary communication. Whether (to recall Emerson) electronic media may come to support a virtual "web of transcendentalism" or increasingly constitute a "heavy cobweb" of programmed interchange and commercial enterprise will persist for some time as an unsettled question. Nevertheless, very definite protocols and expectations have arisen among correspondents for whom electronic conversation has long since become second nature.

For those who accept the conventional proposition that "online *conversations* are really a cross between a letter and a phonecall," e-mail exists as a hybrid genre.[12] Many practitioners look upon e-mail as letter writing made easy, and for that reason, perhaps—as some contend—it has brought about a renaissance of the epistolary habit.[13] Judging by anecdotal evidence, the efficiency of electronic exchange and the comparatively instant gratification of same-day, same-hour, same-minute replies lower the threshold to epistolary activity, and more people are writing (or e-mailing) more people (who e-mail back) than they supposedly were at an earlier time. Such matters of perception are difficult to quantify. E-mail correspondence no doubt builds upon older traditions of letter writing but differs from pre-electronic practice in significant ways. As has already been noted, e-mail involves an exchange of text but not an exchange of materials associated by a metonymy of profound philosophical and theological resonance with the bodies and souls of the partners in the exchange. In the absence of a material exchange there generally exists an absence of record, as few e-mail correspondents appear to download—much less print—their online discussions. In the absence of a permanent record there can be no Walpolian ambition, and often there is little attention, even among literate and otherwise careful writers, to the form and correctness of their electronic prose. One observer suggests that e-mailers exploit the medium more or less consciously to defy the ideology of correctness in the interest of an uninhibited, self-disclosing discourse.[14]

E-mail exchanges, inasmuch as they rarely generate a permanent record and inasmuch as they encourage spontaneous talk-on-the-screen that people supposedly do not revise (although many undoubtedly do, if only to seem more spontaneous), indeed represent a partial merging of the familiar letter and the telephone conversation, an idea reflected technologically by the transmission of e-mail via telephone lines. But whereas the telephone conversation enlists the interlocutors' bodies as synchronous vocal presences, e-mail conversations retain the aspect of inscribed voices emanating from illuminated glass veils. An equivocal effort to put off the veil may be observed in the development of the emoticon, a genre of cybernetic expressiveness in which marks of punctuation simulate the human face in various stereotypic emotional states. As numerous online glossaries attest, the production and variation of emoticons accrues to a pidginized affective vocabulary. Yet the emoticon draws attention to the uniform, impersonal, and minimally personalizable scene of e-mail inscription: the computer screen, endlessly customizable but ever impervious to the impress of the body, private but ever subject to interception by the gaze of concealed third parties. For those, however, who believe in the metonymy of electronic community, the computer is coextensive with the body, and in an era that has seen continual and sophisticated mergings of person and machine, this hardly represents a novel instance in which humans have accepted and naturalized prosthetic extensions.

E-mail, it may be said, succeeds in preserving electronic communication as writing, and if the machine constitutes an extension of the written self it also serves as a rhetorically resistant epidermis. It remains to be seen whether the compelling direction of electronic contact is away from writing and more toward such electronically assisted investments of bodily presence as have long been with us in the form of the telephonic voice and televisual image. The personal computer has every capacity to merge telephone and television, yet it is difficult to imagine users abandoning the option of writing or the idea that they are more truly represented by a textual rather than an aural-visual metonymy. The interactive prosthesis of an immersive virtual reality— enabled by display helmet and wired bodysuit—is further still from any authentically epistolary motive. Granted that electronic contact continues to allow the option of written relationships, the truer question may be this: If epistolarity consists in a transmissible language, does it cease when the language is dominated by computer discourse, systemically omnipresent, prewritten as so many parameters, protocols, routines? Does the online computer itself constitute a self-designating presence to which users are obliged to come into relation, gaining identity and contiguity as they do so? Is that relation any more rigid than those letter writers have always been obliged to negotiate with letter sheet, ink, and the myriad conventions of the genre? Further: Does epistolarity require interaction with a "person," or is it enough to engage with some programmed response, be it advice concerning investments or sexually oriented chat?[15]

Given its efficiency in delivering simulacra of presence, one must ask finally how electronic epistolarity represents absence, love, and death, those features of common experience that occasion the letter genre and condition its themes. The absence of the beloved persists as a matter of lament; at least in that regard e-mail does not reinvent the love letter. Nor is the tradition reinvented by correspondents who fantasize elaborate fictions of romantic and erotic meeting, making reference to them as though they constituted a shared past experience, but whose relationships exist (by mutual preference) solely as a correspondence. Reviving the genres of epistolary fiction, some authors have begun to explore the poetics of e-mail romance, with emphasis chiefly upon the loneliness and delusion of those who would make a reality of electronic fantasy.[16] (Must it not prove inevitable that corresponding literary couples will explore the possibility of publishing their fantasized romances as online novels in open-ended serial form?) If the love letter has been innovated by e-mail, the novelty perhaps has to do with the reduction of temporal intervals between dispatches, the dense instantaneity of incoming and outgoing mail creating speaking presences qualitatively different from those produced by two persons writing and responding in the slower rhythms of a material exchange. Such speaking presences are very powerful: the disruptive potential of e-mail "affairs" is evinced by the existence of support groups for people who have been drawn into addictive Internet relationships. Such relationships no doubt conjure absences that they proceed to fill with the drama of a regular and invigorating exchange.

Just as the love letter has moved to the Internet, so too the condolence. Anecdotal evidence suggests that news of a death prompts e-mail messages bearing traditional formulas in statements variously brief and voluble; we may assume that these expressions support the bereaved in the general ways that personal condolences have always done so. For innovation one must look to the appearance of Internet pages that generate condolences, such as the Web site through which American citizens were invited to express sympathy with the Israeli people following the assassination of Yitzhak Rabin or those through which the international community was provided the opportunity to grieve alongside the British following the death of Princess Diana. The massive accumulation of messages in such formats raises the question of audience: Are there individuals, not to mention collective entities (the Israeli people, the British people), who read these condolences and are moved by them? Is there something inherently condoling in the sheer number of messages pouring in from abroad? Clearly the sum of all those individual messages is greater than the parts: in the Diana Web sites especially, the spectacle of millions of people focused on a seemingly singular grief blurs the line between condoler and condoled, and those who write the brief messages are given the option to read a selection of previous condolences.[17]

The blurring of addresser and addressee, sender and receiver, is similarly if less spectacularly evident in the dozens of memorial "walls" rushed onto the Internet at any celebrity's demise. What people write at such sites commonly takes epistolary form: "Allen," a mourner contributes to one of several walls commemorating the life of Allen Ginsberg, "We look to you deep in the Earth's atmosphere. Thank you."[18] Yet any life, given the freedom of the Internet, may be the subject of electronic celebration, and the anonymous surfer is invited to intrude upon what seem to be the private occasions of oddly publicized grief. The already numerous online memorials, modeled in part on those traditionally published in the classified section of local newspapers, generally combine homage to the deceased as a departed third person with some gesture of addressing the dead as "you." The Internet, however, introduces an element of mysticism: "I will always miss her and I hope she has a way of reading this because I love you mum." This expression appears on a page at the Virtual Heaven Web site, one of several "cemeteries in cyberspace" that allow grieving parties to establish "virtual gravesites." Virtual Heaven does not claim to reunite loved ones, but it does establish a place for the inscription of memory and grief; as "place," it is sufficiently immaterial and utopian that mourners use it to write letters to the dead as though it served as a post office to the next world: "Remember dad I said one day I would get a computer? I did but I never thought that I could write you in heaven. I know you are both there. I miss you a lot. Maybe this will help, that I can talk to you this way."[19]

What people actually "believe" and what they entertain as consoling if improbable notions may not in the end be very different. That the Internet is readily invested with mystical properties is not surprising given its essential immateriality, its global reach, and its insistent self-designation as utopian image and other-world alternative. Underlying its magnetic glamour, its appeal as a window of sensuous and spiritual escape, is its enticing unknowability: one never knows who or what one may encounter, or what force directs one in the path of a meeting, although one person's desire for companionship and fantasy is bound to be confirmed and requited by another's. The mystical appeal of the Internet derives in large measure from our inability to comprehend its reality and possibility—the intellectual incapacity of any one person (as Jameson has observed) "to map the great global multinational and de-centered communicational network in which we find ourselves caught as individual subjects."[20] To be "caught" in such a seemingly nonbind-ing "web" converts unknowability into ostensible liberation; the meta-phors of "web" and "net" emphasize the act of weaving, of creating contiguities, rather than the fate of being entrapped, and the libera-tionist thesis is reinforced by such figures as "surfing" and "navigat-ing," what "individual subjects" equipped with "personal computers" are empowered to do. Thus we enter this finite epistolary medium whose limits never cohere in a recognizable boundary. Ideologically, the Internet avoids producing images of the entrapments by which it, as any medium, encases those who look to it for assurances of identity and purpose. It is far too committed to convincing its users of their infinite mobility and connectedness to represent itself as a field of material constraints.

The dream of instantaneous contact is, we have seen, an old one. To overcome the body's mortal confinement to time and space, to over-come the body, to reconstitute it as a soul that can extend at will through time and space as though the heaven of eternal meeting were almost at hand, is a longed-for condition in much of the writing we have examined. We may question whether our telecommunications technology could ever facilitate a nearer realization of that ideal. Yet it is clear that the ideal itself affords measures of intrinsic satisfaction— that for e-mail adepts as for Emerson, Dickinson, and Adams, episto-lary solitude is often preferable to the face-to-face contact that one projects but ventures to achieve only at considerable peril. One could readily argue that e-mail and Internet contacts perfect the process by which human relations are rendered into simulacra, answering the desire for an imperious privacy populated by evidence of other lives. But one could argue as well that epistolary practices have always traded in simulacra more or less representative of the conditions and aspira-tions of those who correspond, have always relied on utopian fantasy, and have always imaged relations that can only exist in and by virtue of the epistolary text. Correspondence in any form does not concern truth but contiguities mediated by a metonymy of contacts. E-mail as currently practiced would certainly seem to confirm the decline if not the death of a preservable literary tradition. As a social genre, however, it should be judged as any epistolary medium should be judged: by the complexity and satisfaction of contact, by its power to organize and cultivate relations, and by the space it provides for imagining the ways in which one may exist in reciprocity with others.

Notes

· · · · · · · ·

INTRODUCTION

1. A useful history of the American postal service and its effect on life in the United States is provided in Wayne E. Fuller, *The American Mail: Enlarger of the Common Life*.

2. On the emergence of instantaneous communications in American life, see Kern, *The Culture of Time and Space: 1880–1918*, especially 65–70. See also Pool, *Social Impact of the Telephone*, especially Suzanne Keller, "The Telephone in New (and Old) Communities."

3. In *Gossip* (83–85), Patricia Meyer Spacks discusses the "prurience" and "moral vertigo" involved in the reading of other people's mail, as well as the legitimation of such reading effected by the "fact of publication." However, there are different facts of publication, and the legitimation Spacks refers to is less apt to be questioned when it takes the form of a scholarly edition of letters than, say, the cannibalization of a personal correspondence such as takes place in Robert Lowell's poem sequence, *The Dolphin* (1973). In *A Letter Book* (1922), George Saintsbury, referring to love letters in particular, articulates the complacency that commonly accompanies the violation of epistolary privacy: "There are, it is to be hoped, few people who read such letters (unless they are of such a date that Time has exercised his strange power of resanctifying desecration and making private property public) without an unpleasant consciousness of eavesdropping" (90). In publishing and perusing correspondence in any form, we appropriate without necessarily respecting what the letter writers themselves often held to be an inviolably private realm. On the firm distinction in nineteenth-century America between public and private worlds, see Lystra, *Searching the Heart: Women, Men, and Romantic Love in Nineteenth-Century America*, 17–18, 88–120.

4. Charles Vandersee notes that "a sampling of the language of assessment" of familiar letters "exposes it as paltry and even embarrassing. Letters are 'engaging,' 'revealing,' 'charming,' often 'informal' and 'chatty.' They are 'witty,' 'lively,' 'spontaneous.' They are 'vivid,' 'brilliant,' 'evocative.' They 'fill in gaps' in the author's life; they 'show the circumstances' behind the creation of the author's well-known works—novels, plays, treatises. They 'remove the facade' and show the author 'at home,' 'unbuttoned,' 'exposed to our scrutiny.' They welcome us into her drawing room, her boudoir even, her kitchen, the privacy of her 'inner circle'" ("Theorizing the Letter: An Editor's Speculations," 5).

5. See Altman, "The Letter Book as a Literary Institution, 1539–1789: Toward a Cultural History of Published Correspondence in France," 19. On the transformation of letters when they appear in print, see Spacks, *Gossip*, 70–71, who cites the relevance to this matter of Walter Benjamin's well-known observations in "Art in an Age of Mechanical Reproduction."

6. For a discussion of the letter as reflection and instrument of destabilized systems of social identity in late nineteenth- and early twentieth-century America, see Jacobson, *Authority and Alliance in the Letters of Henry Adams*, 3–6, 114–32. As Jacobson observes, for Henry Adams and his contemporaries, "the letter straddled a set of rhetorical boundaries which were crucial to the conditions of transition taking place during this period: between public and private; between literary and nonliterary; between elite and democratic discourse. If its location at these boundaries clouded the letter's formal status, that marginality also gave the letter substantial advantages in the management of transition, especially as a source of strategies of resistance and control" (3–4). In addition to demonstrating the letter's social and political instrumentality in the correspondence of Henry Adams, Jacobson also examines its deployment in the hands of Walt Whitman and Alice James. Another fascinating example of the letter providing "a source of strategies of resistance and control" is *Sister to Sister: Letters Written by Fannie Reed to Her Twin Sister Eliza Crawford, 1894–1904*, edited by Janis L. Pallister. These very nonliterary letters document the efforts of a middle-class midwestern woman to hold her life and family together against the tuberculosis that kills her husband and eventually herself and the poverty into which she, her husband, and children progressively fall. The collection is accompanied by Suzanne L. Bunkers's excellent "Reading and Interpreting the Letters of Fannie Reed."

7. See Derrida, *The Post Card*, 64–67; Landow, *Hypertext: The Convergence of Contemporary Critical Theory and Technology*.

8. Jakobson writes: "Following the path of contiguous relationships, the Realist author metonymically digresses from the plot to the atmosphere and from the characters to the setting in space and time" (111). See "Two Aspects of Language and Two Types of Aphasic Disturbances," in Roman Jakobson, *Language in Literature*, 95–114.

9. Derrida, *The Post Card*, 124. In the final paragraphs of "Bartleby the Scrivener," Herman Melville suggests what the specter of the dead-letter office might have been for nineteenth-century Americans: "Dead letters! does it not sound like dead men? . . . by the cart-load they are annually burned. Sometimes from out the folded paper the pale clerk takes a ring:—the finger it was meant for, perhaps, moulders in the grave; a bank note sent in swiftest charity:—he whom it would relieve, nor eats nor hungers any more; pardon for those who died despairing; hope for those who died unhoping; good tidings for those who died stifled by unrelieved calamities. On errands of life, these letters speed to death" (*The Piazza Tales and Other Prose Pieces, 1839–1860*, 45).

10. See Barbara Herrnstein Smith, *On the Margins of Discourse*, 23–24, and Redford, *The Converse of the Pen: Acts of Intimacy in the Eighteenth-Century Familiar Letter*, 9.

11. In "The Veto of the Imagination: A Theory of Autobiography," Renza (building implicitly on Paul de Man's argument in "Autobiography as De-facement") discusses the preemption of the unique individual's narrative by the generic first-

person discourse of autobiographical narrative and of the various strategies by which the first-person writer insists "on the self-referentiality of his 'I' made in the face of writing's law of gravity: namely, that writing about his own existence iron- ically entails a denial of this existence *as* his own and thus as a secure referential source for such writing" (279). Writing in one of the most formatted of auto- biographical genres, letter writers exhibit many strategies to resist what Renza calls "writing's law of gravity," even as they willingly join the commonality—the release from onerous uniqueness—that a first-person genre promotes. The theoretical is- sues involved in the convergence of autobiographical narrative and letter writing are explored in chap. 6, "Writing the Life in Dialogue: Letters, Epistolary Novels, and Imaginary Conversations," of Grubgeld's *George Moore and the Autogenous Self: The Autobiography and Fiction*.

12. Derrida, *The Post Card*, 48.

CHAPTER ONE

1. With no apology and with little thought of a possible confusion of genres, Henry Clay Bear, a private in the 116th Illinois Voluntary Infantry from 1862 to 1865, explains to his wife that he will keep a notebook diary to be sent to her when completed: "My little woman, I intend to fill this book up with things that take place, that is evry day occurances. I then intend to send it to you in an envelope as a letter." All that was involved in converting the book to a letter was the removal of a back cover that would prevent it from fitting inside the envelope (*The Civil War Letters of Henry C. Bear*, 6, 9). Bear sent several such "books" to his wife during the war.

2. Redford, *The Converse of the Pen: Acts of Intimacy in the Eighteenth-Century Familiar Letter*, 8.

3. Jameson, *The Political Unconscious: Narrative as a Socially Symbolic Act*, 106. Jame- son goes on to observe that contemporary genre criticism appears to divide between semantic (visionary, thematic) and syntactic (structural) approaches to identifying genre (107). (In *Epistolarity: Approaches to a Form*, Janet Gurkin Altman places these two major approaches among several others; see 190–93.) My discussion reflects both approaches but privileges, finally, the semantic inasmuch as I believe that the epistolary occasion (and the visions of the world that proceed therefrom) remains uneffaced when authentic letters become published texts, although the process involves semantic as well as syntactic transformations.

4. A more elaborate definition of the genre is offered by Charles A. Porter in the foreword to his important collection of essays in *Yale French Studies*, *Men / Women of Letters*.

5. The travel letters of the young Samuel Clemens to his family in Missouri rarely advert to spatiotemporal anxiety. Many of Henry Adams's travel letters, early and late, evince confidence and joy in their writer's existing at vast removes from family and friends.

6. Over the past two decades there has been much outstanding work on episto- lary fiction and on the inscription of the female voice in both authentic and fictional epistolary forms. See Altman, *Epistolarity: Approaches to a Form*; Kauffman, *Discourses of Desire* and *Special Delivery*; and Goldsmith, *Writing the Female Voice*.

7. See Altman, "The Letter Book as a Literary Institution, 1539–1789," 53, and

Showalter, "Authorial Self-Consciousness in the Familiar Letter: The Case of Madame de Graffigny," 123.

8. Examining works like Richardson's *Clarissa* and Hannah Foster's *The Coquette* after reading authentic correspondence, one immediately notices an absence among fictional letters of the insistent spatiotemporal referencing that characterizes a genuine epistolary exchange.

9. For a discussion of "the generic crossing between letter-writing manuals and conduct books," see Bodenheimer, *The Real Life of Mary Ann Evans: George Eliot, Her Letters and Fiction*, 10–11. Despite a decline in the volume of routine, personal correspondence mediated by hand-inscribed letter sheet, conduct and advice books continue to take epistolary form in the late twentieth century; for example, Gladys Denny Shultz, *Letters to a New Generation: For Today's Inquiring Teen-Age Girl* (1971); G. Kingsley Ward, *Letters of a Businessman to His Son* (1990).

10. In *The Letters of the Republic: Publication and the Public Sphere in Eighteenth-Century America*, Michael Warner identifies the epistolary pamphlet as one of the two "most popular genres for political debate" during the colonial era, but is careful to distinguish such writings from anything like private correspondence. "The pamphlet is not a personal letter, and *must* not be, in the conditions of the public sphere of representational politics. Writing's unrestricted dissemination appears here as the ground of politics because in its very contrast with personal presence it allows a difference between public discourse and private correspondence." Correspondents in such debate "encounter the exchange *not as a relation between themselves as men, but rather as their own mediation by a potentially limitless discourse*" (40). Warner's distinction usefully highlights the contemporary public engagement of epistolary pamphlets, letters to editors, open letters to public officials or prominent "private" individuals, and the like. Nevertheless, the present study argues that the familiar letter, a socially constructed, publishable, if also personal and private form, is itself always "a potentially limitless discourse" that serves in the short term to mediate writers. A curious additional hybrid that blurs the line between private and public is the letter exchange published without authorization to embarrass a public figure. A notable example is *Correspondence between the Hon. John Adams, Late President of the United States, and the Late Wm. Cunningham, Esq. beginning in 1803, and ending in 1813*—an exchange in which John Adams writes derogatorily but in presumed confidence of Thomas Jefferson—published in 1823 in an effort to sabotage John Quincy Adams's campaign for the presidency (see Cappon, *The Adams-Jefferson Letters*, 2:600–602).

11. Dublin, *Farm to Factory: Women's Letters, 1830–1860*, 42. Statements regarding the necessary confidentiality of romantic and erotic utterance commonly appear in nineteenth-century love letters; as Lystra notes, secrecy enhanced the eros of the epistolary exchange (*Searching the Heart*, 90–91).

12. Early and late in their correspondence, John Adams and Thomas Jefferson were aware of the susceptibility of their letters to interception, whether by foreign agents monitoring the activities of American diplomats (some of their dispatches of the war period are written in code) or by local postmasters wishing to eavesdrop on the conversation of the two former presidents. "I presume that our correspondence has been observed at the post offices, and thus has attracted notice," Jefferson writes to Adams in a letter of August 10–11, 1815. "Would you believe that a printer has had the effrontery to propose to me the letting him publish it? These people think

they have a right to everything however secret or sacred." "That our correspondence has been observed is no Wonder," Adams replies in a letter of August 24, "for your hand is more universally known than your face. No Printer has asked me for copies: but it is no Surprize that you have been requested" (Cappon, *The Adams-Jefferson Letters*, 2:453, 455). The unauthorized publication of letters is a contingency for which prominent persons become more or less prepared; see n. 10.

13. In his capacity as editor of his friend John Hay's letters, Henry Adams writes Whitelaw Reid in February 1907: "I feel no great hesitation in ignoring the order to 'burn when read,' because I believe it meant only as a safe-guard during his life-time, and if I wrote it on letters of my own, I should regard it as equivalent to 'personal' or 'private'" (LHA 6:46). "'Brûle mes lettres'" Martine Reid quotes Stendhal as constantly repeating to his sister Pauline, "only to order her immediately thereafter to preserve them carefully, and above all to shun all prying eyes" ("Correspondences: *Stendhal en toutes lettres*," 153).

14. See Altman, "The Letter Book as a Literary Institution, 1539–1789," 32–33, and Hornbeak, *The Complete Letter-Writer in English 1568–1800*.

15. Showalter, "Authorial Self-Consciousness in the Familiar Letter," 114.

16. See *Selected Letters of Samuel Richardson*, 64. Richardson, for whom the embodiment of the letter writer in the letter was of absorbing interest, provides astute commentary on this matter. Ever aware of the degree to which correspondence may proceed from the libido, he suggests that the autograph may invoke a platonic if emphatically physical presence and foster a celibate if nevertheless eroticized relationship. Writing to Sophia Westcomb, he observes that, while he reads her letter, "I have you before me in person: I converse with you, and your dear Anna, as arm in arm you traverse the happy terrace: kept myself at humble distance, more by my own true respect of you both, than by your swimming robes"; on such grounds he celebrates the "pen that makes distance, presence" (65). In a subsequent letter that acknowledges the sexual field into which an unscrupulous male correspondent may draw his female partner, Richardson asks Westcomb whether "a virtuous and innocent heart [should still] be afraid of having its Impulses *embody'd*, as I may say?" (68). The implication is that the letter embodies virtue and innocence in a form that remains comparatively inviolable.

17. See Ellmann, *Selected Letters of James Joyce*, 160–95.

18. See Altman, "The Letter Book as a Literary Institution, 1539–1789," 35. In the United States such commemoration has been informed by an ideology in which the unique person at some level embodies universal democratic individuality.

19. For a brief history of documentary editing, literary and historical, see Kline, *A Guide to Documentary Editing*, chap. 1.

20. Davis, *Memoirs of Aaron Burr*, vi. That an editor would thus congratulate himself on destroying a part of a correspondence is apt to shock readers of a later era, but it is well to recall the sacrosanct character that the nineteenth century ascribed to the private life as well as the genteel disposition to protect a person's honor. Acts of more or less radical suppression were intended to protect privacy and honor from scandal sheet reductiveness. It is noteworthy that when Charles Eliot Norton published what must strike us as his heavily edited *Correspondence of Thomas Carlyle and Ralph Waldo Emerson* in 1883, he was criticized for not having systematically omitted proper names and for printing unflattering commentary about persons still living (see CEC 68).

21. Adams explains that the emphasis of *The Life of Albert Gallatin* is on Gallatin's "political and public career, which is to be best treated by itself and is the main object of this work" (68).

22. Burnett, *Letters of Members of the Continental Congress*, xiv.

23. See Kline, *A Guide to Documentary Editing*, 4–6.

24. Comparison of virtually any passage in Edward Emerson's edition of the Emerson-Sterling correspondence with its counterpart in the Rusk and Tilton edition of Emerson's letters reveals the heavy-handed editorial intervention of the earlier volume. Comparison of the letters in Charles Eliot Norton's edition of the Emerson-Carlyle correspondence with those of the later (and far more inclusive) edition of Joseph Slater reveals the same thing. Yet even fairly recent volumes bear the marks of invasive shaping: the letters of Wallace Stevens, edited by his daughter, the letters of Flannery O'Connor, edited by a friend with whom she maintained a long correspondence, and the letters of Sylvia Plath, edited by her mother, all offer selected and in many cases partial texts of letters.

25. Standard expositions of the principles and preferred techniques of modern textual editing may be found in Bowers, "Transcriptions of Manuscripts: The Record of Variants"; Tanselle, "The Editing of Historical Documents" and "Textual Scholarship"; and Kline, *A Guide to Documentary Editing*.

26. Viola Hopkins Winner states explicitly what the design of the six-volume Harvard edition everywhere suggests: that Adams's letters constitute "a major literary work equal to, if not surpassing, *The Education of Henry Adams* and *Mont-Saint-Michel and Chartres*" ("Style and Sincerity in the Letters of Henry Adams," 91). Charles Vandersee, proposing that we view letters less as "'portal' to a congenial hearth or private boudoir" and more as "load-bearing wall," declares that "the letters of a human being are a necessary part of the structure of the person's achievement in art and thought" ("Theorizing the Letter: An Editor's Speculations," 5).

27. In conjunction with their efforts to recover the aesthetics and ideology of the Dickinson holograph, Martha Nell Smith and others have recently raised serious objections to Thomas Johnson's standard edition of the Dickinson letters. See *Rowing in Eden: Rereading Emily Dickinson*.

28. See Clemens, *Mark Twain's Letters*, 1:xxvi.

29. My observations here are indebted to George P. Landow, who, in *Hypertext: The Convergence of Contemporary Critical Theory and Technology*, explores hypermedia as the practical realization of the Derridean view of the text as open-bordered and commended to reader domination. Letter texts, like texts generated within word-processing protocols, embrace an unstable and emphatically readerly textuality irreconcilable with the materiality and ideology of the book. That epistolary writing and hypertext converge in e-mail should not be surprising.

30. Hawthorne, *The Letters, 1813–1843*, 1:461.

31. "Tears are signs, not expressions," writes Barthes from the point of view of the speaking (not necessarily inscribing) lover, and affirms that his addressee thereby "receives the 'truest' of messages, that of my body, not that of my speech" (*A Lover's Discourse*, 182). Invoking Barthes, Linda Kauffman traces the motif of the tear- and bloodstained missive in "amorous epistolary discourse" to Roman and Greek antiquity. See *Discourses of Desire*, 36–37, 39.

32. Hawthorne, *The Letters, 1813–1843*, 1:449.

33. *The Letters of Margaret Fuller*, 1:303. "The sight of your well known hand writing in your favour of 25. Feb. last," John Adams writes to Thomas Jefferson on March 10, 1823, "gave me great pleasure, as it proved your arm to be restored and your pen still manageable" (Cappon, *The Adams-Jefferson Letters*, 2:590). "Tho' my hand is shaking (as you sadly notice)," Carlyle writes to Emerson on June 14, 1865, "I determine to write you a little Note today" (CEC 543). "My nerves are a wreck and I sleep as I best can," Henry Adams writes to Elizabeth Cameron on December 1, 1916, in the last letter he inscribed before adopting the practice of dictating his letters. "You can see all this in my hand, but I cling to these signs of my actual health so as to relieve myself of the trouble of talking about it" (LHA 6:741).

34. Handwriting of course does more than image bodily presence. Before the typewriter came into common use in business and personal writing, penmanship was invested with moral and social significance. In chapter 4, "Literacy, Education, and the Reader," of *Revolution and the Word: The Rise of the Novel in America*, Cathy N. Davidson discusses the popular cultivation in the early republic of this particular manifestation of personal literacy: "A fine hand, the writing masters all insisted, not only proclaimed a fine character, but also improved one's prospects in life" (68). It is not unusual to find letters abounding in nonstandard features written with a perfect hand.

35. In "Giving Weight to Words: Madame de Sévigné's Letters to Her Daughter," Goldsmith observes that "Seventeenth-century authors of epistolary manuals [in French] regularly tell their readers that in writing a letter they must imagine they are speaking" (96). In Crèvecoeur's *Letters from an American Farmer*, James, the fictional Pennsylvania farmer, is encouraged to correspond with Mr. F.B. by the latter's assurance "that writing letters is nothing more than talking on paper" (13). In his influential *Lectures on Rhetoric and Belles Lettres* (1783), Hugh Blair articulates the Ciceronian view of Augustan correspondents when he defines letter writing as "conversation carried on upon paper, between two friends at a distance" (2:297). On the letter as written conversation in the eighteenth century and after, see Redford, *The Converse of the Pen*, 1–7, and Spacks, *Gossip*, 77. Nineteenth-century American letter writers commonly affect conversation in their intimate correspondences. Beginning a letter to his future wife, Emily Norcross, Edward Dickinson rejoices "at an opportunity of holding even a short & hasty *paper interview* with one for whom I feel so peculiar an interest," and Emily Norcross begins a letter to Edward thus: "Late as it is I cannot excuse myself without conversing awhile with you" (*A Poet's Parents: The Courtship Letters of Emily Norcross and Edward Dickinson*, 28, 87). Writing to her cousin, Louisa Sawyer, a Lowell, Massachusetts, factory worker, remarks: "It is a long time since I have seen or heard from you but believing I am not forgotten I will chatt awhile this eve with you" (Dublin, *Farm to Factory*, 69). "My Dear Darling: This is the sixth letter I have commenced to you this week," writes Warren Akin, a Georgia representative in the Congress of the Confederate States of America meeting at Richmond, Virginia, to his wife Mary in December 1864. ". . . Are you not mistaken when you sometimes say I dont talk to you? I'm sure I have held sweet converse with you every day this week, to a considerable extent" (*Letters of Warren Akin: Confederate Congressman*, 63). For more examples of familiar letters of common people affecting conversation, see Lystra, *Searching the Heart*, 21–22. In *The Real Life of Mary Ann Evans*, Bodenheimer observes that "the state of solitary writing is essentially dif-

ferent from the action of dialogue. The act of writing creates by its nature a different kind of self-representation than a conversation" (10). As the discussion in chapters 2–5 recurrently demonstrates, letter writers—both more and less literate—recognize this difference, however eagerly they may conflate letter writing and face-to-face dialogue, and thus prize what they often project as the utopian clarity and intimacy of the communication that the written exchange allows.

36. Examples: To Henry V. Emmons (LED 1:246); to Eudocia C. Flynt (LED 2:414); to Mrs. Henry Hills (LED 3:788).

37. *The Poetical Works and Other Writings of John Keats*, 7:157, 8:4. Discussing *Memoirs of a Woman of Pleasure*, *Clarissa*, *Ulysses*, *Liaisons dangereuses*, as well as Flaubert's correspondence, Julia Epstein explores the ways in which "letters circulate as icons of sexual desire. The suspended impatience of epistolary anticipation, delay, and receipt stand in textually for sexual tension and its release" ("Fanny's Fanny: Epistolarity, Eroticism, and the Transsexual Text," 139). Keats's phrase, "make it rich as a draft of poppies," lends to the kiss a dimension of euthanasia developed in the odes, while the preterite phrasing of "where yours have been" concedes that such a letter comes bearing an action already past. In connecting, the correspondents have nevertheless missed one another.

38. "The original letter, in the Dilke Collection," writes Keats's editor, "is very much discoloured, perhaps through the operations of the Health Office" (8:248). Writing in quarantine during his month-long smallpox inoculation, John Adams implores Abigail Smith to be sure that the letters he sends her—which he smokes at his end before dispatching—are smoked again before they are read (John Adams to Abigail Smith, April 13, 1764; AFC 1:29). Henry Clay Bear provides another striking example of the letter artifact exporting the bodily trace. "You see the edges of this book is colored," he writes his wife in the December 13, 1862, entry of his first diary letterbook to her. "It is colored by my swet. When we stoped here there was not a dry stich on my shirt. I had it in my shirt pocket and it was perfectly wet when I took it out" (*The Civil War Letters of Henry C. Bear*, 8).

39. Holmes, *Covered Wagon Women: Diaries and Letters from the Western Trails, 1840–1890*, 1:35, 38.

40. Dublin, *Farm to Factory*, 45.

41. *The Correspondence of Henry David Thoreau*, 199, 203.

42. Ibid., 205.

43. Ibid., 207. Cf. Derrida: "I will swim in your name without turning back, but you will never be your name, you never have been, even when, and especially when you have answered to it. The name is made to do without the life of the bearer, and is therefore always somewhat the name of someone dead" (*The Post Card*, 39).

44. Hawthorne, *The Letters, 1813–1843*, 1:492.

45. Ibid., 606.

46. *The Death and Letters of Alice James*, 107–8. An example of death not so much enabling as forcibly compelling epistolary communication is the condolence Abigail Adams writes to Thomas Jefferson on the occasion of his daughter Mary Jefferson Eppes's death in 1804, the initiation of an agonized, short-lived correspondence that aired differences but achieved no reconciliation. Having nursed a bitter resentment to her former friend over issues both political and personal, Adams is moved in spite of herself when she learns of the death of the young woman for whom she had

served briefly as foster parent seventeen years earlier in London: "It has been some time since that I conceived of any event in this Life, which could call forth, feelings of mutual sympathy. But I know how closely entwined around a parents heart, are those chords which bind the filial to the parental Bosom, and when snaped assunder, how agonizing the pangs of seperation" (Cappon, *The Adams-Jefferson Letters*, 1:269). As she mourns the loss of one whom she had known as "a child of nine years of age . . . seperated from her Friends, and country," Adams tacitly recalls the death of her son Charles four years earlier.

47. See Cox, "Henry Adams and the Apocalyptic Never," 144.

48. For Elizabeth Cameron's response to such letters, see chap. 5 at n. 24.

49. Slater provides detailed accounts of Emerson's anticipation of a published edition of his exchange with Carlyle and of Conway's successful efforts to copy the texts of stolen letters still in the possession of black market dealers. See CEC 64–66.

50. Henry James, *Letters*, 4:541.

51. Ibid., 806.

52. Henry James, "The Correspondence of Carlyle and Emerson."

53. See Sewall, *The Life of Emily Dickinson*, 2:750–51.

54. Adams at this time begs Cameron not to leave his letters "knocking about, as a mash for the female pigs who feed out of the magazine-troughs at five dollars a page, to root in, for scandal and gossip" (LHA 5:103). This misogynistic projection of the potential readership of his letters sharply contrasts with that of 1860, in which he imagines readers (gender not specified) who will turn to his letters out of a dignified interest in a great republic's history.

CHAPTER TWO

1. Quoted in Bradford, *Of Plymouth Plantation 1620–1647*, 179.

2. See Wayne E. Fuller, *The American Mail*, 12–15, 47–48, and chap. 3. John Adams notes what he considers to be the surprising efficiency in the passage of mail between Quincy and Monticello soon after he and Thomas Jefferson have resumed epistolary relations in 1812 (Cappon, *The Adams-Jefferson Letters*, 2:293–94). In 1813 he remarks to Jefferson that "it is a pleasure to discover that We are only 9 days apart" (2:333).

3. *War Letters of William Thompson Lusk*, 197–98.

4. Van Doren, *The Letters of Benjamin Franklin and Jane Mecom*, 81.

5. Woolman, *The Journal and Major Essays*, 183–84.

6. Wayne E. Fuller, *American Mail*, 47–48, 66–67.

7. See Cott, *The Bonds of Womanhood: "Woman's Sphere" in New England, 1780–1835*, chap. 3, "Education"; and Davidson, *Revolution and the Word: The Rise of the Novel in America*, chap. 4, "Literacy, Education, and the Reader." In the "Memoir" of his grandmother that he appends to the second edition of *Letters of Mrs. Adams* (1840), Charles Francis Adams reflects upon the home curriculum of Abigail Adams and the valuable "species of exercise" that letter writing constituted (1:xxix). See chap. 5, n. 4, below.

8. Wayne E. Fuller, *American Mail*, 42–45.

9. In this book I draw examples from five volumes of Civil War letters that together represent most of the divided country's major regions as well as a broad

range of class and education. Surviving letters from African American soldiers to their families are extremely rare; in *A Grand Army of Black Men: Letters from African-American Soldiers in the Union Army, 1861–1865*, Edwin S. Redkey reprints a selection of letters written to black newspapers such as the *Christian Recorder* and the *Weekly Anglo-African*. Excerpts from prefaces of two privately printed editions of Civil War letters have much to say regarding the cultural use of such texts:

> These letters have been put into print, that a story of heroism might be handed down. . . . Threaded through them is a sturdy philosophy which puts forward the bright side of life to face all obstacles. (*War Letters of William Thompson Lusk*, 1)

> As you read, you will see that this was a family of earnest Americans, having no other thought at that time, than to give themselves and their possessions freely— as thousands of other families did—to the service of the men in the field. Some of you were little children then, most of you were not born. You know nothing of the history of the great national sin, slavery, which led to the war, and can never understand the spirit with which a great multitude, ourselves among them, en-tered into this struggle, unless you can detect it in the first chapter of this story. . . . To you your own land is made sacred by the death of half a million steadfast men, and by the thought of the thousands and thousands of broken-hearted women at home, who quietly acquiesced in sacrifice out of love and loyalty to their country's flag. (Bacon and Howland, *Letters of a Family during the War for the Union, 1861–1865*, viii)

10. A passage from the preface to *Frost's Original Letter-Writer* (1867) gives one a good idea of the audience to whom letter-writers were marketed: "in spite of the universal need and craving for such intercourse, there are vast numbers of people who seldom write or read a letter, and who, when the want is felt, are deeply sensible of their own deficiency. Many who handle the saw or hammer daily, will shrink from attempting to wield a pen, and feel that their own want of practice will cause them to make blunders that will excite the ridicule of their correspondent. It is to these more especially that this little book is dedicated, hoping that it will fill a long felt void" (13).

11. *The Journal of Christopher Columbus*, 168–69.

12. Zamora, "Christopher Columbus's 'Letter to the Sovereigns': Announcing the Discovery," 3–7.

13. Ibid., 7.

14. Lane, "To Sir Francis Walsingham," 202–3.

15. Lane, "To Sir Philip Sidney," 204–5.

16. Everett Emerson, *Letters from New England: The Massachusetts Bay Colony, 1629–1638*, 70.

17. Ibid., 72.

18. Ibid., 71.

19. Ibid., 63.

20. Ibid., 64.

21. Ibid., 65.

22. Ibid., 66.

23. Ibid., 68.

24. Ibid., 64.

25. Ibid., 66.

26. Ibid., 87.

27. Ibid., 45.

28. Ibid., 85–86.

29. Quoted in Bradford, *Of Plymouth Plantation*, 368. Such letters were received with eagerness and gratitude. "I desire that you will be as frequent in your letters as you may," James Cudworth of Massachusetts Bay writes to John Stoughton in December 1634, ". . . for they put a great deal of quickening life and edge unto my affections, and you know the best in this life are subject to grow cold in our perfection that we daily need some exhortation and consolation, both to provoke to the practice of holy things and to support us in the time of temptation or affliction" (Emerson, *Letters from New England*, 139–40). The model of the Pauline epistle is evident in the many letters John Woolman wrote as a recorded minister reproving slaveholding Friends as well as in the yearly meeting epistles authored collectively by Quaker elders. "It having pleased the Lord to draw me forth on a visit to some parts of Virginia and Carolina," Woolman begins a letter of May 29, 1757, "you have often been in my mind, and though my way is not clear to come in person to visit you, yet I feel it in my heart to communicate a few things as they arise in the love of Truth" (Woolman, *The Journal and Major Essays*, 67–68).

30. Woolman, *The Journal and Major Essays*, 39.

31. *The Papers of Thomas Jefferson*, 1:5.

32. Burstein, *The Inner Jefferson: Portrait of a Grieving Optimist*, 117. Chap. 4, "Letter Writing and Friendship," ably explores conventions of elite letter writing in colonial America, especially as they mirror practices current in Augustan England.

33. Cappon, *The Adams-Jefferson Letters*, 2:576, 529.

34. Van Doren, *The Letters of Benjamin Franklin and Jane Mecom*, 193–94.

35. Ibid., 208.

36. Ibid., 224.

37. Ibid., 204.

38. Ibid., 227.

39. Dublin, *Farm to Factory*, 43.

40. Starobin, *Blacks in Bondage*, 58. The holograph is among the Charles Colcock Jones Papers, Howard-Tilton Memorial Library, Tulane University. Letters written by slaves inevitably reflect their authors' subject status but nevertheless manifest significant variety. In *Slave Testimony: Two Centuries of Letters, Speeches, Interviews, and Autobiographies*, John W. Blassingame includes letters representing a broad range of experience, literacy, and expressiveness.

41. Holmes, *Covered Wagon Women*, 1:73.

42. Ibid., 74.

43. Ibid., 80.

44. Ibid., 80–81.

45. Ibid., 82.

46. Ibid., 19–20.

47. Ibid., 8:25–26.

48. John McDonough Papers, Howard-Tilton Memorial Library, Tulane University. What appears to be the challenging tone of the letter of March 7, 1848, written at least five years into Washington McDonough's Liberian residency, contrasts with the assiduously congenial tenor of a letter dated February 18, 1846, in which

McDonough also petitions for aid. The letter (see page 93 for a photograph of the first page of the manuscript) commences as follows:

Honoured Parent

I improve this opportunity to express the sense of gratitude I feel for the many benefits you have ever been pleased to confer upon me I have abundant reason to thank you for the opportunities with which you have so liberally favoured me, of acquiring a correct and useful Education, and I hope by my future exertions to be able to render you ample satisfaction for these and all other privileges which through your goodness I have received. I received your very kind letter and am happy to learn that you still continue to enjoy good health by the blessings and goodness of God. Dear sir you need not think that I shall ever forget your kind advice to me[.]

Although the cursive style in the letter of February 18, 1846, is nearly identical to that in the letter of March 7, 1848, the earlier letter (written while McDonough was visiting his mother) exhibits a much more careful hand; the signature in the later letter omits the *u* in McDonough. It is possible that one or both of the letters were dictated.

Washington McDonough's spiritual contrasting of America and Africa in the letter of March 7, 1848, is interesting for the way that it inverts such moral geography as Phillis Wheatley inscribes in a letter of May 19, 1772, to Obour Tanner, a slave in the home of James Tanner of Newport, Rhode Island: "let us rejoice in and adore the wonders of God's infinite Love in bringing us from a land Semblant of darkness itself, and where the divine light of revelation (being obscur'd) is as darkness. Here, the knowledge of the true God and eternal life are made manifest; But there, profound ignorance overshadows the Land" (*Poems of Phillis Wheatley*, 190). The question of whether the slave trade was justifiable on the grounds that it rescued Africans from heathenism was of course an old one; Samuel Sewall addresses it as early as 1700 in *The Selling of Joseph, A Memorial*. Wheatley's position was more ambivalent than this quotation alone suggests.

49. Gornick, "Letters Are Acts of Faith; Telephone Calls Are a Reflex," *New York Times Book Review*, July 31, 1994, p. 3.

50. *The Civil War Letters of Henry C. Bear*, 23. Although a recurrent epistolary expression, "land of the living" is also a recurrent Old Testament phrase (Job, Psalms, Isaiah, Jeremiah, and Ezekiel), and almost certainly would have been familiar as such to Glenn, McDonough, and Bear. The opening sentences of McDonough and Glenn feature other epistolary formulas that break down as follows: "I have taken this opportunity," "after so long a silence," "I am again permitted," "addressing you a few lines," "to write a few lines."

51. *The Ladies' and Gentlemen's Model Letter-Writer*, 105.

52. *A New Letter-Writer, for the Use of Gentlemen*, 53–54.

53. *A New Letter-Writer, for the Use of Ladies*, 74.

54. Thaddeus Hurlbut Capron Papers, American Heritage Center, University of Wyoming.

55. Ibid.

56. Dublin, *Farm to Factory*, 164. Another example of passing ironic self-reflexivity may be seen in a December 1895 letter written by Fannie Mathilda Reed in

Pasadena, California, to her sister in Minneapolis, Minnesota: "We haven't heard from Ward's folks for a long time. I suppose it will be, 'I wish you would write oftener,' when we do hear" (Pallister, *Sister to Sister: Letters Written by Fannie Reed to Her Twin Sister Eliza Crawford, 1894–1904*, 22–23).

57. Since Annette Kolodny's editing of the manuscript in 1987, Elizabeth House Trist has become well-known for the diary of her travel across the Alleghenies and down the Ohio and Mississippi Rivers in 1783 and 1784 in a disappointed quest to join her husband.

58. Hawkins, *Letters, Journals and Writings*, 1:89, 163, 164.

59. *War Letters of William Thompson Lusk*, 161.

60. Ibid., 66.

61. Greene, *The Ewing Family Civil War Letters*, 31; *The Civil War Letters of Henry C. Bear*, 24.

62. *Letters of Celia Thaxter* (1895); Dodge, *Gail Hamilton's Life in Letters* (1901); *Letters of Susan Hale* (1919).

63. On Alice James's letters, see Jacobson, *Authority and Alliance in the Letters of Henry Adams*, 120–26. In *The Education of Mrs. Henry Adams*, Eugenia Kaledin discusses Clover Adams's habits as a correspondent who maintained a regular correspondence with her father in Boston and who wrote rhetorically performative accounts of European travel and Washington life. As Kaledin notes, "the gregarious Dr. Hooper with fatherly pride would read Clover's letters aloud to gathered relatives and friends, making her all the more self-conscious as a writer" (57). Kaledin also examines psychologically complicated youthful letters not collected in Ward Thoron's edition of *The Letters of Mrs. Henry Adams*.

CHAPTER THREE

1. The earliest evidence of Emerson's epistolary activity suggests that he wrote a letter in 1807 to Mary Moody Emerson just after the death of his brother John (LRWE 7:101).

2. An interesting parallel to this period in the Emerson family correspondence may be found in the correspondence of the young Samuel Clemens and his siblings.

3. Cf. the twenty-one-year-old Henry Adams to Charles Francis Adams, February 9, 1859: "What one writes is considerably influenced by the accidental state of his mind at the instant of writing, and it is not strange if, among so many letters, when I am hurrying to put down the first thing that comes into my head, and fill out a sentence as quickly as possible, it is not strange, I say, if I say many silly things" (LHA 1:18).

4. Evelyn Barish addresses in detail the formative influence of Emerson's correspondence with Mary Moody Emerson. See *Emerson: The Roots of Prophecy*, especially 53, 66–71. Many of the letters Emerson received "from the vale" are reprinted in Simmons, *The Selected Letters of Mary Moody Emerson*. Simmons's preface to Mary Moody Emerson's letters of the 1820s (125–33) discusses this period in the exchange between nephew and aunt and examines her correspondence with Ralph Waldo Emerson in the context of an extensive and inveterate epistolary practice.

5. Some examples of Emerson on conversation: "Conversation is a game of circles. In conversation we pluck up the *termini* which bound the common of silence on

every side. The parties are not to be judged by the spirit they partake and even express under this Pentecost. . . . When each new speaker strikes a new light, emancipates us from the oppression of the last speaker, to oppress us with the greatness and exclusiveness of his own thought, then yields us to another redeemer, we seem to recover our rights, to become men" ("Circles," CW 2:184). "All good conversation, manners, and action, come from a spontaneity which forgets usages, and makes the moment great" ("Experience," CW 3:39). Disappointed conversation is represented in a journal entry of 1838 that is revised for inclusion in "Friendship": "Of a commended stranger only the good report is told by others. . . . We talk better than we are wont. We have no obstructions. For a long time we can continue a series of sincere, graceful, rich communications drawn from the oldest secretest experience. . . . But as soon as the stranger begins to intrude his partialities, his definitions, his defects into the conversation, it is all over" (JMN 7:76; CW 2:114). Cf. JMN 5:386, 468.

6. Mary Moody Emerson aggressively identifies her nephew as party to her preference of epistolary over face-to-face conversation: "Indeed *we* can only commune by pen," she writes in September 1826. "You are more sensitive than ever— that dolefull shake of head & grim look I had when you interested me thursday in parlour disgusts you so that you wont talk—all the way going you said nothing that you might. That destiny of which the freedom of our wills seems but an obedient member, forbids me to enter fine society at the peril of constant & hopeless disgrace from the ebullition of vanity & confidence w'h lies so dead in solitude— Therefore write I say if you can & I will write to remember that I have self existence of some sort" (Simmons, *The Selected Letters of Mary Moody Emerson*, 221). Ralph Waldo Emerson's preference of written over spoken conversation materializes— and confesses itself—as debility in his 1835 epistolary proposal of marriage to Lydia Jackson: "And think it not strange, as you will not, that I write rather than speak. In the gravest acts of my life I more willingly trust my pen than my tongue. It is as true. And yet had I been master of my time at this moment. I should bring my letter in my own hand" (LRWE 7:232–33). The sublimity of the preference is reasserted in a journal entry of March 1840. "Some men can write better than they speak," Emerson observes, generalizing from his own experience and developing the notion that writing speaks to the divine immanence as well as the human addressee. "Of such I had rather see the manuscript than see the man. For what he speaks he says to me but what he writes he says to God" (JMN 7:490).

7. My reference is to Rousseau's phrase after which Derrida entitles part 2, chapter 2, of *Of Grammatology*. With reference to Derrida's discussion, Martine Reid in "Correspondences: *Stendhal en toutes lettres*" suggests that the letter "may remain as the last avatar of naturalism and 'representation.' A formalization from the very outset, the letter dreams constantly however of a speech whose exact copy it would be, whose ideal nature would assure it a truthful character. The letter claims to *take the place of* speech and through this link with speech, presumed more true than writing, assures itself—in spite of its history, which formalizes and fictionalizes it straightaway—of the same benefits as speech" (166). Certainly it may be said of Emerson's letter writing that it dreams "of a speech whose exact copy it would be, whose ideal nature would assure it a truthful character." To the degree that Reid's commentary ascribes to the letter genre and its practitioners a categorical naïveté, however, it is ill-equipped to recognize the sophistication of Emerson—or, for that

matter, of Emily Dickinson, Henry Adams, and other self-studying practitioners of the epistolary genre who never simply presume speech to be "more true" than writing, and whose practices greatly complicate the binary opposition of writing to speech.

8. Explaining his reluctance to take part in a symposium of like-minded individuals who would go on to form the Transcendental Club, Emerson cites "an influence even baleful upon my power of conversation" exerted by the argumentative talkers that he should expect to meet. "The men of strong understanding are a menacing rapid trenchant race," he writes to Frederic Henry Hedge in July 1836, "—they cut me short—they drive me into a corner—I must not suggest, I must define" (LRWE 2:29). In his letter of December 1840 to George Ripley itemizing reasons why he was unsuited to join the Brook Farm experiment, he mentions his "little skill to converse with people" (LRWE 2:370)—meaning perhaps that he should not find the conversation at Brook Farm congenial.

9. For an account of the place of oratory in the curriculum and culture of antebellum New England, see Buell, *New England Literary Culture: From Revolution through Renaissance*, chap. 6, "New England Oratory from Everett to Emerson," 137–65. In the *First Series* essay "Spiritual Laws," Emerson's critical view of oratory is exhibited in his observation that "a public oration is an escapade, a noncommittal, an apology, a gag, and not a communication, not a speech, not a man" (CW 2:88).

10. On Emerson's vernacularization of his public discourse, see Buell, *New England Literary Culture*, 156–58. Buell observes that Emerson's rhetorical "staple remained the pungent, compressed, detached aphorism" (144); aphoristic utterance is by no means inconsistent with the recursive and paratactic tendencies of spoken and written conversation.

11. Joseph Slater identifies the "quasi-commercial relationship between the two men" as "the strongest buttress of their friendship" (CEC 16).

12. Ellen Emerson, *One First Love: The Letters of Ellen Louisa Tucker to Ralph Waldo Emerson*, 11, 18, 105–6.

13. The point with regard to the *First Series* essays is made more explicitly in the journal entry that Emerson draws upon for the passage. "I have been writing with some pains Essays on various matters as a sort of apology to my country for my apparent idleness," he writes on October 7, 1840. "But the poor work has looked poorer daily as I strove to end it. My genius seemed to quit me in such a mechanical work, a seeming wise, —a cold exhibition of dead thoughts. When I write a letter to any one whom I love, I have no lack of words or thoughts: I am wiser than myself & read my paper with the pleasure of one who receives a letter, but what I write to fill up the gaps of a chapter is hard & cold, is grammar & logic; there is no magic in it; I do not wish to see it again" (JMN 7:404–5).

14. Mary K. Cayton's account of the disappearance in the New England of the 1830s of an organic community held together through a system of deference and obligation is instructive when considering Emerson's spiritual retreat from an audience to whom he is vigorously merchandizing lectures. See *Emerson's Emergence: Self and Society in the Transformation of New England, 1800–1845*.

15. " 'Never' strikes us as the likelier case," writes David M. Robinson in *Emerson and the Conduct of Life: Pragmatism and Ethical Purpose in the Later Work* (37). Robinson

discusses the impossible idealism as well as the experience in bereavement that shaped the generally unrealizable conditions of the human bond that Emerson theorizes in "Friendship." See 35–40.

16. In "Veiled Ladies: Dickinson, Bettine, and Transcendental Mediumship," Barton Levi St. Armand remarks that "the name 'Bettine' was like a magic wand evoking all that was most intense and elusive in the youthful adolescence of the newness that was American Transcendentalism" (12). Bettina von Arnim's vogue among the transcendentalist literati is usefully outlined in Robert D. Richardson Jr., *Emerson: The Mind on Fire*, 327–28. Richardson suggests that the friendship between Emerson and Caroline Sturgis "was colored, if not actually created by Bettina von Arnim's *Goethe's Correspondence with a Child*," with Emerson playing Goethe and Sturgis the young adult female "child." The observation is just, and enhances our perception of the self-consciously philosophical-literary experiment of this epistolary friendship. Emerson and Sturgis, however, are much more inclined to approach one another as equals than von Arnim and Goethe. Moreover, as we would expect in an authentic epistolary discourse, the varied contingencies of their respective lives ultimately exert stronger influence on the tenor of relations than their readings in von Arnim's *Correspondence*; over time their conversation unfolds in reference to events peculiar to their historical, regional, and personal conditions.

17. A letter that served a public purpose was a letter that Emerson found ways to regret if not disown. Having written to President Martin Van Buren protesting the removal of the Cherokees (LRWE 7:303–6)—the letter is one of Emerson's most famous political statements—he confides in his journal that it was not his "impulse" to make such statements, "& therefore my genius deserts me, no muse befriends, no music of thought or of word accompanies" (JMN 5:479). Substituting the third person for the first, Emerson would use this sentence to conclude the second paragraph of "Self-Reliance."

18. For example, "The Divinity School Address," July 15, 1838; "Emancipation in the British West Indies," August 1, 1844; "The Fugitive Slave Law" (two versions), May 3, 1851, March 4, 1854; "John Brown," November 18, 1859.

19. *The Early Lectures of Ralph Waldo Emerson*, 3:187–88.

20. Letters written by members of Emerson's circle show abundant evidence of the customary sharing of epistolary texts; the receiving and circulation of letters is an event that correspondents frequently depict. "Yesterday was truly our lucky day—three letters from you—one from Lucy and one from Mr Cutler which for your dear sake delighted us 'silly' women to an extraordinary degree," Lidian Jackson Emerson writes her husband in March 1842. ". . . On the fourth page of the other sheet is an extract from a letter Henry sent this week to Lucy. I did not know it was there till I had written some lines—but will not tear it from the sheet since you may like it as well as I do—& if so it will cheer your loneliness" (*The Selected Letters of Lidian Jackson Emerson*, 107–8). The sharing of letters did require discretion and the setting of protocols. It is thus that Fuller writes forwarding letters to Sturgis: "You are at liberty to show Mr E's letters to Jane and Marianne, requesting them not to mention them to any one, as I do not wish to have it told about that I show Mr E's letters—From the others you may read to them and if you wish, to your sister Ellen also any critiques on lit[eratur]e art, or character carefully omitting everything personal" (*The Letters of Margaret Fuller*, 2:36).

21. *The Letters of Margaret Fuller*, 1:327, 2:159.

22. In a journal entry of September 26, 1840, Emerson addresses that sexual tension, writing the letter that he could not send to Margaret Fuller: "You would have me love you. What shall I love? Your body? The supposition disgusts you. What you have thought & said? Well, whilst you were thinking & saying them, but not now. I see no possibility of loving any thing but what now is, & is becoming; your courage, your enterprize, your budding affection, your opening thought, your prayer, I can love,—but what else?" (JMN 7:400).

23. Slater explores in great detail the troubled phases of the Emerson-Carlyle friendship and its effect on their correspondence. See CEC 30–52.

24. See Allen, *Waldo Emerson*, 351–52. Joel Myerson includes a biographical sketch of Caroline Sturgis in *The New England Transcendentalists and the "Dial": A History of the Magazine and Its Contributors*, 206–8. See also Robert D. Richardson Jr., *Emerson: The Mind on Fire*, 327–31.

25. This affirmation contrasts tellingly with what Emerson writes on the same day (September 25, 1840) to Margaret Fuller: "you & I are not inhabitants of one thought of the Divine Mind, but of two thoughts, that we meet & treat like foreign states, one maritime, one inland, whose trade & laws are essentially unlike" (LRWE 2:336). A month later, Fuller composed a stinging critique of Emerson's capacity for friendship, to which Emerson responded by affirming their friendship but requesting that Fuller's relentless analysis of its—and his—inadequacies cease. The quarrel with Fuller deepened his commitment to his friendship with Sturgis, who shared some of Fuller's reservations about Emerson, but who never assumed Fuller's hectoring tone, and whose personality appealed to Emerson in ways that Fuller's never could.

26. Some additional passages from typical letters to Lidian Jackson Emerson:

(Concord, approximately July 27, 1843)
> Mother says that Edie has no more cold than a bird though she sobs most bewitchingly at breakfast & dinner. Nelly is as curious & as busy & as much in papa's eyes nose & mouth as a fly: and the household proceeds after its customary laws: And here are ten dollars
> All which is affectionately submitted;
> R Waldo (LRWE 3:192)

(Perth, February 21, 1848)
> The kind letters you send me loaded with so many benedictions from that strange selfaccusing spirit of yours, (afflicting you, benefitting me,) and with all these touching anecdotes & now drawings & letters of my darlings—duly come to my great joy and ought to draw answers to every letter & almost to every piece of information. But I cannot yet answer but with most ungrateful brevity. I live in these days in a whirl from town to town & in strange houses and can ill command the short hour that is needed to write a letter. But you shall have a short chronicle of my late journeys, for fear I shall not have time to send them to you in any other form. . . . (LRWE 4:17)

Lidian Emerson's letters to her husband when he is absent from home typically provide detailed accounts of the children, discuss domestic finances, report news of family and friends, mentioning and sometimes quoting from letters received. Always observing a measure of formality (Emerson is addressed as "dear husband"), they nonetheless engage in intimate disclosures, as when Lidian writes of "a pleasant dream" in which she opens little Waldo's coffin (*The Selected Letters of Lidian Jackson Emerson*, 134–35). Such intimacy is perhaps never quite requited on Emerson's side of the correspondence.

27. *The Letters of Margaret Fuller*, 2:183.

28. The inability of the *Dial* to win a broad sympathetic audience is documented in Myerson, *The New England Transcendentalists and the* Dial, chaps. 2–4. The other (related) form that the desire for alternative community took was of course Brook Farm, the materialization of what Emerson and his friends initially imagined as (to quote Robert D. Richardson Jr.) "a sort of free university" (337). See Richardson, *Emerson: The Mind on Fire*, chap. 56.

29. Emerson's mature attitude toward lapses in correspondence is summed up in a remark that he makes to Henry James Sr. in 1843: "a friendly silence is more grateful than inadequate communion, as most Communions are" (LRWE 7:542).

30. "I have now for more than a year, I believe, ceased to write in my journal, in which I formerly wrote almost daily," Emerson observes in 1859. "I see few intellectual persons, and even those to no purpose, and sometimes believe that I have no new thoughts, and that my life is quite at an end" (JMN 14:248). On Emerson's growing weariness and decline, see Robert D. Richardson, *Emerson: The Mind on Fire*, 539, 543–71.

CHAPTER FOUR

1. In "The Female World of Love and Ritual: Relations between Women in Nineteenth-Century America," in *Disorderly Conduct: Visions of Gender in Victorian America* (53–76), Carroll Smith-Rosenberg discusses the close and seemingly homoerotic bond among late-eighteenth-century and nineteenth-century women as evidenced (among other documents) by their correspondences. Dickinson's passionate letters to Abiah Root, Jane Humphrey, Catherine Anthon, and especially Susan Huntington Gilbert may be considered as variations, however extreme, on well-established conventions that encouraged the flow of emotionally warm and even sexually charged missives between female friends. Smith-Rosenberg suggests that the romantic (although not overtly nor even necessarily lesbian) love of one woman for another may have been influentially modeled by the correspondence of Bettina von Arnim with Karoline von Gunderode (*Disorderly Conduct*, 39). For qualifications of Smith-Rosenberg's thesis in view of what Martha Nell Smith sees as the undeniably lesbian eroticism of Dickinson's correspondence with Susan Gilbert Dickinson, see *Rowing in Eden: Rereading Emily Dickinson*, 25.

2. Barton Levi St. Armand writes that *Goethe's Correspondence with a Child* (an 1859 edition of which was found at Austin and Susan Gilbert Dickinson's home inscribed with the latter's maiden name) and "especially the 1842 *Gunderode* translated by Margaret Fuller and published by Elizabeth Palmer Peabody, obviously were used as the basis of a 'code' between the young Sue and Emily, just as Dickens and Shakespeare provided scenarios for the poet's later correspondence with such intimate friends as Samuel Bowles and Otis Phillips Lord" ("Veiled Ladies: Dickinson, Bettine, and Transcendental Mediumship," 11). St. Armand also suggests that "in her letters to Higginson, Dickinson—with her references to noiseless noises, mysterious

lights, and angelic presences—sounds very much like an American version of this most Transcendental of German romantics" (14–15). This point is well taken, although Dickinson's concision and parataxis contrast strikingly with the prolixity and hypotaxis of von Arnim.

3. The interest in Dickinson's correspondence has grown steadily in the past two decades, as may be seen in the work of Lillian Faderman, "Emily Dickinson's Letters to Sue Gilbert"; Suzanne Juhasz, "Reading Emily Dickinson's Letters"; Vivian R. Pollak, *Dickinson: The Anxiety of Gender*; Barton Levi St. Armand, *Emily Dickinson and Her Culture: The Soul's Society*; Cynthia Griffin Wolff, *Emily Dickinson*; Cristanne Miller, *Emily Dickinson: A Poet's Grammar*; Judith Farr, *The Passion of Emily Dickinson*; and Martha Nell Smith, *Rowing in Eden: Rereading Emily Dickinson*. Juhasz's "Reading Emily Dickinson's Letters" argues that "Dickinson's letters are always love letters" (171) encoding diverse messages to various recipients, but consistently striving to elicit some token of reciprocal affection. In *Dickinson: The Anxiety of Gender*, Pollak draws extensively on the letters in her examination of the state of "erotic bereavement" (17) from which, as she argues, much of Dickinson's poetic achievement derives. In *Rowing in Eden: Rereading Emily Dickinson*, Smith, noting that at least a third of Dickinson's poems were inscribed in or as letters, examines the centrality of the circulating manuscript to the composition and "publication" of Dickinson's poetry. Pollak has underscored the importance of epistolary language to Dickinson studies in *A Poet's Parents: The Courtship Letters of Emily Norcross and Edward Dickinson*, as has St. Armand in " 'Your Prodigal': Letters from Ned Dickinson, 1879–1885," in which he draws attention to stylistic peculiarities that run in the family.

4. Jay Leyda, in *The Years and Hours of Emily Dickinson*, draws extensively on the letters. The extent to which Dickinson's poems may be read as (or for) biographical evidence is a longstanding matter of debate. Not only does Dickinson embed poems in letters, but she also makes slight alterations to fit the epistolary occasion, and this affirms her willingness that the poems be read (at least by her addressee) within autobiographical frames of reference. But this does not mean that the autobiographical reference is necessarily "factual" in the way that a biographical reference would aspire to be. Although the poem, in such instances, is subordinated to the immediately epistolary motive, the latter is not necessarily less performative than the motive of the poem. "In practical terms," writes Cristanne Miller in *A Poet's Grammar*, "letters and poems appear to be complementary forms of the same kind of communication" (10). Miller provides valuable analysis of Dickinson's ability to change "from prose to verse in mid-sentence" (10–12). See also Martha Nell Smith, *Rowing in Eden*, 107–8.

5. See Sewall, *The Life of Emily Dickinson*, 2:750–51.

6. Prior to 1858, Dickinson's dating commonly refers to day of week and time of day, but seldom to month and year (a not uncommon practice, as one can see, for example, in Louisa May Alcott's dating of her letters). For many letters Johnson and Ward provide approximate dates, guided largely by Dickinson's handwriting, which they judge to have undergone almost yearly change throughout her life.

7. In *Rowing in Eden*, Martha Nell Smith challenges the Johnson and Ward edition in its representation of erasures and mutilations (22) and insertions (113) as well as what she considers to be misleading contextualizations, among them the suggestion that the "Master" letters were addressed to the Reverend Charles Wadsworth (124) and that certain exchanges are sarcastic and apologetic in tone (145–46, 149–50).

8. I borrow the phrase from Judith Farr, who in *The Passion of Emily Dickinson* endeavors to construct a "narrative of Sue" and "narrative of Master" from biographical-critical readings of the poems and letters.

9. Barthes theorizes a threefold split: "the one *who speaks* (in the narrative) is not the one *who writes* (in real life) and the one *who writes* is not the one *who is*" ("An Introduction to the Structural Analysis of Narrative," 261).

10. Where the poem begins and the letter leaves off has been pointedly challenged by scholars who propose an edition of Dickinson's writings that would restore verses and letters to an originary, mutually dependent context. At the same time, recent efforts to derive "new poems" from the letters reflect a conviction that veins of verse pervade the letters' ostensible prose. Two publications recast Dickinson's epistolary prose as poems: Shurr, *New Poems of Emily Dickinson*, and Turco, *Emily Dickinson, Woman of Letters: Poems and Centos from Lines in Emily Dickinson's Letters*.

11. Martha Nell Smith gives a detailed account of the fetishization of these documents—much of it dubiously productive—in *Rowing in Eden*, 97–127.

12. A selection of Dickinson household correspondence (including letters written by Edward, Lavinia, and Austin Dickinson, although not in response to Emily's letters) is printed in Bingham, *Emily Dickinson's Home*.

13. Lystra, *Searching the Heart*, 13–15. Advice books aimed specifically at young people, like Eliza W. R. Farrar's *The Youth's Letter-Writer* and *The Young Lady's Friend*, and Lydia Sigourney's *Letters to Young Ladies*, prescribe on matters ranging from the proper content of letters and the crispness of ink on the letter sheet to the correct disposal of accumulated correspondence. Such advice indicates the ways in which youthful letter writing resists regulation. The garrulous, insouciant, and passionate letters of the young Emily Dickinson, which glory in satire and revel in inkblots, would seem to exemplify everything that Farrar wishes to upbraid.

14. Seen in a broader context, this passage, with its conflation of eroticism with illness, is consistent with the Victorian association of sexual transgression with bodily ailment, the iconography of which is discussed in Dijkstra, *Idols of Perversity* (see especially 64–65).

15. As is well-known, Dickinson—virtually alone among the young women of her acquaintance—steadfastly resisted the revivalism that swept through the Connecticut Valley of her youth.

16. The poems are J 109, 169, 334, 441, 487, 494, 636, 1035, 1089, 1290, 1459, 1639. Many other poems, however, are relevant to the question of epistolary relations, among them 1209, 1319, 1398.

17. The phrase "simple News" clearly contrasts the renewals of a female, domestic, and natural cycle against the ostensibly more complex news of historical events that define the patriarchal realm. At one level we must read this poem as Dickinson's ambivalent statement of her ambition as a woman of letters, a poet who identifies her work as female and deriving from a feminized Nature, but who would be read by a "World" of "country*men*," a more inclusive readership than the contemporary audience of women's poetry. On Dickinson's unusual ambition in the context of the literary endeavor of women in mid-nineteenth-century America, see Dobson, *Dickinson and the Strategies of Reticence: The Woman Writer in Nineteenth-Century America*; Bennett, *Emily Dickinson: Woman Poet*; and Reynolds, *Beneath the American Renaissance*,

387–437. On affinities and differences between Dickinson's and Emerson's respective construction of "Nature," see Diehl, *Dickinson and the Romantic Imagination*, 162–65; and Wolff, *Emily Dickinson*, 224–25, 286–87. In J 441, "Nature" is at once empowering and debilitating, the latter in proportion as it proposes a submissive relationship to "countrymen." To be preempted by a patriarchally determined feminine nature is to be put in the position of addressing men with little hope of answer—of being an object seldom addressed as subject.

18. In a letter to Austin, Dickinson vividly depicts a scene in which she selectively reads portions of her brother's letters aloud to their father (LED 1:136–37); in other letters she and Sue figure as the rapturous recipients and sharers of Austin's epistolary attentions (LED 1:241, 245).

19. Dickinson was hardly alone in seeking securely private space before reading an intimate letter. The seeking of privacy represented in "The Way I read a Letter's—this" bears striking resemblance to the way Lidian Jackson Emerson is reported to have read letters from her husband; see Robert D. Richardson Jr., *Emerson: The Mind on Fire*, 193. As well, it resembles Lucy's search for private space in which to read a letter from Dr. John in Charlotte Brontë's *Villette* (chap. 22, "The Letter"). Nor does the poem describe an exclusively female way of reading. "I long to get home," Nathaniel Hawthorne writes Sophia Peabody from the Boston Custom House in April 1840 upon receiving a letter from her, "that I may read it again and again; for in this uncongenial region, I can but half comprehend it—at least, I feel that there is a richness and sweetness in it, too sacred to be enjoyed, save in privacy" (*The Letters*, 1:449). "Whenever I get one of your letters," writes Eldred Simkins, a Confederate army officer, in 1864 to Eliza Trescot, "I always look to the end to see how long Lize has talked to me and then lock my door and have you all to myself. I cannot bear to read your letters near anybody but will keep it in my pocket until I am by myself. In fact I treat your letters as I would yourself" (quoted in Lystra, *Searching the Heart*, 22).

20. The heaven, even, of sexual consummation; see St. Armand, *Emily Dickinson and Her Culture*, 137–46. This notion of heaven is also present in the last paragraph of the third "Master" letter: "nobody else will see me, but you—but that is enough—I shall not want any more—and all that Heaven only will disappoint me—will be because it's not so dear" (LED 2:392).

21. The difference between "feels to me like" (LED 2:460) and "seemed to me like" (LED 3:752) may be accounted for by the fact that the latter (in the past tense) bases the recognition on a maturer experience. The sensuous apprehension of death and the afterlife is, however, by no means absent from the letter of 1882, as in it Dickinson writes of what her mother's death "feels to me like."

22. Wolff is most thorough in her treatment of this topic. Considering whether Dickinson underwent psychotic episodes, John Cody cites her "fears that the beloved one no longer exists whenever he is not physically present. There seems to be an attenuated form of this delusion in many of Emily Dickinson's letters" (*After Great Pain: The Inner Life of Emily Dickinson*, 337–38). I would suggest that epistolary writing encourages the production of such fears. Dread that materializes in consequence of a separation exacerbated by a possible lapse in contact is articulated in a letter Henry Adams writes from Havana to Elizabeth Cameron: "Your letter, which I looked for, and found, immediately, gave me a sort of confidence; for I am always in deadly fear that you will get into some mischief the moment I turn my back" (LHA

4:249). In the context of his troubled and increasingly epistolary relationship with Cameron, the often ironic Adams is in earnest when he speaks here of "deadly fear."

23. Cf. J 1053: "He asked if I was his— / I made no answer of the Tongue / But answer of the Eyes—."

24. Fearing that she should not again see her correspondent, Dickinson could imagine death as a means of approaching the lost but still living beloved. In the fury of the second "Master" letter, she confesses, "I used to think when I died—I could see you—so I died as fast as I could" (LED 2:374).

25. On Dickinson's friendship with Otis Phillips Lord, see Sewall, *The Life of Emily Dickinson*, 2:642–67. A passage from the partially mutilated pencil draft in which Dickinson identifies "no" as "the wildest word we consign to Language" reads as follows: "to lie so near your longing—to touch it as I passed, for I am but a restive sleeper and often should journey from your Arms through the happy night, but you will lift me back, wont you, for only there I ask to be—I say, if I felt the longing nearer—than in our dear past, perhaps I could not resist to bless it, but must, because it would be right" (LED 3:617).

26. On Victorian domestic conceptions of heaven, see St. Armand, *Emily Dickinson and Her Culture*, chap. 4.

27. Although few writers approach Dickinson's passionate statement of it, the idea itself is a period commonplace. "If in my present life I love one person truly," explains Louisa May Alcott in an 1884 letter to Maggie Lukens, "no matter who it is, I believe that we meet somewhere again, though where or how I dont know or care, for genuine love is immortal" (*The Selected Letters of Louisa May Alcott*, 279).

28. Letter-writers of the day showcase period commonplaces of the condolence letter. In the following selection from a model condolence, "To a Friend on the Death of a Father," death is identified as a release from suffering and the promise of reunion in the next life is affirmed as a matter of course: "Deeply as I sympathize with you in your heavy loss, I cannot but be grateful that your dear father is relieved from the frightful agony of the past three months, and is in the happy home of the redeemed, enjoying the reward of his pure Christian life" (*Frost's Original Letter-Writer*, 93). In the model condolence "On a Child's Death" quoted in chap. 2 at n. 53, on the other hand, reunion of mother and child in an afterlife provides the sole basis of consolation.

29. "When Jesus tells us about his Father," Dickinson writes her Amherst neighbor Mrs. Henry Hills, the recipient of a long series of condolences following the death of her infant son in 1879, "we distrust him. When he shows us his Home, we turn away, but when he confides to us that he is 'acquainted with Grief,' we listen, for that also is an Acquaintance of our own" (LED 3:837). The statement counters such banalities as the model condolence "On a Child's Death" quoted in chap. 2 articulates.

30. Again, Pollak gives an instructive account of Dickinson's conversion of eroticism "into a preoccupation with death" (Dickinson, *The Anxiety of Gender*, 58).

31. "Is Heaven a Place—a Sky—a Tree?" So Dickinson asks in J 489. "Location's narrow way is for Ourselves— / Unto the Dead / There's no Geography—"; see also J 1691.

32. Diehl rightly points out that such a view of the child was alien to the poet's own early experience. "Examining her past and her childhood, Dickinson recalls no

privileged sanctuary. Taught to perceive children as lost souls who must find grace before they can be freed from guilt, she feels exiled . . . from the 'prenatal' possibility of grace" (*Dickinson and the Romantic Imagination*, 16). In reaction to such Calvinist austerities, the culture in which Dickinson came of age was only too willing to celebrate the "visionary gleam" of childhood. See St. Armand, *Emily Dickinson and Her Culture*, 43. Also, note how this letter incorporates certain motifs present in the model condolence "On a Child's Death" quoted in chap. 2.

33. In this same otherworldly vein: in a letter written two years later to Mabel Loomis Todd, Dickinson refers to the words of Jesus as "the Letter he wrote to all mankind" (LED 3:882).

34. *Called Back* concerns a man and a woman who are retrieved respectively from blindness and amnesia and who subsequently come to the realization that they were both present at the scene of a murder. Once the dark libidinal past has been clarified, they are free to know and to love one another.

CHAPTER FIVE

1. In 1840, Charles Francis Adams published *Letters of Mrs. Adams*; in 1875, the year before the nation's centennial, he published *Familiar Letters of John Adams and His Wife, during the Revolution*. For a discussion of the Adams family archive and Charles Francis Adams's decision to make private papers public, see Harbert, *The Force So Much Closer Home: Henry Adams and the Adams Family*, especially 11–17.

2. In Walpole, Adams would have found the example of a correspondent deeply engaged in the public events of his time who was nonetheless adept at assuming a detached perspective from which to construct self-consciously performative accounts of those events. For a discussion of Walpole's massive subordination of the content of his letters to his art as a letter writer, and particularly his tendency to fashion distinct epistolary identities for each of his major correspondences, see Redford, *The Converse of the Pen*, chap. 4.

3. For a sampling of such acknowledgments see Jacobson, *Authority and Alliance in the Letters of Henry Adams*, 9. The dust jackets of the 1982–88 Harvard edition carry testimony that "Adams is one of the best letter-writers in the language" (Marcus Cunliffe, in a commentary on the first three volumes, published in 1982) and that "Adams was one of the great letter writers of the English language" (Otto Friedrich, reviewing the first three volumes for *Time*).

4. In the "Memoir" that serves as preface to the second edition of *Letters of Mrs. Adams*—a publication of significance to the family's construction of an epistolary tradition inasmuch as it represents the making public of family letters—Charles Francis Adams cites the didactic value of youthful letter writing: "Perhaps there is no species of exercise, in early life, more productive of results useful to the mind, than that of writing letters. Over and above the mechanical facility of constructing sentences, which no teaching will afford so well, the interest with which the object is commonly pursued, gives an extraordinary impulse to the intellect" (1:xxix).

5. "If I call this volume a letter," Adams writes in the preface to this work, "it is only because that literary form affects to be more colloquial or more familiar than the usual scientific treatise; but such letters never require a response, even when they invite one; and in the present case, the subject of the letter involves a problem which

will certainly exceed the limits of a life already far advanced, so that its solution, if a solution is possible, will have to be reached by a new generation." For an account of the efforts of a few recipients to respond to the *Letter*, see Decker, *The Literary Vocation of Henry Adams*, 85–93.

6. Far more than the present chapter, which focuses on the self-reflexive theme of presence and absence in Adams's correspondence, Jacobson's *Authority and Alliance in the Letters of Henry Adams* studies the variety and motivation of Adams's correspondence as well as the role letter writing played in his positioning of himself within the context of family and national politics.

7. I cite Jack London and Ernest Hemingway as authors whose class and regional origins differ significantly from Adams's but whose correspondences also demonstrate inveterate and facile geographic mobility and whose use of the genre likewise exhibits aggressive subordination of the world to the self.

8. Commenting on Horace Walpole's lengthy account of the trial and execution of Lawrence, Earl Ferrers, in letters to Horace Mann, Redford observes that "Mann *per se* drops out completely—or rather, is subsumed into Walpole's hypothetical reader of the future" (*The Converse of the Pen*, 144). In neither the letters Adams wrote to Charles Francis Adams Jr. during the secession crisis and subsequently nor really to anyone at any other time do we discern a total absorption of the addressee into such hypothetical future readership.

9. Family correspondence of the war years is collected in the two-volume collection, *A Cycle of Adams Letters, 1861–1865*, edited by Worthington Chauncy Ford.

10. Certain attitudes, like the one Adams assumes in this letter, may well be modeled on the valetudinarian and indifferent posture recurrently evident in Walpole's letters. The following sentences, from a letter dated September 22, 1765, that Walpole wrote from Paris to George Montagu in Greatworth, anticipate a whole class of such utterances found in the letters of the young, middle-aged, and elderly Henry Adams: "It is true, amusements do not always amuse when we bid them. I find it so here; nothing strikes me; everything I do is indifferent to me" (*Horace Walpole's Correspondence*, 10:174–75). "Instead of laughing, I sit silently reflecting, how everything loses charms, when one's own youth does not lend it gilding. When we are divested of that eagerness and illusion with which our youth presents objects to us, we are but the *caput mortuum* of pleasure" (10:176). "In short, I have done with the world, and only live in it, rather than in a desert, like you" (10:177).

11. Adams's account of Louisa's death in *The Education of Henry Adams* obviously draws on not only the ultimately traumatic vigil at his sister's deathbed but also the shock of Clover's suicide. See Decker, *The Literary Vocation of Henry Adams*, 64–65.

12. Adams's activities as the *North American Review* editor (which involved extensive and international epistolary networking) are characterized in Samuels, *The Young Henry Adams*, 218–34, 275–89. See also Henry Adams, *Sketches for the "North American Review."*

13. For a photograph of five-of-hearts letter sheet (Henry Adams to John Hay, April 8, 1883) see LHA 2:facing p. 497. Other objects that reified group identity include a tea service and menu cards. For photographs of such items see O'Toole, *The Five of Hearts*, 69, 87.

14. The fullest account of the anti-Semitic voice in Adams's writing is Levenson,

"The Etiology of Israel Adams: The Onset, Waning, and Relevance of Henry Adams's Anti-Semitism."

15. In addition to *A Letter to American Teachers of History* there is the historical speculation known as "The Tendency of History," which takes the form of an open letter addressed to Professor Herbert Baxter Adams and intended to be read before the historians assembled for the American Historical Association's annual convention in December 1894. Henry Adams, that year's reluctant association president, submitted the letter as his presidential address; at the time of the convention he was traveling in Mexico. The tone of the letter is admonitory, warning colleagues of American society's necessarily ideological resistance to what they should teach as the unwelcome truths of "scientific history." "In these remarks," Adams observes in closing, adverting to the epistolary form of his communication, "which are only casual, and offered in the paradoxical spirit of private conversation, I have not ventured to express any opinion of my own; or, if I have expressed it, pray consider it as withdrawn" (LHA 4:233). For this text's place among Adams's other historical speculations, see Decker, *The Literary Vocation of Henry Adams*, chap. 3.

16. On Clover's suicide as a gossip column topic, see Samuels, *Henry Adams: The Middle Years*, 273–76.

17. Following the demise of the five of hearts, Adams's innermost circle consisted of Elizabeth Cameron, John Hay, and Anna Cabot Mills Lodge, a group that (as Chalfant points out) referred to itself as "the family." Alluding to the romance between John Hay and Anna Lodge and the less easily defined relationship between Adams and Cameron, Chalfant observes that "in reality they were two pairs, each with their own secrets" (*Better in Darkness: A Biography of Henry Adams. His Second Life—1862–1891*, 593).

18. Tehan, *Henry Adams in Love: The Pursuit of Elizabeth Sherman Cameron*, provides detailed biographical information regarding Elizabeth Cameron's membership in a powerful Ohio family and the disappointments that shaped her relationship with Henry Adams.

19. See Samuels, *Henry Adams: The Middle Years*, 244.

20. Concerning the textual character of the Adams-Cameron friendship, Jacobson observes that their correspondence constituted neither "a substitute for personal contact or even simply a means of avoiding it. Instead, the letters created a discourse with an integrity of its own, whose balance between intimacy and neutrality could not survive outside the correspondence" (*Authority and Alliance in the Letters of Henry Adams*, 76).

21. Chalfant suggests that these lines may have been written at a time when Adams was ridding the Quincy household of old possessions, his diplomatic uniform of the London years among them. See *Better in Darkness*, 547.

22. On August 23, 1890, before boarding the *Zealandia*, Adams wrote Elizabeth Cameron: "When I am tired I am homesick, and a sudden spasm came over me, that I *must* see Martha. I got over it with the help of a bottle of Champagne and a marvelous dinner at the Club, but I am at best homesick enough for Beverly" (LHA 3:264). His most lavish indulgence of homesickness is the six-stanza poem dated "Apia. November 25, 1890. 4 o'clock, A.M." See n. 23.

23. The last three stanzas are as follows:

John Hay is hurrying from his house to meet us;
   My sister Anne is coming up the stair;
But still I strain to see the street beneath us,
   To catch the whiteness of the dress you wear.

It is the surf upon the coral streaming,
   The white light glimmering on the village lawn;
The broad banana-leaf reflects the gleaming;
   The shadowy native glides across the dawn.

Death is not hard when once you feel its measure;
   One learns to know that Paradise is gain;
One bids farewell to all that gave one pleasure;
   One bids farewell to all that gave one pain. (LHA 3:340)

24. Elizabeth Cameron, letter of January 10, 1891, in *Microfilms of the Henry Adams Papers, 1843–1938*, reel 7.

25. See LHA 3:481.

26. For accounts of the 1891 Paris reunion of Henry Adams and Elizabeth Cameron, see Samuels, *Henry Adams: The Major Phase*, 64–74, and Chalfant, *Better in Darkness*, 618–41.

27. Even in his own time, Adams could not maintain the private status of these books. Through the efforts of Ralph Adams Cram and with the sponsorship of the American Institute of Architects, Houghton Mifflin brought out *Mont Saint Michel and Chartres* in 1913. From 1907 on, Ferris Greenslet of Houghton Mifflin recurrently pressured Adams to let his firm publish *The Education of Henry Adams*. See Samuels, *Henry Adams: The Major Phase*, 539–40, 559–69.

28. Two quotations from *The Education of Henry Adams* characterize Adams's thought on politics and friendship and together suggest what was for him the nonideological nature of the latter: "Politics, as a practice, whatever its professions, had always been the systematic organization of hatreds" (7); "Friends are born in archaic horizons; they were shaped with the *Pteraspis* in Siluria; they have nothing to do with the accident of space" (311). An example of Emerson's insistence that private friendship transcends ideology is his refusal to admit openly that his conflicts with Fuller stemmed from the politics of gender. See chap. 3 at n. 22.

29. Ever an ironic and theoretical epistolary practitioner, Adams himself resists the term "condolence." "Do not try to answer this letter," he writes Elizabeth Kilgour Anderson, widow of his lifelong friend Nicholas Longworth Anderson, in September 1892; "it is not one of condolence, for death is beyond condolence; it is only to show that friends do not forget you" (LHA 4:66).

30. Another striking articulation of this position occurs in a letter of July 31, 1905, to Richard Watson Gilder: "Thanks for your letter. Life, towards its end, becomes singularly fantastic. I no longer distinguish between the live and the dead. Saint Simon tells of one of the Condé's of his time who never would admit that anybody was dead, and promptly kicked out of Chantilly anyone who tried to convince him that any friend of his had died. I agree with him. Anyway they are as much alive as I am myself, who have been dead these twenty years except to them" (LHA 5:698–99).

CONCLUSION

1. The presence of a telephone at 1603 H Street, which we might surmise, is confirmed by Edward Chalfant, who learned of its existence from Ailene Tone. Chalfant speculates that the telephone, which Adams himself did not use, was installed in 1908, the year that his Washington residence was wired for electricity (letter to the author, September 20, 1996). The telephone exchange system serves as the matrix for subsequent telecommunications; electronic correspondence, the "information superhighway," and the communities one joins via computer screen—all depend on phone lines. "The telephone network now interconnecting the continents is by far the largest integrated machine in the world," wrote Colin Cherry in 1976, the centenary of the invention of the telephone ("The Telephone System: Creator of Mobility and Social Change," 123). In the last twenty years of the twentieth century the magnitude of the machine and complexity of its integration have, of course, increased vastly.

2. On the nineteenth- and early twentieth-century international standard time movement, see Kern, *The Culture of Time and Space*, 10–15. As Kern points out, the wireless telegraph provided the means "of determining and maintaining accurate time signals and transmitting them around the world" (13).

3. *The Correspondence of Henry David Thoreau*, 199.

4. The occasion was that of Otis Lord's illness in early May 1882. See LED 3: 730–31.

5. Henry James, *Portrait of a Lady*, 1:13.

6. Henry James, *Letters*, 4:625.

7. Clemens, *Mark Twain's Letters*, 1:363.

8. *The Death and Letters of Alice James*, 192.

9. This person was my tenth-grade French teacher. One evening he invited the class to his residence, and while the group was gathered around the fireplace the small, black rotary telephone on a corner table began to ring. Glancing at his watch he hushed the students and studied the telephone intently; the whole class joined him in the scrutiny of an object that he had made enigmatic by letting it ring unanswered. When it fell silent he explained that the call was from abroad. He was clearly pleased with the message and proud of the manifest cleverness of its conveyance. This man evidently also maintained a prolific written correspondence, as his desk contained stacks of airmail envelopes.

10. Wiesel, *All Rivers Run to the Sea: Memoirs*, 47.

11. In *Dead Man Walking*, Helen Prejean writes in detail of the visual, tactile, and emotional experience of receiving mail from her death row correspondents as well as the initial hesitancy and subsequent conviction with which she wrote and sent her replies. See also Gilpin, "A Letter-Writing Ministry," and Arriens, *Welcome to Hell: Letters and Writings from Death Row*. Web sites devoted to soliciting correspondents for inmates include "Penn-Pals Prison Inmate Services Network" (http://www. pennpals.com), "Prison Pen Pals.Com~Ea" (http://www.prisonpenpals.com), and "The Prison Pen-Pal Homepage" (http://www.rcf.usc. edu/~Ealaa/prison/index. html). Usually, initial contact with the prisoner is made via e-mail directed to the Web site with which the prisoner has registered; thereafter, the correspondence proceeds either as an old-fashioned exchange of letter sheet or via e-mail for the

party outside the prison wall and inscribed letter sheet for the party inside. Comparatively few prisoners have direct access to e-mail and the privilege of a fully electronic correspondence.

12. This statement is made in a brief disquisition entitled "On Line Emotion— emoticons," a page at "The Emoticon Shop" Web site where, in addition to learning about emoticons (once but now unfashionably known as "smilies"), one may purchase T-shirts featuring emoticons. Evidently the fetish value of an object or expression is measurable by the marketability of its T-shirt publication—an interesting conjunction of body and language. "The very nature of communicating on the Internet," one reads at this site, "allows people to express thoughts and feelings with an openness and frankness unusual in face to face or phone conversations." This suggests that the old epistolary dream of transparent disclosures and real, transmissible, albeit mediated presence is alive and well.

13. See, for instance, Ellen Strenski, "Electronic Epistolarity: E-Mail as Gift Exchange," a paper presented at the fourth annual Cultural Studies Symposium, Kansas State University, and subsequently published on the Internet.

14. Strenski, fundamentally in agreement with the vision of e-mail promoted at "The Emoticon Shop," asserts that "e-mailers value spontaneity. They do not want to revise. For instance, the Pine mailing system . . . offers an easy-to-use spellchecker that writers usually ignore, more so than with ordinary word-processed prose. The result is associative, open-ended discourse that prompts self-disclosure" (ibid., n.p.). What we observe in such "spontaneity" is simply a fresh simulacrum of self-disclosure.

15. In *The Wired Neighborhood*, an intelligently constructed critique of the much vaunted democratizing and community-building merits of the Internet, Stephen Doheny-Farina observes that "much of the net is a Byzantine amalgamation of fragmented, isolating, solipsistic enclaves of interest based on a collectivity of assent" (55) that suppresses difference and authentic dialogue. "I can watch as I create and manipulate my selves within the confines of the virtual world I've entered," Doheny-Farina writes with reference to his participation in a MUD (multiuser dimension) site/event. "But does this game really connect me to others? Or is this primarily a navel-gazing exercise that enables me to look at these abstract selves I've created set against the personas I've encountered scrolling up my screen?" (65).

16. See, for instance, Dick, "Minitel 3615" (1989), and Fletcher, *E-Mail: A Love Story* (1996).

17. Diana Web sites, official and nonofficial: <http://www.royal.gov.uk/vbk />, <http://www.pcbjr.com/diana.htm>, <http://www.i8acorns.deomn.co. uk./index.html>.

18. This and many other epistolary messages have been left at "Allen Ginsberg Memorial Page": <http://www.buffnet/~Edeadbeat/ginsberg/>.

19. Virtual Heaven pages (available via <http://www.cyberspace. com/~Eais/ heaven.html>) are generally unsigned or signed with a first name only. Other similar sites: World Wide Cemetery, World Gardens.

20. Jameson, *Postmodernism, or, The Cultural Logic of Late Capitalism*, 44.

Bibliography

· · · · · · · · · · · · ·

For bibliographical information on works cited by page number in the text, see the abbreviations list on page xiii.

Adams, Charles Francis, ed. *Letters of Mrs. Adams.* 2 vols. Boston: C. C. Little and J. Brown, 1840.

———. *Familiar Letters of John Adams and His Wife, during the Revolution.* Boston: Houghton, Mifflin and Company, 1875.

Adams, Henry. *The Life of Albert Gallatin.* Philadelphia: J. B. Lippincott and Company, 1879. Rpt. New York: Peter Smith, 1943.

———. *The Education of Henry Adams.* Ed. Ernest Samuels. Boston: Houghton Mifflin, 1973.

———. *Microfilms of the Henry Adams Papers, 1843–1938.* Massachusetts Historical Society, 1979.

———. *Sketches for the "North American Review."* Ed. Edward Chalfant. Hamden, Conn.: Archon Books, 1986.

Adams, Marian. *The Letters of Mrs. Henry Adams, 1865–1883.* Ed. Ward Thoron. Boston: Little, Brown, and Company, 1936.

Akin, Warren. *Letters of Warren Akin, Confederate Congressman.* Ed. Bell Irvin Wiley. Athens: University of Georgia Press, 1959.

Alcott, Louisa May. *The Selected Letters of Louisa May Alcott.* Ed. Joel Myerson, Daniel Shealy, and Madeleine B. Stern. Boston: Little, Brown, 1987.

Allen, Gay Wilson. *Waldo Emerson: A Biography.* New York: Viking, 1981.

Altman, Janet Gurkin. *Epistolarity: Approaches to a Form.* Columbus: Ohio State University Press, 1982.

———. "The Letter Book as a Literary Institution, 1539–1789: Toward a Cultural History of Published Correspondence in France." *Men / Women of Letters,* ed. Charles A. Porter, special issue of *Yale French Studies* 71 (1986): 17–62.

Arriens, Jan, ed. *Welcome to Hell: Letters and Writings from Death Row.* Boston: Northeastern University Press, 1997.

Bacon, Georgeanna Woolsey, and Eliza Woolsey Howland, eds. *Letters of a Family during the War for the Union, 1861–1865.* 2 vols. Privately printed, 1899.

Bakhtin, M. M. *The Dialogic Imagination.* Trans. Caryl Emerson and Michael Holquist. Austin: University of Texas Press, 1981.

Barish, Evelyn. *Emerson: The Roots of Prophecy.* Princeton, N.J.: Princeton University Press, 1989.

Barthes, Roland. "An Introduction to the Structural Analysis of Narrative." *New Literary History* 6, no. 2 (1975): 237–72.

——. *A Lover's Discourse: Fragments.* Trans. Richard Howard. New York: Hill and Wang, 1978.

Bear, Henry C. *The Civil War Letters of Henry C. Bear.* Ed. Wayne C. Temple. Harrogate, Tennessee: Lincoln Memorial University Press, 1961.

Bennett, Paula. *Emily Dickinson: Woman Poet.* Iowa City: University of Iowa Press, 1990.

Bianchi, Martha Gilbert. *Life and Letters of Emily Dickinson.* Boston: Houghton Mifflin Company, 1924.

Bingham, Millicent Todd. *Emily Dickinson's Home: Letters of Edward Dickinson and His Family.* New York: Harper and Brothers, 1955.

Blair, Hugh. *Lectures on Rhetoric and Belles Lettres.* 2 vols. London: Strahan and Cadell, 1783. Rpt. Carbondale: Southern Illinois University Press, 1965.

Blassingame, John W., ed. *Slave Testimony: Two Centuries of Letters, Speeches, Interviews, and Autobiographies.* Baton Rouge: Louisiana State University Press, 1977.

Bodenheimer, Rosemarie. *The Real Life of Mary Ann Evans: George Eliot, Her Letters and Fiction.* Ithaca, N.Y.: Cornell University Press, 1994.

Bowers, Fredson. "Transcriptions of Manuscripts: The Record of Variants." *Studies in Bibliography* 29 (1976): 212–64.

Bradford, William. *Of Plymouth Plantation 1620–1647.* Ed. Samuel Eliot Morison. New York: Knopf, 1966.

Buell, Lawrence. *New England Literary Culture: From Revolution through Renaissance.* New York: Cambridge University Press, 1986.

Burnett, Edmund C., ed. *Letters of Members of the Continental Congress.* 8 vols. Washington, D.C.: Carnegie Institution of Washington, 1921–36.

Burstein, Andrew. *The Inner Jefferson: Portrait of a Grieving Optimist.* Charlottesville: University Press of Virginia, 1995.

Cabot, James Elliot. *A Memoir of Ralph Waldo Emerson.* 2 vols. Boston: Houghton, Mifflin and Company, 1887.

Cappon, Lester J., ed. *The Adams-Jefferson Letters: The Complete Correspondence between Thomas Jefferson and Abigail and John Adams.* 2 vols. Chapel Hill: University of North Carolina Press, 1959.

Casson, Herbert N. *The History of the Telephone.* Chicago: A. C. McClurg and Company, 1910.

Cayton, Mary Kupiec. *Emerson's Emergence: Self and Society in the Transformation of New England, 1800–1845.* Chapel Hill: University of North Carolina Press, 1989.

Chalfant, Edward. *Both Sides of the Ocean: A Biography of Henry Adams. His First Life—1838–1862.* Hamden, Conn.: Archon Books, 1982.

——. *Better in Darkness: A Biography of Henry Adams. His Second Life—1862–1891.* Hamden, Conn.: Archon Books, 1994.

Cherry, Colin. "The Telephone System: Creator of Mobility and Social Change." In *Social Impact of the Telephone*, ed. Ithiel de Sola Pool, 112–26. Cambridge, Mass.: Harvard University Press, 1977.

Child, Lydia Maria Francis. *Correspondence between Lydia Maria Child and Governor Wise and Mrs. Mason, of Virginia.* New York: American Anti-Slavery Society, 1860.

Clemens, Samuel L. *Mark Twain's Letters.* Ed. Edgar Marquess Branch, Michael B.

Frank, and Kenneth M. Sanderson. Berkeley: University of California Press, 1988.

Cody, John. *After Great Pain: The Inner Life of Emily Dickinson*. Cambridge, Mass.: Harvard University Press, 1971.

Columbus, Christopher. *The Journal of Christopher Columbus*. Trans. Cecil Jane. New York: Clarkson N. Potter, 1960.

Conway, Hugh [pseud. of Frederick John Fargus]. *Called Back*. London: Griffith and Farran, 1884.

Cott, Nancy F. *The Bonds of Womanhood: "Woman's Sphere" in New England, 1780–1835*. New Haven: Yale University Press, 1977.

Cox, James M. "Henry Adams and the Apocalyptic Never." *American Literary History* 3, no. 1 (Spring 1991): 136–52.

Crèvecoeur, J. Hector St. John de. *Letters from an American Farmer*. Ed. Susan Manning. New York: Oxford University Press, 1997.

Davidson, Cathy N. *Revolution and the Word: The Rise of the Novel in America*. New York: Oxford University Press, 1990.

Davis, Matthew L., ed. *Memoirs of Aaron Burr with Miscellaneous Selections from His Correspondence*. 2 vols. New York: Harper and Brothers, 1836–37. Rpt. New York: Da Capo Press, 1971.

Decker, William Merrill. *The Literary Vocation of Henry Adams*. Chapel Hill: University of North Carolina Press, 1990.

de Man, Paul. "Autobiography as De-facement." *Modern Language Notes* 94 (1979): 919–30.

Derrida, Jacques. *The Post Card: From Socrates to Freud and Beyond*. Trans. Allan Bass. Chicago: University of Chicago Press, 1987.

Dick, Leslie. "Minitel 3615." In *Erotic Literature: Twenty-Four Centuries of Sensual Writing*, ed. Jane Mills. New York: Harper Collins, 1993.

Diehl, Joanne Feit. *Dickinson and the Romantic Imagination*. Princeton, N.J.: Princeton University Press, 1981.

Dijkstra, Bram. *Idols of Perversity: Fantasies of Feminine Evil in Fin-de-Siècle Culture*. New York: Oxford University Press, 1986.

Dobson, Joanne. *Dickinson and the Strategies of Reticence: The Woman Writer in Nineteenth-Century America*. Bloomington: Indiana University Press, 1989.

Dodge, Mary Abigail. *Gail Hamilton's Life in Letters*. Ed. H. Augusta Dodge. 2 vols. Boston: Lee and Shepard, 1901.

Doheny-Farina, Stephen. *The Wired Neighborhood*. New Haven: Yale University Press, 1996.

Dublin, Thomas, ed. *Farm to Factory: Women's Letters, 1830–1860*. New York: Columbia University Press, 1993.

Ellmann, Richard, ed. *Selected Letters of James Joyce*. New York: Viking, 1975.

Emerson, Ellen Louisa Tucker. *One First Love: The Letters of Ellen Louisa Tucker to Ralph Waldo Emerson*. Ed. Edith W. Gregg. Cambridge, Mass.: Harvard University Press, 1962.

Emerson, Everett, ed. *Letters from New England: The Massachusetts Bay Colony, 1629–1638*. Amherst: University of Massachusetts Press, 1976.

Emerson, Lidian Jackson. *The Selected Letters of Lidian Jackson Emerson*. Ed. Delores Bird Carpenter. Columbia: University of Missouri Press, 1987.

Emerson, Ralph Waldo. *The Early Lectures of Ralph Waldo Emerson*. Ed. Stephen E. Whicher, Robert E. Spiller, and Wallace E. Williams. Cambridge, Mass.: Harvard University Press, 1959–72.

Epstein, Julia. "Fanny's Fanny: Epistolarity, Eroticism, and the Transsexual Text." In *Writing the Female Voice: Essays on Epistolary Literature*, ed. Elizabeth C. Goldsmith. Boston: Northeastern University Press, 1989.

Faderman, Lillian. "Emily Dickinson's Letters to Sue Gilbert." *Massachusetts Review* 28 (Summer 1977): 197–225.

Farr, Judith. *The Passion of Emily Dickinson*. Cambridge, Mass.: Harvard University Press, 1992.

Farrar, Eliza W. R. *The Youth's Letter-Writer*. New York: Bartlett and Raynor, 1834.

——. *The Young Lady's Friend*. Boston: American Stationers' Company, 1836. Rpt. New York: Arno Press, 1974.

Fletcher, Stephanie. *E-Mail: A Love Story*. New York: Donald I. Fine Books, 1996.

Ford, Worthington C., ed. *A Cycle of Adams Letters, 1861–1865*. 2 vols. Boston: Houghton Mifflin, 1920.

Frost, S. A. *Frost's Original Letter-Writer*. New York: Dick and Fitzgerald, 1867.

Fuller, Margaret. *Memoirs of Margaret Fuller Ossoli*. Ed. R. W. Emerson, W. H. Channing, and J. F. Clarke. Boston: Phillips Sampson, 1852.

——. *The Letters of Margaret Fuller*. Ed. Richard N. Hudspeth. 6 vols. Ithaca, N.Y.: Cornell University Press, 1983.

Fuller, Wayne E. *The American Mail: Enlarger of the Common Life*. Chicago: University of Chicago Press, 1972.

Furness, Horace Howard. *Records of a Lifelong Friendship, 1807–1882: Ralph Waldo Emerson and William Henry Furness*. Boston: Houghton Mifflin Company, 1910.

Gilpin, Mariellen O. "A Letter-Writing Ministry." *Friends Journal* 42, no. 6 (June 1996): 14–16.

Goldsmith, Elizabeth C. "Giving Weight to Words: Madame de Sévigné's Letters to Her Daughter." In *The Female Autograph*, ed. Domna C. Stanton. Chicago: University of Chicago Press, 1984.

——. *Exclusive Conversations: The Art of Interaction in Seventeenth-Century France*. Philadelphia: University of Pennsylvania Press, 1988.

——, ed. *Writing the Female Voice: Essays on Epistolary Literature*. Boston: Northeastern University Press, 1989.

Gornick, Vivian. "Letters Are Acts of Faith; Telephone Calls Are a Reflex." *New York Times Book Review*, July 31, 1994.

Greene, John T., ed. *The Ewing Family Civil War Letters*. East Lansing: Michigan State University Press, 1994.

Grubgeld, Elizabeth. *George Moore and the Autogenous Self: The Autobiography and Fiction*. Syracuse, N.Y.: Syracuse University Press, 1994.

Hale, Susan. *Letters of Susan Hale*. Ed. Catherine P. Atkinson. Boston: Marshall Jones Co., 1919.

Harbert, Earl N. *The Force So Much Closer Home: Henry Adams and the Adams Family*. New York: New York University Press, 1977.

Hawkins, Benjamin. *Letters, Journals and Writings of Benjamin Hawkins*. Ed. C. L. Grant. 2 vols. Savannah, Ga.: Beehive Press, 1980.

Hawthorne, Nathaniel. *The Letters, 1813–1843*. Ed. Thomas Woodson, L. Neal

Smith, and Norman Holmes Pearson. 4 vols. Columbus: Ohio State University Press, 1984.

Holmes, Kenneth L., ed. *Covered Wagon Women: Diaries and Letters from the Western Trails, 1840–1890*. 10 vols. Glendale, Calif.: Arthur H. Clark, 1983–91.

Hornbeak, Katherine Gee. *The Complete Letter-Writer in English 1568–1800*. Northampton, Mass.: Smith College Studies in Modern Languages, 15, nos. 3–4 (April–July 1934).

Jacobson, Joanne. *Authority and Alliance in the Letters of Henry Adams*. Madison: University of Wisconsin Press, 1992.

Jakobson, Roman. *Language in Literature*. Ed. Krystyna Pomorska and Stephen Rudy. Cambridge, Mass.: Harvard University Press, 1987.

James, Alice. *The Death and Letters of Alice James: Selected Correspondence*. Ed. Ruth Bernard Yeazell. Berkeley: University of California Press, 1981.

James, Henry. "The Correspondence of Carlyle and Emerson." *Century Magazine* 26 (June 1883): 265–72.

——. *The Portrait of a Lady*. 2 vols. New York: Charles Scribner and Sons, 1908.

——. *Letters*. Ed. Leon Edel. 4 vols. Cambridge, Mass.: Harvard University Press, 1974–84.

Jameson, Fredric. *The Political Unconscious: Narrative as a Socially Symbolic Act*. Ithaca, N.Y.: Cornell University Press, 1981.

——. *Postmodernism, or, The Cultural Logic of Late Capitalism*. Durham, N.C.: Duke University Press, 1990.

Jefferson, Thomas. *The Papers of Thomas Jefferson*. Ed. Julian P. Boyd et al. 25 vols. to date. Princeton, N.J.: Princeton University Press, 1950–.

Juhasz, Suzanne. "Reading Emily Dickinson's Letters." *ESQ* 30, no. 3 (1984): 170–92.

Kaledin, Eugenia. *The Education of Mrs. Henry Adams*. Philadelphia: Temple University Press, 1981.

Kauffman, Linda S. *Discourses of Desire: Gender, Genre, and Epistolary Fictions*. Ithaca, N.Y.: Cornell University Press, 1986.

——. *Special Delivery: Epistolary Modes in Modern Fiction*. Chicago: University of Chicago Press, 1992.

Keats, John. *The Poetical Works and Other Writings of John Keats*. Ed. H. Braxton Forman. 8 vols. New York: Scribner and Sons, 1938.

Keller, Suzanne. "The Telephone in New (and Old) Communities." In *Social Impact of the Telephone*, ed. Ithiel de Sola Pool, 281–98. Cambridge, Mass.: Harvard University Press, 1977.

Kern, Stephen. *The Culture of Time and Space: 1880–1918*. Cambridge, Mass.: Harvard University Press, 1983.

Kline, Mary-Jo. *A Guide to Documentary Editing*. Baltimore: Johns Hopkins University Press, 1987.

The Ladies' and Gentlemen's Model Letter-Writer: A Complete Guide to Correspondence on All Subjects, With Household & Commercial Forms. London: Frederick Warne and Co.; New York: Scribner, Welford and Co., 187–.

La Farge, John. *An Artist's Letters from Japan*. New York: The Century Company, 1897.

Landow, George P. *Hypertext: The Convergence of Contemporary Critical Theory and Technology*. Baltimore: Johns Hopkins University Press, 1992.

Lane, Ralph. "To Sir Francis Walsingham." In *The Roanoke Voyages, Vol 1*. 2d series, no. 104, pp. 199–204. London: The Hakluyt Society, 1955.

——. "To Sir Philip Sidney." In *The Roanoke Voyages, Vol 1*. 2d series, no. 104, pp. 204–6. London: The Hakluyt Society, 1955.

Levenson, J. C. *The Mind and Art of Henry Adams*. Boston: Houghton Mifflin, 1957.

——. "The Etiology of Israel Adams: The Onset, Waning, and Relevance of Henry Adams's Anti-Semitism." *New Literary History* 25 (1994): 569–600.

Leyda, Jay. *The Years and Hours of Emily Dickinson*. New Haven: Yale University Press, 1960.

Lingis, Alphonso. *Abuses*. Berkeley: University of California Press, 1994.

London, Jack. *The Letters of Jack London*. Ed. Earle Labor, Robert C. Leitz III, and I. Milo Shepard. 3 vols. Stanford: Stanford University Press, 1988.

Lowell, Robert. *The Dolphin*. New York: Farrar, Straus and Giroux, 1973.

Lowry, Howard F., and Ralph Leslie Rusk, eds. *Emerson-Clough Letters*. Cleveland: The Rowfant Club, 1934.

Lusk, William Thompson. *War Letters of William Thompson Lusk*. Privately printed, 1911.

Lystra, Karen. *Searching the Heart: Men, Women, and Romantic Love in Nineteenth-Century America*. New York: Oxford University Press, 1989.

Melville, Herman. *The Piazza Tales and Other Prose Pieces, 1839–1860*. Evanston, Ill.: Northwestern University Press, 1987.

Miller, Cristanne. *Emily Dickinson: A Poet's Grammar*. Cambridge, Mass.: Harvard University Press, 1987.

Miller, Randall M., ed. *"Dear Master": Letters of a Slave Family*. Ithaca, N.Y.: Cornell University Press, 1978.

Myerson, Joel. *The New England Transcendentalists and the "Dial": A History of the Magazine and Its Contributors*. Rutherford, N.J.: Fairleigh Dickinson University Press, 1980.

A New Letter-Writer, for the Use of Gentlemen. Philadelphia: Porter and Coates, ca. 1860.

A New Letter-Writer, for the Use of Ladies. Philadelphia: Porter and Coates, ca. 1860.

Norcross, Emily, and Edward Dickinson. *A Poet's Parents: The Courtship Letters of Emily Norcross and Edward Dickinson*. Ed. Vivian R. Pollak. Chapel Hill: University of North Carolina Press, 1988.

Norton, Charles Eliot, ed. *The Correspondence of Thomas Carlyle and Ralph Waldo Emerson, 1834–1872*. Boston: James R. Osgood, 1883.

——. *Letters from Ralph Waldo Emerson to a Friend, 1838–1853*. Boston: Houghton, Mifflin and Company, 1899.

"On Line Emotion—emoticons." Available via <http://wwws.enterprise.net/fortknox/emoticon/smiley.html>.

O'Connor, Flannery. *The Habit of Being*. Ed. Sally Fitzgerald. New York: Farrar, Straus and Giroux, 1979.

O'Toole, Patricia. *The Five of Hearts: An Intimate Portrait of Henry Adams and His Friends, 1880–1918*. New York: Clarkson Potter, 1990.

Pallister, Janis L., ed. *Sister to Sister: Letters Written by Fannie Reed to Her Twin Sister Eliza Crawford, 1894–1904. Turn-of-the Century Women: A Special Issue* 4, no. 1 (Summer 1987).

Plath, Sylvia. *Letters Home: Correspondence 1950–1963.* Ed. Aurelia Schober Plath. New York: Harper and Row, 1975.

Pollak, Vivian R. *Dickinson: The Anxiety of Gender.* Ithaca, N.Y.: Cornell University Press, 1984.

Pool, Ithiel de Sola, ed. *Social Impact of the Telephone.* Cambridge, Mass.: Harvard University Press, 1977.

Porter, Charles A. Foreword. *Men/Women of Letters,* ed. Charles A. Porter, special issue of *Yale French Studies* 71 (1986): 1–14.

Prejean, Helen, C.S.J. *Dead Man Walking: An Eyewitness Account of the Death Penalty in the United States.* New York: Vintage Books, 1994.

Redford, Bruce. *The Converse of the Pen: Acts of Intimacy in the Eighteenth-Century Familiar Letter.* Chicago: University of Chicago Press, 1986.

Redkey, Edwin S. *A Grand Army of Black Men: Letters from African-American Soldiers in the Union Army, 1861–1865.* New York: Cambridge University Press, 1992.

Reid, Martine. "Correspondences: *Stendhal en toutes lettres.*" *Men/Women of Letters,* ed. Charles A. Porter, special issue of *Yale French Studies* 71 (1986): 149–68.

Renza, Louis A. "The Veto of the Imagination: A Theory of Autobiography." In *Autobiography: Essays Theoretical and Critical,* ed. James Olney, 268–95. Princeton, N.J.: Princeton University Press, 1980.

Reynolds, David S. *Beneath the American Renaissance: The Subversive Imagination in the Age of Emerson and Melville.* New York: Knopf, 1988.

Richardson, Robert D., Jr. *Emerson: The Mind on Fire.* Berkeley: University of California Press, 1995.

Richardson, Samuel. *Familiar Letters on Important Occasions.* New York: Dodd, Mead, 1928.

———. *Selected Letters of Samuel Richardson.* Ed. John Carroll. London: Oxford University Press, 1964.

Robinson, David M. *Emerson and the Conduct of Life: Pragmatism and Ethical Purpose in the Later Work.* New York: Cambridge University Press, 1993.

St. Armand, Barton Levi. *Emily Dickinson and Her Culture: The Soul's Society.* New York: Cambridge University Press, 1984.

———. "'Your Prodigal': Letters from Ned Dickinson, 1879–1885." *New England Quarterly* 61, no. 3 (September 1988): 358–80.

———. "Veiled Ladies: Dickinson, Bettine, and Transcendental Mediumship." *Studies in the American Renaissance* (1987): 1–51.

Saintsbury, George. *A Letter Book: Selected with an Introduction on the History and Art of Letter-Writing.* London: G. Bell and Sons, Ltd., 1922.

Samuels, Ernest. *The Young Henry Adams.* Cambridge, Mass.: Harvard University Press, 1948.

———. *Henry Adams: The Middle Years.* Cambridge, Mass.: Harvard University Press, 1958.

———. *Henry Adams: The Major Phase.* Cambridge, Mass.: Harvard University Press, 1964.

Sewall, Richard B. *The Life of Emily Dickinson.* 2 vols. New York: Farrar, Straus and Giroux, 1974.

Showalter, English, Jr. "Authorial Self-Consciousness in the Familiar Letter: The Case of Madame de Graffigny." *Men/Women of Letters,* ed. Charles A. Porter, special issue of *Yale French Studies* 71 (1986): 113–30.

Shultz, Gladys Denny. *Letters to a New Generation: For Today's Inquiring Teen-Age Girl.* Philadelphia: Lippincott, 1971.

Shurr, William H., ed. *New Poems of Emily Dickinson.* Chapel Hill: University of North Carolina Press, 1993.

Sigourney, Lydia H. *Letters to Young Ladies.* New York: Harper and Brothers, 1837.

Simmons, Nancy Craig. *The Selected Letters of Mary Moody Emerson.* Athens: University of Georgia Press, 1993.

Smith, Barbara Herrnstein. *On the Margins of Discourse: The Relation of Literature to Language.* Chicago: University of Chicago Press, 1978.

Smith, Martha Nell. *Rowing in Eden: Rereading Emily Dickinson.* Austin: University of Texas Press, 1992.

Smith-Rosenberg, Carroll. *Disorderly Conduct: Visions of Gender in Victorian America.* New York: Knopf, 1985.

Spacks, Patricia Meyer. *Gossip.* New York: Knopf, 1985.

Starobin, Robert S., ed. *Blacks in Bondage: Letters of American Slaves.* New York: New Viewpoints, 1974.

Stevens, Wallace. *Letters of Wallace Stevens.* Ed. Holly Stevens. New York: Knopf, 1966.

Strenski, Ellen. "Electronic Epistolarity: E-Mail as Gift Exchange." Paper presented at fourth annual Cultural Studies Symposium, Kansas State University, April 11, 1995, available via <http://eee.oac.uci.edu/faculty/strenski/kansas.html>.

Tanselle, G. Thomas. "The Editing of Historical Documents." *Studies in Bibliography* 31 (1978): 1–56.

———. "Textual Scholarship." In *Introduction to Scholarship in Modern Languages and Literatures*, ed. Joseph Gibaldi. New York: Modern Language Association, 1981.

Tehan, Arline Boucher. *Henry Adams in Love: The Pursuit of Elizabeth Sherman Cameron.* New York: Universe Books, 1983.

Thaxter, Celia. *Letters of Celia Thaxter.* Boston: Houghton Mifflin, 1895.

Thoreau, Henry David. *The Correspondence of Henry David Thoreau.* Ed. Walter Harding and Carl Bode. New York: New York University Press, 1958.

Trist, Elizabeth House. *The Travel Diary of Elizabeth House Trist: Philadelphia to Natchez, 1783–84.* Ed. Annette Kolodny. In *Journeys in New Worlds: Early American Women's Narratives.* Ed. William L. Andrews. Madison: University of Wisconsin Press, 1990.

Turco, Lewis. *Emily Dickinson, Woman of Letters: Poems and Centos from Lines in Emily Dickinson's Letters.* Albany: State University of New York Press, 1992.

Vandersee, Charles. "Theorizing the Letter: An Editor's Speculations." Unpublished essay.

Van Doren, Carl, ed. *The Letters of Benjamin Franklin and Jane Mecom.* Princeton, N.J.: Princeton University Press, 1950.

Walpole, Horace. *Horace Walpole's Correspondence.* Ed. W. S. Lewis et al. 42 vols. New Haven: Yale University Press, 1937–83.

Ward, G. Kingsley. *Letters of a Businessman to His Son.* Rocklin, Calif.: Prima Publications, 1990.

Warner, Michael. *The Letters of the Republic: Publication and the Public Sphere in Eighteenth-Century America.* Cambridge, Mass.: Harvard University Press, 1990.

Webster, Daniel. *Correspondence between Mr. Webster and His New Hampshire Neighbors*. Washington, D.C.: Gideon and Company, Printers, 1850.

Wheatley, Phillis. *The Poems of Phillis Wheatley*. Ed. Julian D. Mason Jr. Chapel Hill: University of North Carolina Press, 1989.

Wiesel, Elie. *All Rivers Run to the Sea: Memoirs*. New York: Knopf, 1995.

Winner, Viola Hopkins. "Style and Sincerity in the Letters of Henry Adams." In *Essaying Biography: A Celebration for Leon Edel*, ed. Gloria G. Fromm. Honolulu: University of Hawaii Press, 1986.

Wolff, Cynthia Griffin. *Emily Dickinson*. New York: Knopf, 1986.

Woolman, John. *The Journal and Major Essays of John Woolman*. Ed. Phillips P. Moulton. Richmond, Ind.: Friends United Press, 1989.

Young, John. *The Letters of Agricola on the Principles of Vegetation and Tillage*. Halifax: Holland and Co., 1822.

Zamora, Margarita. "Christopher Columbus's 'Letter to the Sovereigns': Announcing the Discovery." In *New World Encounters*, ed. Stephen Greenblatt. Berkeley: University of California Press, 1993.

Index

· · · · · · · ·

Dickinson, John, 24
Dickinson, Susan Gilbert. *See* Dickinson, Emily—correspondence with: Susan Gilbert Dickinson
Dodge, Mary Abigail ("Gail Hamilton"), 102
Doheny-Farina, Stephen, 270 (n. 15)

Editing of letters (principles and procedures), 7–8, 27–35
E-mail, 3–4, 36, 39, 234, 235, 236–41; and condolence, 238–39; and love, 238
Embodiment of writer in letter artifact, 15, 38–41, 42
Emerson, Charles, 135
Emerson, Edward Bliss, 135
Emerson, Ellen Louisa Tucker, 135
Emerson, Lidian (Lydia) Jackson, 263 (n. 19). *See also* Emerson, Ralph Waldo—correspondence with: Lidian Jackson Emerson
Emerson, Mary Moody. *See* Emerson, Ralph Waldo—correspondence with: Mary Moody Emerson
Emerson, Ralph Waldo: anticipated readership of letters, 9; and beginning of telecommunications era, 230; and condolence, 168; congeniality as feature of epistolary rhetoric, 115–16; decline as letter writer, 137–40; and *Dial*, 115, 124, 126, 132; discontinuity between public and private discourse, 114, 117, 119–24, 132; editing of Ralph Waldo Emerson's letters, 8, 30–31, 32; erotic correspondence, 116–17, 126–29; as exemplary practitioner, 11–13; friendship as written relationship, 116, 117–19, 123–24, 126–30, 134–36; and generic definition, 18–20; intellectual friendship with brothers, 110, 125; letter as alternative literary genre, 119, 121–22, 124; letter as metonym, 119, 123; mentorship of Mary Moody Emerson, 110, 111,

113–14; preference of written to spoken conversation, 111–13, 115; privatization of discourse, 119; solitude as fundamental epistolary condition, 105, 127, 136, 138–40; telepathic aspirations, 128; transcendentalist epistle, 122–23; utopian imagination, 105, 126, 127–28, 135–36
—correspondence with: brothers, 104, 105–6, 107, 108, 109, 110, 116, 125; Thomas Carlyle, 27, 40, 43–45, 50, 51, 52, 111, 115, 116, 126, 128, 136, 138, 139; Ellen Louisa Tucker Emerson, 105, 116–17, 129; Lidian Jackson Emerson, 130–31, 138; Mary Moody Emerson, 105, 110–11, 113–14, 115, 138, 139; William Emerson, 138, 139–40; Margaret Fuller, 111, 116, 122, 123, 124–26; Caroline Sturgis, 116, 123, 126–37, 139; Henry David Thoreau, 45–47, 50, 230
—works: "The Divinity School Address," 111, 114; *Essays: First Series*, 114, 117, 121; "Experience," 134; "Friendship," 117–18, 127, 134–35; *Nature*, 106–7, 109, 111, 114, 115, 119; "The Over-Soul," 111
Emerson, Waldo (son), 133, 135
Emerson, William. *See* Emerson, Ralph Waldo—correspondence with: William Emerson
Emoticon, 237
Eros and correspondence, 26–27, 38, 42, 47–48, 80, 238. *See also* Adams, Henry: erotic correspondence; Dickinson, Emily: erotic correspondence; Emerson, Ralph Waldo: erotic correspondence
Ethics of third-party reading of letters, 5–6, 9–10
Ewing, George H. (Civil War soldier), 101–2

Farrar, Eliza W. R., 262 (n. 13)
Franklin, Benjamin, 59, 76–78